New Perspecti

EUROPEAN JOYCE STUDIES

7

General Editor: Fritz Senn
Associate Editor: Christine van Boheemen

NEW PERSPECTIVES
ON
DUBLINERS

Edited by

Mary Power
and
Ulrich Schneider

Amsterdam - Atlanta, GA 1997

∞ The paper on which this book is printed meets the requirements of "ISO 9706:1994, Information and documentation - Paper for documents - Requirements for permanence".

ISBN: 90-420-0385-5 (bound)
ISBN: 90-420-0375-8 (paper)
©Editions Rodopi B.V., Amsterdam - Atlanta, GA 1997
Printed in The Netherlands

Contents

INTRODUCTION TO *NEW PERSPECTIVES ON DUBLINERS*

Is a rationale needed for another critical book on *Dubliners*? We feel that it is appropriate to look at these stories as the millennium nears in the light of new information and critical theories that are available to us. We also feel that the text of these stories is so rich, allusive and unexpected that it almost compels further study and commentary.

When *Dubliners* first appeared in 1914, the stories were regarded as something unmistakably new, but were not always understood because they did not seem to fit the established literary patterns of Poe or Maupassant. They were spare and bleak; some readers thought they lacked a plot. They came to be regarded as the early work of the man who was later to undertake the grand experiments of *A Portrait of the Artist as a Young Man, Ulysses* and *Finnegans Wake*. It took considerable time for readers to become aware of the understated artistry and narrative power of *Dubliners*. The surface of these stories may seem transparent, but more and more readers have discovered underlying complexities and debated the meaning of symbols and extolled the richness of these deceptively simple texts. As the short story collection gained acclaim and won a major place in the Joycean canon, critics began to read it through *Ulysses* and *Finnegans Wake*. In fact, this is currently a major trend in *Dubliners* scholarship. It is also clear that *Dubliners* is not to be dismissed as juvenilia, but is as distinguished as Joyce's later fiction.

There have been a number of books about *Dubliners* from various critical vantage points to date — Warren Beck, Bernard Benstock, Peter Garrett, Clive Hart, Garry Leonard, Robert Scholes and A. Walton Litz, Ulrich Schneider, Donald

Torchiana, and Craig Werner.[1] Scholarly journals have devoted special issues to *Dubliners — Style,* and *The James Joyce Quarterly* in 1991 and *Studies in Short Fiction, 1995.* There have been several new editions of *Dubliners* recently, most notably John Wyse Jackson and Bernard McGinley's *James Joyce's Dubliners: An Annotated Edition* (London, Sinclair-Stevenson, 1993). The annotations of Jackson and McGinley provide many new possibilities for reading the texts beyond the glosses of Don Gifford and Robert Seideman's *Notes for Joyce* (Berkeley: University of California, second edition 1982). A number of new translations of *Dubliners* have appeared since the copyrights have expired, and John Huston's stunning film of "The Dead" (1988) sparked enormous popular interest. All these developments prompted us to write.

We offer pluralism of interpretation in keeping with recent critical developments. We hope that these essays will extend readers' knowledge of the stories, and will lead to further discussion and debate. Our contributors invoke Lacan, Cixous, Deleuze, Girard, Derrida, Jameson, Paul De Man, Hartmann, Lyotard, Foucault and others. The approaches vary from the hermeneutics and supreme good sense of Fritz Senn to the work of Margot Norris and John Gordon in reading *Dubliners* stories

---

[1]   Warren Beck, *Joyce's Dubliners: Substance, Vision, Art* (Durham: University of North Carolina Press, 1969); Bernard Benstock, *Narrative Con/texts in Dubliners* (Urbana: University of Illinois Press, 1994); Peter Garrett, *Twentieth Century Interpretations of Dubliners* (Englewood Cliffs,N.J.: Prentice-Hall, 1986); Clive Hart, *James Joyce's Dubliners: Critical Essays* (New York: Viking, 1969); Garry Leonard, *Reading Dubliners Again: A Lacanian Perspective* (Syracuse, N. Y.; Syracuse University Press, 1993); Ulrich Schneider, *James Joyce: Dubliners* (Munich: Wilhelm Fink,1982); Robert Scholes and A.Walton Litz, *James Joyce: Dubliners,* The Viking Critical Library (New York, Viking, 1969); Donald T. Torchiana, *Backgrounds for Joyce's Dubliners* (Boston: Allen and Unwin, 1986); Craig Hansen Werner, *Dubliners: A Pluralistic World* (Boston: Twayne,1988).

through Joyce's later fiction. We also offer Marie Dominique Garnier's Feminist Theory, the New Historicism of Carol Schloss, the Discourse Analysis of Wolfgang Wicht, the Biblical Exegesis of Ulrich Schneider, the Structuralism of Wolfgang Karrer and Post-Structuralism of Laurent Milesi. Jana Giles, a young creative writer, provides a view of Joyce's editing. If there is any special emphasis in this collection, it lies in corresponding arguments for the cyclical structure of *Dubliners* advanced by Karrer and Power. Karrer makes a strong, reasoned case for the cohesiveness of the first three stories — the stories of childhood — and Power argues that the stories of public life are more tightly connected than has previously been shown.

Many of the stories in *Dubliners* are discussed, though we make no special effort to be inclusive. "Grace," the next to the last essay in the collection, is the subject of two essays — one by Ulrich Schneider, one by Yvonne Studer — because we feel that it is unexpectedly rich and interesting, and has often been overlooked.

We would like to thank Helga Byrne, Helen Damico, Don Fennema, Michael Fischer, Bob Fleming, David Jones, Charlene McDermott, Elvira Pulitano, Charlotte Schneider, Debbie Schneider, Lorenz Schneider, and Julianne White for their help and encouragement. We are especially grateful to Glenn Norman and Matthew Allen for their patience, lynx eyes and computer expertise.

U. S.

M. P.

July 1995

In Memoriam

Uli Schneider died 1 December 1995 before this volume was finished, yet his spirit guided the project from start to finish. Uli's special scholarly concentrations were James Joyce and popular music at the turn of the century. These interests are reflected in his books, *Die Funktion der Zitate in Ulysses, James Joyce: Dubliners,* and *Die Englishe Music Hall und Ihre Song.* He also compiled and co-edited with Laurence Senelick and David Chesire, *British Music-Hall, 1840-1923: A Bibliography and Guide to Sources,* and is the author of many influential articles. In addition, Uli was an excellent teacher, and brought many scholars together through his enthusiasm for James Joyce and Irish Literature. Uli generously shared information on the music hall, and demonstrated his delight in Joyce's writing and the wealth of popular culture surrounding his work.

DYNAMIC ADJUSTMENTS IN *DUBLINERS*
"(as Joyce clearly states)"

FRITZ SENN

The subtitle of this paper is an unauthorized borrowing from a review of a book about Joyce. In it the ghost of Father Flynn's (as well as Joyce's) hypothetical syphilis again appears. Our concern here is not syphilis, but by what evidence or procedure such questions (if considered relevant) might be settled. The "conclusive" evidence offered in the above mentioned essay is a trustful: "Fr. O'Flynn [sic] did not have syphilis either; it was a stroke (as Joyce clearly states)."[1]

As we all know, the problems involved in arriving at knowledge are intriguing. What does Joyce clearly *state?* What does *Joyce* clearly state? What does Joyce *clearly* state? Readers seek certitude and Joyce is elusive. The dilemma is written into all the stories, but the first, "The Sisters" provides some particularly good examples. An early remark of an unnamed woman, the boy/narrator's aunt, will serve as a starting point. Most readers do not remember exactly what she contributes to the conversation; it may not seem memorable at first. We should assert that there are immediately and strikingly memorable things women say in *Dubliners*, notably Gretta's final words, the book's last spoken ones: "O, the day I heard that, that he was dead!" (*D* 221); this emotional outburst almost names the last

---

[1] Peter Costello, "Syphilis and Symbol," review of J. B. Lyons, *Thrust Syphilis Down to Hell and Other Rejoyceana, Irish Literary Supplement*, 8 (1988), 22. The collocation of what Joyce "clearly states" and the renaming of Father Flynn anticipates some of the comments to follow in this essay.

story.[2] We also remember Gretta's forthright: "I was great with him at that time" (*D* 220), or Lily's unsettling outburst about men being "only all palaver" (*D* 178). But in the opening scene of "The Sisters" the aunt's entry, after one pious exclamation, is low key. She seems to intrude on a conversation of the uncle and Mr Cotter. Quietly asserting herself, the aunt is a minor disturbance to the men. She requests clarification (as we do) about why Mr Cotter would like children not to become too close to "a man like that" — referring to Father Flynn:

— How do you mean, Mr Cotter? asked my aunt. (*D* 10)

The request is taken up: "What I mean is ... it's bad for children." This is not much of an elucidation, so the aunt persists (softening, by the way, "bad" to "not good"): "But why do you think it's not good for children, Mr Cotter?" Mr Cotter's answer is still tautological: it's bad because seeing "things like that" has an effect. Like so many questions in *Dubliners,* hers is never answered except by evasion. The aunt may be irritating and intrusive to her husband and Mr. Cotter, but she asks the right questions, and has an inquisitive mind. The visit to the house of mourning later in the story owes something to her curiosity.

The aunt is on the reader's side, and in the reader's position. Her question is basic and implies the scrupulousness of the author. How do you mean? How does Mr Cotter — how does Joyce – how do we *mean*? Soon afterwards we find the boy, baffled by words and puzzled about how "to extract meaning from ... unfinished sentences" (*D* 11); to him Father Flynn had "explained ... the meaning of the different ceremonies of the Mass" (*D* 13). In a similar manner, we find Jimmy Doyle, in

---

[2]   The phrase "that he was dead" also plays its minute part in the mirrored circularity of *Dubliners*: the phrase echoes (and varies) the initial "if he was dead, I thought..." (*D* 9).

"After the Race," guessing at the meaning of quick phrases (*D* 44). This practice continues until the question — "What do you mean, sir?" — is anecdotally addressed to Johnny the horse in "The Dead" (*D* 208).[3] The horse may not mean anything, but it does provide expansive meaning ("*how*?": by circling round King Billy's statue) and, by extension, on the whole story, on Gabriel, on Dublin, on Irish politics, history and human behavior.

So for our purpose, the aunt's "How do you mean?" is dissociated from its initial environment, and is made absolute. Its emphasis is changed in the light of an overall search for significance: *How* do you mean? It is not so much in the confines of a particular story, or the whole collection as ("a chapter in the moral history of my country"?), or even of special cruxes like "paralysis" or those absences and silences we hear so much about, but of smaller units, sentences, simple statements. No serious reader today thinks that simple statements are simple; but there are things that in fact "Joyce clearly states." So, in this essay, we will look at a few statements that have the appearance of narrative objectivity — such as sentences with a seemingly external point of view. Few of them have objectivity; there is a narrative slant or a tinge of innuendo almost everywhere. The topic is the relation between what we say or write and that mysterious entity called truth. It is called up very early. Words, like a phrase of Father Flynn's may be judged "...idle. Now I knew they were true" (*D* 9). The true/idle dichotomy is inscribed into the first paragraph.

The second story, "An Encounter," strongly asserts a truth about Joe Dillon — an adventurous and enterprising boy who introduced "the Wild West" to other boys and arranged Indian

---

[3]   The question is a rhetorical one, anyway, and Johnny would have been unable to give an answer. But it is typical that, where the horse remains silent, critics step in and spell out the meaning of the scene in a sophisticated fashion.

battles. He had a higher spiritual purpose and the next paragraph is devoted to his unexpected metamorphosis:

Everyone was incredulous when it was reported that he had a vocation for the priesthood. Nevertheless it was true. (*D* 19)

This is the last we hear of Dillon. The narrative assurance of "Nevertheless it was true" replaces a first reaction of incredulity. How dependable a truth is this? What the statement expresses may be something like an acknowledgement that, contrary to boyish appearances, Joe Dillon announced that he had a religious vocation and that, no doubt, he became (and remained) a priest. There is no need to question this; but the perspective is an external one taken over by the first person narration. The claim of truth refers not to a future career, perceptible to many, but to a vocation, an inner call. The trouble is that no outside perspective can possibly verify such a spiritual fact. It is a matter between Joe Dillon and his maker. Definitions of "vocation" emphasize this. *A Catholic Dictionary*, for example, defines vocation as "a disposition of Divine Providence ... whereby persons are invited to serve God in some special state — e.g. as ecclesiastics or religious. The ecclesiastical vocation is manifested by the pious desires of the heart, by innocence of life, by the sincere love of Christ, by pure zeal for God's glory and the salvation of souls."[4] *A Portrait* devotes whole passages to a Jesuit advising Stephen to make very sure he has a vocation: "To receive that call ... is the greatest honour ... But you must be quite sure, Stephen, that you have a vocation because it would be terrible if you found

[4]   William E. Addis and Thomas Arnold, *A Catholic Dictionary*, revised with additions by T. B. Scannell (London: Kegan Paul, Trench, Trübner, 1903), p. 932.

afterwards that you had none ... It is a solemn question..." (*P* 158-60).

The question of a religious vocation was raised, after all, in "The Sisters," a story which refracts the career of a priest, — Father Flynn — someone who once must have felt he had a vocation, though his later conduct did not patently accord with whatever the divine call[5] implies: the duties it entailed were "...too much for him"; he was sitting wide-awake in his confession-box, "laughing-like softly to himself." Such conduct suggests a disturbance of some sort. It is possible to read "The Sisters" as probing into a priest's vocation through hindsight. The first story implicitly questions what in the second is outwardly asserted. Since a vocation is a very special, divine, "call" — but one nobody else can hear — it may be worth noting that the release from a menacing encounter is initiated by a loud, repeated, call at the end of the story (*D* 28), and that what precedes the vocation to the priesthood is a call of notable *in*significance: Joe Dillon yells, "Ya! yaka, yaka, yaka!" (*D* 19). The noise does not invalidate the statement which, in its market place sense, and with no evidence to the contrary, may be sound enough, but in its nature a true vocation is one intrinsically incommunicable to anyone outside. So "it was true" boils down to something like a summary of what may have been public comment.

Reading is a matter of trust and adjustment. One of the most concise statements in the whole collection consists of just three words, in "A Mother," in what appears to be a thumbnail synopsis of Mrs Kearney: "She had tact" (*D* 138). The context determines what her tact consists of:

---

[5]   Interestingly enough, it was when Father Flynn "was wanted for to go on a call" (*D* 17) that they could not find him— but this is a different kind of a call. Notice also that "The Sisters," for what it is worth, has "vacation" in its first paragraph, and that this is also an entirely different notion.

As Mr Holohan was a novice in such delicate matters as the wording of bills and the disposing of items for a programme Mrs Kearney helped him. She had tact. She knew what *artistes* should go into capitals and what *artistes* should go into small print. (*D* 138)

Tact, in this case, implies dexterity and judgment in setting social or theatrical hierarchies by means of precedence or type size. Mrs Kearney possesses useful diplomatic skills in this narrow sphere. Her tact may be appreciated by those around her. The phrase "She had tact" goes beyond her ability to assemble a programme; it sums up and continues what we already know of her. The story, however, will demonstrate the failure of such skill, even in the superficial sense of "tact"; her sense of what is appropriate and strategically fitting, deserts her; she no longer achieves the desired results. There is general disapproval, and her daughter's career is pronounced finished. "A Mother" shows the breakdown or superficiality of Mrs Kearney's tact, and furthermore, the story demonstrates that Mrs Kearney does not have any of the more refined aspects of this virtue, such as a "delicate sense of what is fitting, skill, judgement" (as is specified in the *OED*). In that larger sense, Mrs Kearney is conspicuously deficient; the term "tact"[6] itself might serve as a touchstone. In some particular sense she has it (and loses it), but never in any other. A meaning absent is that pertaining to music; fittingly, concern for the music itself, its artistic (no italics) quality, the overt purpose of all the concerts, is nowhere in evidence. Even etymologically, Mrs Kearney ends

---

[6]   "A little tact was necessary," we read elsewhere (*D* 54) This is Lenehan, a "leech" of adroitness and eloquence; his tact is not discretion, reticence or renunciation, but a strategy towards a selfish goal: "He did not wish to ruffle his friend's temper" (*D* 53). What his "tact" leads him to come up with is: "She's a fine decent tart." In "The Dead" Aunt Kate's "brisk tact" serves to deflect conversation from domestic tension (*D* 181).

up being out of "touch" with events. On the other hand, it becomes possible to reconsider her much-admired "playing and ivory manners" (*D* 136); that intriguing phrase, "ivory manners," seems to combine the notion of frigid superiority with the touch of fingers to the white keys of a piano.

Semantic or contextual divarications often show in translation. One might think a mere three syllables (or ten letters) would come out more or less the same in different versions done into a language like Italian; but the solutions offered and published are remarkable in their diversity. The existing Italian wordings are here arranged in a rising quantitative scale:

She had tact:

Aveva tatto.[7] – Lei aveva tatto.[8] – Aveva tatto, lei?[9] – Lei, aveva tatto.– Aveva molto tatto.[10] – Era una donna di tatto, lei![11] – Lei sì che era una donna di tatto.[12]

---

[7] James Joyce, *Gente di Dublino*, traduzione di Marina Emo Capodilista, (Rome: Newton Compton Editori, 1974), p. 132. [Capodilista]

[8] James Joyce, *Gente di Dublino*, traduzione di Marco Papi, (Aldo Garzanti Editore, 1976), p. 131. [Papi]

[9] James Joyce, *Gente di Dublino*, traduzione di Franca Cancogni, (Turin: Einaudi, 1964), p. 137. [Cancogni]

[10] James Joyce, *Gente di Dublino*, tradutto da Annie e Adrian Lami, Milan: Dall'Oglio, Editor, p. 182. [Lami]. The version is identical with that of *Gente di Dublino*, traduzione di Maria Pia Balboni, Milano: Fratelli Fabbri Editori, 1970, p. 157. [Balboni]

[11] James Joyce, *Dublinesi*, traduzione di Margherita Ghirardi Minoja, Milan, Rizzoli Editore, 1961), p. 154. [Minoja]

[12] James Joyce, *Gente di Dublino*, traduzione di Attilio Brilli, (Milan: Arnoldo Mondadori Editore, 1987), p. 126. [Brilli]

There are six different versions in the seven renderings. Translators find themselves at idiomatic crossroads and go variant ways. Disagreement is not a lexical concern — the noun "*tatto*" remains constant — but the framing varies considerably. We see translators hard at work on the most appropriate slant and tone.

Words change with their context and then help to change the context. Just imagine a sentence *without* the embedding characteristic of Joyce. Suppose we came upon "*Mr Chandler has the gift of easy and graceful verse*" in isolation, and not within the framework of a daydreamed review of a book of poems never to be written or at best vaguely conceived (*D* 74). Our impressions would be wholly different if our reading didn't show how totally ill at ease Little Chandler is with himself and others. The context of multiple subordination or staggered relativity, translatable into a series of *that* and *if* clauses, bristles with qualifications.

Before Little Chandler thinks of giving expression to his melancholy, he passes through a group of children in Henrietta Street. Then clearly, unambiguously the text reads: "Little Chandler gave them no thought" (*D* 71). Unless this is distanced narrative, a strictly outside point of view (as at the beginning of "Two Gallants"), the sentence contradicts its own context. For what preceded the dismissal is:

> A horde of grimy children populated the street. They stood or ran in the roadway or crawled up the steps before the gaping doors or squatted like mice upon the thresholds. Little Chandler gave them no thought.

Little Chandler sees a great many children, and notices their griminess. He tries to ignore their individuality and humanity; he transforms them into a devaluative "horde" and, above all, bestows upon them the dismissive simile "squatted like mice" (assuming that mice squat). This commentary, if it represents

Chandler's mental response, is emphatically *not* giving them *no* thought. The sequence bears this out: "He picked his way deftly through all that minute vermin-like life"; where the deictic "that" alone betrays an effort to keep something at a distance, something that already is in his mind. What the sentence expresses is not the absence of thought, but an internal command to ignore the vermin-like life that intrudes too much. It signals repugnance, repression, and assumed grandeur; it suggests a pose of not dignifying the life around him by the attention it has already commanded. Little Chandler's impulse of superiority is in keeping with his appointment with Gallaher; it represents to Little Chandler the elevation into an apparently higher sphere of society ("It was something to have a friend like that," *D* 70). Chandler's "thought" has become something to be ceremoniously "given": bestowed, vouchsafed, conferred. We see that the next stage of Little Chandler's commentary contains a deliberate exclusion and deliberate uplift, a transformation of "all that minute vermin" into a more noble past: "the shadow of the gaunt spectral mansions in which the old nobility of Dublin had roistered." The language of Little Chandler's thought puts on its best costume, a refined one, with literary or obsolescent words such as "spectral, gaunt, roistered."

As readers, we tend to deduce something from what is on the page, yet we may also add more than was contextually included. As the story progresses, readers see that the sentence about Dublin's children provides a valid characterization of Little Chandler; it has implications for his personal life. At the end Chandler, preoccupied as he is with his own situation and indulging in self-pity, will give his own child "no thought." He has no concern for its being and, instead of love, Chandler feels dissatisfaction. He regards a lot of thought (and emotion) as a mere intrusion. His own child is being drawn into the irritating circle of "horde," " mice," "vermin," and even the parental gender seems to show his distance: "he tried to hush it" (*D* 84).

This may be worth a short digression on verbal

sham-disaffirmation. Subsequently Joyce was to develop this technique, which is not, of course, a new one, to show instant self-deception. A sample of studied non-perception can be isolated from *Ulysses*. This is Gerty MacDowell on the beach:

> And Gerty, rapt in thought, scarce saw or heard her companions or the twins at their boyish gambols or the gentleman off Sandymount green . . . (*U* 13:304)

She shows not a total disregard, but a disdainful "scarce saw or heard," something, presumably, of little importance. But in the rest of the sequence all attention is illogically devoted to what Gerty hardly perceives, and the peripheral gentleman usurps the mental presentation. The text reads:

> that Cissy Caffrey called the man that was so like himself passing along the strand taking a short walk. You never saw him in any way screwed but still and for all that she would not like him for a father because he was too old or something or on account of his face (it was a palpable case of Dr Fell) or his carbuncly nose with the pimples on it and the sandy moustache a bit white under his nose.

This epic abundance with its many visual details is an odd implementation of the dismissive "scarce": it now stands revealed as a posed pretence.[13] The gentleman now prevails so much that he is compared to Gerty's father (who was on Gerty's mind a few moments before). It becomes possible to dwell on

---

[13]   Little Chandler and Gerty MacDowell, both dissatisfied and aiming for higher things, have similar attitudes; for one, they share poetic aspirations: Gerty "felt that she too could write poetry if she could only express herself like that poem" (*U* 13:644); Chandler "tried to weigh his soul to see if it was a poet's soul . . . If he could give expression to it [melancholy] in a book of poems" (*D* 73).

"scarce" as something exquisite and literary, which reinforces the air of pretence, or displays a refusal to take in the vexatious manifestations of the external world. Narrative self-contradiction signals subjective, unconscious repression with more economy than might otherwise be possible.

There are cases when language must be neutral, unslanted, and as free as possible from presuppositions. Legal discourse aims at such an ideal. *Dubliners* contains at least one instance of it — the newspaper report of an inquest in "A Painful Case" (*D* 113-5). Its language ("cautious words of a reporter," *D* 115) is careful, precise, formulaic, and deliberately bare of connotations. Statements are designated as such: the witnesses "stated ... deposed ... said." Occasionally there is a muted euphemistic paraphrase: "his wife began to be rather intemperate in her habits." The jury returns a "verdict" ("truth-saying") that exonerates the railway company of blame. Correctively, as readers we tend to isolate the appended summation, "No blame attached to anyone," and to reinvest it with connotative turbulence.

The language of the law is exceptional and precarious in *Dubliners*. Many of the stories are in the nature of inquests; each reader forms a separate opinion by sifting evidence and weighing probabilities. Language never conforms to the factual ideal. Statements refuse to remain static. Mrs Sinico, witnesses agree, was killed "attempting to cross the lines" (*D* 114). It is hard not to force metaphorical import on the phrase (and its variations).

In contrast, no legal niceties are involved at the beginning of "The Dead" when the scene is set:

It was always a great affair, the Misses Morkan's annual dance. Never once had it fallen flat. For years and years it had gone off in splendid style, as long as anyone could remember. (*D* 175)

We may never quite agree on the narrative perspective of this beginning: it does not come from some neutrally assessing agency (compare "Mrs Mooney was a butcher's daughter"); it is a current opinion, or what the guests are likely to say, sincerely or else out of courtesy. We allow for exaggeration; the code of "great affair" entails a conventional grain of salt. The judgement is *made* true: the evening becomes a great affair by arrangement, like promoting Lily to *garderobière*, with the upstairs bathroom "converted."

But within the framework of the whole story, "always a great affair" acquires overtones. It turns out that, in spite of a successful speech, the evening was not so great for Gabriel Conroy; he has been belittled almost to a vanishing point. Retrospectively, the affair is less than great; he himself has "fallen flat," his own "splendid style" debunked to "orating to vulgarians" (*D* 220). Yet ironically, a twisted truth has been presented. In "The Boarding House," the word "affair" has a different ring.[14] At a certain point in the later story, the word might sound strangely in Gabriel's ears; what seems to emerge to him, out of the nowhere of Gretta's past, is what could be described, crudely, as a secret affair. Some readers might need to make a special effort to divest the superficial opening phrase of that meaning. A spectral truth has arisen that is difficult to dismiss.

An adjective like "great" need not carry much weight: we find "great applause," "a great deal of confusion," and a phrase like "a great pity"; all inconspicuously distributed. There are "those great singers" of the past, or "those dead and great ones"

---

[14]   "People in the house began to talk about the affair" (*D* 63); "to patch up such an affair for a sum of money" (*D* 65); "All the lodgers in the house knew something about the affair" (*D* 65); "the priest had drawn out every ridiculous detail of the affair" (*D* 65); "The affair would be sure to be talked of" (*D* 65); "He could imagine his friends talking of the affair and laughing" (*D* 66).

(a rhetorical run, *D* 203); Lily, contrary to code or expectation, speaks "with great bitterness" (*D* 178). But above all, when Gabriel asks Gretta, in a forced "tone of cold interrogation" if she had been in love with "this Michael Furey," she answers with a disarming, forthright, reverberatingly simple: "I was great with him at that time" (*D* 220). In other words, both "great" and "affair" will never quite mean what once we thought they meant. They radiate. One feature of Joyce's works ("The Sisters" and "The Dead" in particular) is *crypto-prolepsis:* that is to say, early, low key, casual, utterances (of the "all palaver" category) that scintillate retroactively.

Dubliners begins, *inter alia*, with the boy/narrator's close study of a geometrical shape which can provide knowledge in a convoluted way: "If he (Father Flynn) was dead, I thought, I would see the reflection of candles on the darkened blind, for I knew that two candles must be set at the head of a corpse" (*D* 9). This is circumstantial evidence at best; there is no stringent, conclusive logical progression from visual reflections to the state of death; but we have to construe our cases from what we perceive. The formula "knew/must" will be repeated in "The Dead," in Gabriel's meditation with elusive indirection:

> He had never felt himself like that towards any woman, but he knew that such a feeling must be love. (*D* 223)

What kind of knowledge is that? There is a strong air of self-consciousness and introspection: the act (or illusion) of knowing is foregrounded. Since Joyce has a way of suggesting alternatives not in the text, roads not taken, phrases not chosen (just as "The Dead" resurrects an alternative for Gretta that was no longer for choosing), we might speculate on how and if meaning would be changed if the phrase "but he knew that" were elided, as well it might be. Closer synonymic wordings can be conceived. Does, in other words, Gabriel's knowing that he knows make his knowledge more certain? Our views of what goes on in his mind at this particular complex point would affect — and in turn be affected by — how we understand the whole ending, and it would color our highly divergent notions of one unfailing critical issue: Is Gabriel fixed in his ways or is he capable of change or conversion? In other words, is Gabriel paralyzed or does he experience an epiphany?

The sentence about Gabriel's knowledge of love is no longer "simple" by any means, though its language is basic. So it is revealing to see what happens when such lexical simplicity is translated cinematically. John Huston's filming of "The Dead" necessitated a translation since the visual and aural medium does not accommodate slanted verbal indirection. In the movie, Gabriel's off-stage voice says:

I've never felt that way myself towards any woman, but *I know* that such a feeling must be love.

The change (didactically *italicized* here) is slight ; it is only a transition from "He" to "I" and an adjustment of tense. Yet the shift to the immediacy of a grammatical present and the first person is momentous; in an essential way, the film script is not an adequate translation of Joyce's story (no blame attached to anyone). It would take a great effort to verbalize the altered relationship by the transformation into interior monologue; the precariousness of putting into exact critical terms of what we seem to grasp intuitively may circumscribe the delicacy of Gabriel's state.

Translations in the strict sense also part ways in predictable variety. Three French versions of this passage can be compared:

... mais il savait qu'un sentiment pareil ne pouvait être autre chose que de l'amour. (Fernadez)
... et il savait qu'un tel sentiment ne pouvait être que l'amour. (Vuarnet)
... mais il savait qu'un tel sentiment devait être l'amour. (Aubert)

and seven Italian ones:

> ... ma sapeva che un sentimento simile doveva essere amore. (Minoja, 250) ... e sentiva che quello doveva essere veramente amore. (Cancogni, 222) ... eppure sapeva che quello doveva essere amore. (Balboni, 253) ... ma capiva che un tale sentimento doveva essere veramente amore. (Lami, 301) ... ma sapeva che quel sentimento doveva essere amore. (Papi, 212) ... ma sapeva che un sentimento come quello doveva essere amore. (Capodilista, 202) ... ma sapeva che un sentimento di quel genere doveva essere amore. (Brilli, 206)

That no two versions agree entirely is a comment on the slanted dynamism. The divergences are not in the key terms (except that some signalling of truth is thrown in: "veramente"), but of tone and syntactic gear-shifting, which are guide posts of indirection and supposition. Beyond this, the phrase (in the original or in any of its dislocutions), might be read, recited, or acted out, in different tones and poses as insight, as relief, as shock, as humiliation, as parody, as kitsch, or as resignation....

Perhaps we might hold on to the cue that Gretta herself gives in her story of Michael Furey:

> I never knew rightly. (*D* 220)

That we may never know "rightly"[15] does not mean we do not

---

[15] Typically, Gabriel uses the same adverb, "rightly", in his speech, in the sense, not in accord with factual truths, but related to lawful claims: "living duties and living affections which claim, and rightly claim, our strenuous endeavours" (*D* 204). He will end up not liking some emergent claims of living affections. In some subsidiary way, "The Dead" is also the tale of the collapse of what Gabriel considered rightful claims.

know something, something worth while, and maybe quite a lot. After all, in the text and through the text we know Father Flynn *has* died, and there *was* an incident with a chalice; Mrs Sinico's death makes us think of suicide (whether it was or not); Joe Dillon in some way *had* "a vocation to the priesthood"; Gretta did know a Michael Furey, and so on, unless we want to flaunt an attitude of completely freewheeling textuality. But there is always at least a hint of incertitude. Our qualifications and our quibblings, may be minor, but they are there, and should not be discounted or discredited. The readerly qualifications are specific; they are not just vague doubts, and it often takes a lot of research to justify one's reservations. All the foregoing remarks and examples of semantic postmodification and overlapping contexts are not intended to open the floodgates of total relativity and skepticism or initiate a school of criticism in which anything goes. There is no wholesale license in commentary, criticism, interpretation; there are standards, degrees of plausibility, scales of pertinence and relevance — though we will disagree about those as well.

* * *

What is truth? Everything we have of *Dubliners* (apart from authorial comments) are the words thereof — words which will be mentally processed again. We become entangled in the process as soon as we produce our own formulations. We say everything about the stories at our own risk. Joyce has given us fair warning: restating in words what we think we have grasped is tricky: all we can hope for is that the conclusions we (must) jump to have some communicable plausibility. The difficulty becomes poignantly obvious once we try to summarize — sketch a plot, or give the gist of — any of the stories. This is a telling example of what has been done to one of them, from a reference book of supposed objectivity:

Die Schwestern. – Der Knabe steht vor dem im Trauerhaus aufgebahrten Geistlichen James Flynn, seinem ehemaligen Lehrer, und hört das Gespräch oder Geschwätz der beiden Schwestern des Verstorbenen.[16]

It looks easy to voice discomfort at the selection and misrepresentation of such verdicts (especially when they tend to become referential facts); but in practice it will be far less easy to design a working model of a story as intricately layered, as bifocal, as off-center, as oddly titled as "The Sisters." Here is a much more up-to-date thumbnail sketch provided by an expert and critic who explores some borderlines of Joycean indeterminacy:

The priest, who no longer officially represents the Church in Ireland ..., takes a disciple as the main reason for his existence and a reliable source of snuff. Fellow Dubliners are convinced that he is defective both mentally and physically, but what life and mind he has left are dedicated to instructing a neophyte.[17]

The story tolerates such selective judgements. Each item in the synopsis can be traced to textual sources. We cannot help but place subjective stresses on Joyce's story (this essay, for example, stresses semantic qualification and contextual slants, as though little else mattered in *Dubliners*). In this case the boy

---

[16] *Reclams Romanführer*, (herausgegeben von Johannes Beer), Stuttgart: Philipp Reclam (1970), Band III, p.163. "The boy stands in front of the house of mourning, where the priest James Flynn is laid out, his former teacher, and he listens to the talk and gossip of the two sisters of the defunct."

[17] Phillip F. Herring, *Joyce's Uncertainty Principle* (Princeton: Princeton University Press, 1987), p. 15.

18

is considered the center of Father Flynn's life during its last stages; but this perhaps is more than can be cogently deduced from Father Flynn's momentary focal position (for the period covered by the story) in the boy's life. What exactly are Dubliners convinced of? The ones we hear are reluctant to voice their convictions. Inevitably, when we are arranging our opinions in our minds, the ones *we* have, we extract meaning from unfinished and questionable bits of information. It may be revealing that the earliest conversation features "opinion — theory — idea — principle," as though in anticipation of what systematic readers would come to produce in proliferation.

How do we know?[18] "Who do you no tonigh?" This question at the beginning of a chapter in *Finnegans Wake* (FW 126.2) ushers in twelve more questions with twelve corresponding and puzzling answers that seem to state a great deal and determine fairly little. The theme is as old as thinking humanity; it runs through Joyce's prose all the way to Anna Livia's defiant: "They'll never see. Nor know" (FW 227.36). In *Dubliners*, the problem of knowledge is a commonplace that is acted out afresh in each reading, and it creates an inescapable dynamism.

Zurich

---

[18] It is old hat by now, but still worth repeating, that *gnomon* links up to knowing and knowledge (**gn≈mvn**: someone/something that knows: <**gnv**-). Knowledge is diversely written into the first paragraph of Joyce's prose fiction.

DUBLINERS:
"RENEWED TIME AFTER TIME"

FRITZ SENN

from time to time changing the direction (D 143)

My paper will focus on some of the complex interrelationships of time in *Dubliners*. One dimension of my topic concerns the actual writing of *Dubliners* and the way in which the stories show the effects of time. Joyce experienced delays in getting the collection published, and he used the time to revise some of the stories. One of the principal benefits of reworking the stories is that it allowed him to experiment with fictional time more subtly, incisively and artfully than most readers realize. While publishers procrastinated, the collection grew from twelve stories (15 October 1905) to fourteen. Joyce's revisions may indicate an integrating foresight rather than a thrusting of the word in our faces. His manner is in keeping with controlled reticence and an increasing sense of the implicit. In a further delay, Joyce had the inspiration to add "The Dead" as a coda to the collection. This final story provided an ending to the collection and created a resonance which affected everything that had gone before. In other words, the first fourteen stories are changed and amplified when they are read in light of it or through it. For that matter, all the early stories are modified and enriched by later additions to the collection. Another aspect of Joyce's consciousness of time in *Dubliners* is the well known schema which sets the order of the stories. Joyce provided his brother Stanislaus in September 1905 with this outline which lists the stories as a natural chronological progression — childhood, adolescence and mature life — capped by another section called "public life." The following comments single out a few examples of the intricate working of time in the collection, and point toward others.

The temporal stratification of *Dubliners* does not appear to have been examined in detail. The stories vary in the length of time they cover, from a few hours ("Ivy Day") or one evening ("Clay," "The Dead") to several years ("A Little Cloud," "A Painful Case"). Time can be condensed or summarized or else extended at will . The stories differ in their chronographical complexity, even when they seem to follow one another in easy succession. "The Sisters," the earliest story to be conceived, may well be the most intricate. Technically, *Dubliners* offers a survey of narrative time management. How the fifteen tales handle antecedence alone is a topic for research and provisional classification. How is anteriority introduced? In "The Boarding House" there is almost conventional exposition. Mention of Mrs Mooney's marital troubles precedes the events of that momentous Sunday morning. Mr James Duffy is given a long descriptive introduction at the beginning of "A Painful Case," and we learn in a similar way how "Miss Devlin had become Mrs Kearney" in "A Mother." There is some preparation for the day trip in "An Encounter," while Eveline's past is revealed more subjectively, and it is enfolded in associative flashbacks. In "Ivy Day" the presentation is mainly dramatic, and arises from the comments and gossip of men who have nothing else to do. All in all, *Dubliners* is a showcase of methods of managing narrative time.

I would like to come back to the first story, "The Sisters," and show paradoxically that with its headlong plunge into a confusing present and its apparent random release of sketchy and unreliable data, it is the most deviously structured story in the collection. Time is so common an element of life or narration that we may not pay much attention to it, but Joyce seems to thrust it on us, by telling, showing and by pervasively acting it out. He includes the word "time" in the first sentence, and it is worth noting that "time" recurs twice in the opening sentence of *A Portrait*.[1] These are just signals, outward and visible forms of an inward invisible urge, and so is one of the last sentences in the collection: "The time had come for him to set out on his journey westward" (*D* 223). While *Dubliners* begins and ends with time initiating a transition, it is not the same transition.

There are striking changes in temporal effects when an early version of "The Sisters" is compared to the revised one. These dramatic changes have attracted much comment. The early version starts with a focus on time:

Three nights in succession I had found myself in Great Britain Street at that hour, as if by providence.[2]

The storyteller is located in exact space, which is a trademark of *Dubliners*, and also anchored in time. Expectation is implied, and an ominous note is struck by "that hour," and it is combined with conjectural providence. The strange reflexive phrasing "I had found myself" expresses a blend of active urgency and fateful passivity; the phrase, of course, admits another reading, a more absolute one which foreshadows the theme of many of the stories, some self-revelation[3] (to which I promise the

[1]   "*A Portrait*: Temporal Foreplay," *Etudes Irlandaises*, 12 (1987), 65-73.

[2]   *The Irish Homestead*, 13 August 1904, p. 3; identical with a holograph manuscript at Yale (*JJA* 4, 333). It is no more than a coincidence that "OUR WEEKLY STORY" was placed above Cantrell & Cochrane's Mineral Waters, before an advertisement for Dairy Machinery and immediately after a poem whose closing lines were "And, O, God of Grace, it was fine to be / In beauteous Ireland at that time!" Providence provided an ironic context for the as yet unwritten stories – at *that time*!

[3]   In *Ulysses* 9:1046 Stephen Dedalus claims that we are "always meeting ourselves."

stereotyped label *epiphany* will not again be attached in this essay). All of this occurs with an air of self-consciousness, a rhetorical questioning: "as if by providence," invokes supernatural manipulation. The first paragraph continues in this vein, with emphatic recurrence of the key term: "But in spite of the providence which had led my feet ..." (Meanwhile a cautious "as if" has given way to an unquestioned causal connection: "It may have been the same providence that led me there — a whimsical kind of providence — to take me at a disadvantage." This quadrupled "providence" was backed by an echoing "I found myself a prophet" in the same paragraph. The passage both looks ahead and predicts the future. In more ways than the young author could possibly guess, the early version of the story looks ahead.

But the story was changed; that salient fourfold "providence" along with "prophecy" went by the board. Or did it? The word was discarded, but not the sense of looking ahead and having foresight (*pro-videntia*). *Pro-videre* once meant, first, to see ahead, what is in front; then it was transferred to the future, and suggested an ability to foresee what has not yet taken place. It could then develop to mean what we do in view of a future, to consider in advance, take measures, provide (God, of course, does all of that: he foresees and, if all goes well, provides for us). So providence can come to mean a prescient force exercising powers, which may be either arbitrary or whimsical, or else, a Christian divine, benevolent, power. A tangential development of the Latin participle, *providens* shortened to *prudens*, came to mean an ability to calculate consequences — Odysseus was prudent, or Bloom "the prudent member."

"The Sisters," as we now know it, opens with providence in the sense of looking ahead: "There was no hope for him this time"; "no hope" is a prediction of something to come; it suggests imminent certainty and inevitability; "the third stroke" implies foreseeable fatal consequences. Of course, as will be borne out, the opening sentence of "The Sisters" also looks back; it is, like the story itself, both prospective and retrospeculative. The boy is literally looking ahead in the third sentence: "If he [Father Flynn] was dead, I thought, *I would see* the reflection of candles on the darkened blind" (*D* 9; the emphasis is part of my commentary, not the text).

The first story begins with an intricate moment in time: a mature narrator looks back on a crucial moment in his boyhood when he was anticipating the death of his friend and teacher; the rest of the story continues in the near future, the following day, and casts shadows on the more mysterious extended past of a lifetime. Such moments of temporal complexity are very Joycean. For example, the end of *Ulysses* is a promise for a future ("yes I will Yes") given sixteen years before, and remembered in the present which the novel generally tends to put into the past tense. *Finnegans Wake*, of course, conflates tenses, drastically in ambivalences like "scruting foreback into the fargoneahead" (*FW* 426.23). "There was no hope for him this time, it was the third stroke" is a Janus-like "scruting foreback." Joyce's very first prose sentence in the canon, in other words, squints ahead to *Wakean* fusions.

Being conditioned by Joyce's later works, we critical readers have come to observe in "The Sisters" a prediction of actions, of themes and of techniques. Those three strange and fascinating words in the first paragraphs have been abused, and rightly so, for all kinds of critical hindsight prophecies.[4] The first story, then, contains the seeds of much that is yet to come.

---

[4]   The preceding linking of a Wakean ambivalence with the opening of "The Sisters" is a similar abuse.

Vacation Time

There was no hope for him this time. (*D* 9)

This first sentence of "The Sisters" displays a breach of narrative convention: it evokes an unstated antecedent. The reader is facing an immediate present which is the outcome of events as yet unknown. The presentation is unusual in that it assumes there were no readers or listeners there to be brought up to date (or else had been there all along).

By common usage, "this time" implies *that* time *then*. What happened before the story formally begins is the theme and it will be revealed in an oblique, intriguing and defective way. "The Sisters" fuses the personae of the dead priest and the boy who now, years later, tells what he once experienced and tried to learn about Father Flynn's life. The narrator is also "finding himself" in the past. Several stages are conflated in "this time": the present telling is implied, the memory of events before and after the death, along with memories, recollections, conjectures and hints. Time is complicated — it is "folded together"as several pasts are superimposed on the line of the story. Appropriately, "time" is named from the start as something from which one instance ("this") can be set apart from the rest.[5]

Whatever else, the first sentence of "The Sisters" is disquieting. It has an impatience and curiosity about it that will never be quite fulfilled. The story begins at this point, precisely because "this time" is special, decisive, and terminal; "it was the third stroke" adds a portentous ring of the passing of time, with echoes of fairy tales, in which the third attempt is different and

---

[5]   Oddly enough, the first occurrence of "this time" on record, in *Genesis*, is also connected with the third event in a series: "And [Leah] conceived again, and bore a son; and said, Now this time will my husband be joined unto me, because I have borne him three sons" (Gen. 29:34).

decisive.[6] But the other two times are, so far, mere intimations. The technique is one of contrived exclusion, exclusion of the previous two "times." Even at the end there is much more that readers do not know. Our ignorance about unspecified and vague time goads us into new uncertainties.

We speculate, with good reason, on the strange foreign words that appear by way of digression in the opening paragraph — "*paralysis*" (a process through time) — "*simony*" (which is theologically defined as a barter of spiritual for "temporary" things) and "*gnomon.*" A gnomon (someone who knows) was also a pointer on a sundial — one of the oldest instruments on record to measure time: "this time," as it happens, does indicate the time, but leaves us in ignorance, until we can pinpoint the date to some time close to "July 1st, 1895" (*D* 12). Once alerted, we may detect numerous other temporal indicators in the first paragraph: "Night after night ... (it was vacation time) ... night after night ... not long for this world ... I had thought ... Now I knew ... It had always ... But now it sounded," and an early verb "I had passed" which is also the chief activity of time.[7] In wholly conventional fashion, Joyce settles the time of the action at this point, but, unconventionally, he reserves many facts for later, but there is never to be any information about two earlier strokes. The story ends on the same note: "So then, of course, when they saw that, that made them think ..." (*D* 18): "then" marks a point when knowledge became possible. Our understanding of the story depends on such marks; we move between "this time" and "So then, of course" and don't even know how far apart these two points are.

---

[6]   The impact of the first sentence can be measured when we imagine it positioned later in the story, say, after "He was quite resigned" (*D* 15); within such a conventional sequence, it would be entirely unexciting and unremarkable.

[7]   Compare: "Better pass boldly into that other world" (*D* 223).

The marks allow speculation, for example, on what Father Flynn's life might look like if it were arranged in biographical order, a task which we might be able to assemble from hints. It was most probably a sequence of this sort: youth in Irishtown — study at the Irish College in Rome — a long priestly career at St. Catherine's Church — the incident with the chalice — the incident in the confession box — the days spent within the boy's memory — the death. The chronology I guess at is plausible, but unsatisfactory because it omits the dramatic turning points and the logic of cause and effect. Was the "breaking" of the chalice (breaking? chalices are made to last) the cause for what followed,or are we baffled because those events are the result of some previous action outside our reach? A tantalizing web of processes that are spiritual, psychological, or physiological,[8] suggests sequence and consequences, and changes. Observe some of the narrator's shifts or transitions: "I noticed there was something queer coming over him latterly ... it was that chalice he broke.... That was the beginning of it ... After that he began to mope by himself"; all the way to the final "So then, of course." Of course: it is the course of events that eludes us.

Even subsidiary actions show the attrition of time. The boy/narrator's attitude toward Mr. Cotter's storytelling is a case in point: "When we knew him first he used to be rather interesting ...; but I soon grew tired of him and his endless stories about the distillery ..." (*D* 10). That the endless stories annoy the boy, in what looks like an irrelevant early aside, indirectly highlights the lack of an appropriate, expository, beginning: in another sense "The Sisters" is an end-less story: It fades out in an ellipsis where tradition might expect a revelation. Old Cotter's stories that are not passed on were "about the distillery" (the article functions like the opening

---

[8]   The view that Father Flynn may have suffered from venereal disease, proposed, refuted and reproposed at intervals, falls into this category.

"this"): in the distilling process non-essentials are eliminated. Non-essentials in Joyce's retelling are rigorously excluded, but some of the most important facts and events are omitted as well; we must extract them in a scrupulous transformative process.

The phrase "this time" and the parenthetical "(it was vacation time)" were added in the story's revision. They sharpen our temporal awareness. We may now ponder the meaning of "vacation" time: time singled out from some implicit norm, like the demands of school or some other duty. Notice the "duties of the priest" a few pages later (*D* 13), when Father Flynn instructed the young boy (as in a school situation). A priest, of course, is never on vacation from Holy Orders and that is one reason why the dropping of a chalice or solipsistic laughter in a confession box cannot be peripheral or ferial. "The duties of the priesthood," Eliza Flynn remarks in what may well have been Father Flynn's words, "was too much for him" (*D* 17). For the boy, a "vacation" occurs as a relief, "a sensation of freedom, as if I had been freed from something by his death" (*D* 12). Narratively "The Sisters" applies "vacation time" by clearing or emptying a lot of the details and conventions traditional fiction tended to supply. The story has factual gaps for a number of reasons: reports are chancy; grown-ups have scruples in the presence of the young narrator and circumstances surrounding illness and death are blunted out of consideration for the family. If this were not enough, there are also problems caused by defective memory, disgust, and decorum. The vacuum is "filled" by a strange kind of fear, which the first paragraph associates with words (*D* 9). The gnomonic absences and silences and gaps of the story have rightly received much attention recently, and I have here rephrased the problem in terms of the vacation of time and the necessity for further inquiry and study.

Taking His Time

Compared to "The Sisters," a story like "Counterparts" is chronologically simple and mechanically straightforward; in many ways, it is a chain reaction from Mr Alleyne's initial "furious voice" all the way to Farrington venting his fury on the last victim and weakest link, his son Tom. The story is mainly in the present time (and the past tense); there is hardly anything antecedent that would be relevant, almost no use of the pluperfect.

Farrington is running against time at his job, or rather, he is attempting to escape from its rigid grasp. He falls behind, cannot cope, and actually wastes time when he is under stress. This happens not only because he sneaks away during office hours: "Are you going to stand there all day?" he is asked (*D* 88); he spends "a few minutes" in the office just listening, not copying (*D* 90); the chief clerk snubs him in public: "Five times in one day is a little bit ..." (*D* 89). The whole evening turns out to be a waste. Against all this lost time, however, one brief climactic instant of Farrington's story is singled out as though in compensation: "his tongue had found a felicitous moment" (*D* 91).[9] This turning point is underscored by the attention it gets and by its consequences. First of all the "author of the witticism" himself is "astounded," as much as the witnesses. That his tongue "had found" that moment suggests a hiatus in consciousness, the finding itself is not on record: the pluperfect indicates a brief mental absence. The speech, like some automatism, has taken Farrington by surprise. The formulaic introduction of the punch line is unwittingly apt:

---

[9]   One short instant may change all; this is part of the warning in the Hell Fire Sermon of *A Portrait*. "We shall all be changed, in a moment, in the twinkling of an eye," wrote St. Paul (1 Cor. 15:51-2).

— I don't think, sir, he said, that that's a fair question to put to me. (*D* 91)

This unintentionally, but echoingly, answers Mr Alleyne's question: "Do you think me an utter fool?"[10] He did *not* think; there was no conscious time for it. Thinking comes afterwards, with futile regrets. The shock is registered as "a pause in the very breathing of the clerks": a code has been violated. To answer at all is an insubordination: up to that moment Farrington has only allowed himself a submissive "Yes, sir." When he tried to launch into "But Mr Shelley said, sir —," he is interrupted at once (*D* 87). His final impertinence takes the form of a literal answer to a kind of question that is obviously rhetorical and, as such, the exclusive privilege of superiors. The insubordinate changing of the rules challenges the question and implies a comment. All of this is "felicitous," an opportunity has been used to best advantage. But it upsets the hierarchy and threatens the future, and an already shaky position deteriorates further. The narrative flourish "felicitous" — a tone-raising choice, not a likely part of Farrington's own vocabulary — puts further stress on the infraction.

More weight is added by repetition. The climax is told twice. After the factual representation it is fictionalized and modified in Farrington's own retelling. (For all we know, it may well be reiterated again in the future with additional embroidery, according to a live oral tradition.) A witness, Higgins, moreover gives "his version of it," a version of which only the manner of the telling ("with great vivacity," *D* 93) is registered in the text. The two versions at hand are worth comparing. Farrington's revised account, after the fact, is silent; it is a consideration of how he would narrate the incident to the boys. It is a matter of

---

[10]   As it turns out, Farrington's own foolishness consisted precisely in uttering the words, and making them public.

providence, foreseeing; we do not know what he will actually say — the responses he gets are less than enthusiastic. This is the wording he mentally rehearses, in leisurely reconstruction:

— So, I just looked at him — coolly, you know, and looked at her. Then I looked back at him again — taking my time, you know. *I don't think that that's a fair question to put to me, says I.* (*D* 93)

Farrington does not tamper greatly with what he actually said; only "sir" has been left out.[11] What is being falsified is not the wording of the reply but its manner, the performative skill, and the rearrangement of time involved. The alterations concern the stage directions (the tone of voice is likely to have changed as well) and strategic silences. The pause that originally followed the answer is transferred to the moments before, and the pause is divided up for better effect. The man who appeared so flustered and embarrassed, who had "glanced from the lady's face to the little egg shaped head and back again," is now seen in full control of the situation, with strategic delays that are made even more dramatic in the telling. What was an instinctive reply of someone cornered, becomes a consummate performance. Farrington is indeed "taking [his] time" — time that was practically non-existent during the event, when a reply occurred to him "almost before he was aware of it" (*D* 91). Now he reprocesses it and it is masterful as were his stares at office girls (*D* 93). He is a competent, if slightly less than truthful, storyteller, who makes the most of the occasion and restructures the moment, by means of imaginative manipulation, into a

---

[11]   A counterpart can be found in *Ulysses*. When Bloom tells, or remembers, the incident of Parnell´s hat that had been knocked off and retrieved by Bloom, the reply is quoted twice in close succession, once as "*Thank you,*" the second time as "*Thank you, sir*" (*U* 16:1336, 1523). The difference turns on the same honorific.

felicitous and winning one. The sample passage shows that a brief, period of time has been disassembled into its constituent parts. Coterminous sensations have to be rendered by serial reiteration.

What was a subjectively "felicitous moment" when it happened, is now worked into the envisaged performance which, as an artistic counterpart, can be handled "coolly." Farrington's two sentences of magisterial composure have drawn out and replaced the term "moment" in the more objective description, the smallest measure of time. "Moment" was, in the original sense, movement: *movimentum* shortened to *momentum*. Motion, an impulse, is imparted from that instant; from this point on the story gathers momentum, is accelerated by the clash, and ultimately Farrington's son Tom will feel (without knowing about it) the added momentum.

Is it fair to give such weight to this one word "moment" (which, after all, has some sixty other appearances in the book)? It is not fair in the sense that Joyce, taking his time, coolly considered the word in all its possible applications, but it makes sense in the subjective effects of a possible momentum on a reader. It is a preconsidered term within its own context. Instead of a phrase about Farrington's mind, or brain (usually expressed by a simple "he"), Joyce's sentence focuses on "his tongue," the mere instrument of articulation, and now it finds a moment in time.

Farrington's authorial telling has misrepresented part of the incident. Every representation through language is amiss, at least to a degree (as in the inevitable selection of what is worth mentioning): most readers will assume that the primary narration of it, in the distanced third person perspective, is more accurate, or "realistic," than the one offered by Farrington in the attempt to gain belated admiration from his peers. Even that first account, however, contained Farrington's point of view, he considered, no matter how briefly, the moment as favorable, and in his later rendition, he just magnified the assumed felicity.

Soon after the event the felicity of one moment turned out to be spurious and costly; it was certainly not conducive to Farrington's advancement at Crosbie and Alleyne. It was a mis-take.

Farrington "preconsidered the terms in which he would narrate the incident." In this respect he is his author's counterpart, an artist. Joyce used notebooks and drafts for such purposes. As an earlier version proves, the terms of the first story, "The Sisters," were reconsidered at a later stage. In fact, revision became an artistic procedure for Joyce — a revision of the terms to be used, as well as a rearrangement of time. Incidents change with the telling.

General All Over

Dubliners invites its readers to do what some characters are forced to learn: reinterpret, supplement, learn from errors and mistakes, extract meaning. *A Portrait of the Artist As a Young Man* is a novel organized as a series of such insights and reevaluations, and in a novel there is much more scope for modification and adjustment. In *Dubliners*, too, each incident, no matter how small, has an effect, and may alter what went before. "The Dead" offers reinterpretations: in the end Gabriel Conroy reviews the meaning of his marriage, his male prominence, his role, and even his place in the universe. He, too, will redefine what first felt like moments of felicity, remote or recent: "He had felt proud and happy then, happy that she was his" (*D* 215).[12] The spectral appearance of an unknown Michael Furey, dead and glorified, changes all that for Gabriel brings his own being into question. The postponed alterations of meaning are most interesting. Just as the unexpected emergence

---

[12]   See also his "happy eyes" (*D* 180); his "eyes were still bright with happiness" (*D* 213), "he could not eat for happiness" (*D* 213), "his heart was brimming over with happiness" (*D* 217).

of Michael Furey changes Gabriel,[13] so later words actually modify earlier ones. A metaphor like "perished alive" (*D* 177) will widen and deepen its application, and will then have acquired reverberations in a subsequent reading that could not have been there at first. Part of Gabriel's "mistake" (*D* 178) with Lily, the caretaker's daughter,[14] is that he was reading her traditionally, in the light of stereotypes and of casual male patronage, and was not aware of her as a person within her own context, nor of the changes that — unknown to him, of course — had "come over her lately" (*D* 181). He is off the mark in supposing Lily is about to marry: "one of these fine days with your young man" (*D* 178). We can gauge a serious disappointment from her "bitter and sudden retort" about "the men that is now is all palaver." But only later will we associate, perhaps, the easy "fine days" with the present night that turns out to be far from fine. There does not seem to be the expected "young man" for Lily, on the other hand one young man who is entirely unsuspected will begin to haunt Gabriel — one, by the way, who is also remembered by words: "he said he did not

[13]   Michael's first name makes Gabriel's retrospectively more angelic than it would be on its own. If Michael were called Frank or Freddy, religious implications of Gabriel would look far-fetched.

[14]   Even in Lily's presentation we have a possible realignment of accidentals. She is introduced as "the caretaker's daughter"; her father is probably in charge of the house, but "caretaker" suggests associations to cemeteries. Just before Gabriel puts his questions to her she was "folding his overcoat carefully" (*D* 177). Her sudden retort suggests that she was not able to "take care of" herself (as independent, unaccompanied Miss Ivors will say later she can [*D* 195]). Obviously, too, Gabriel, in spite of his friendly remark, did not really care, he was just being sociable. This is similar to his thoughts, "What did he care that his aunts were only two ignorant old women?," (*D* 192). So a merely appositional detail may (but need not) radiate. Gretta, as Gabriel finds out painfully, cares for someone else and, at a moment longingly envisioned, not so much for him. The original sense of care is sorrow. "The Dead" is a story about caretaking.

want to live" (*D* 221), words that did not seem to Gretta to be mere palaver. Lily, we are told, is "not the girl she was at all" (*D* 181): nor will Gabriel ever be the man he was. Michael Furey, we may be certain, never was what he is in Gretta's memory, or in Gabriel's imagination. The words and sentences in the story are not the same when we return to them either.

How do such changes work? The mere framing can be effective, the later re-use of something we noticed in passing, like a remark on the weather: "and I read this morning in the newspapers that the snow is general all over Ireland" (*D* 211). What could be more trivial than such a report? When the phrase occurs later, its significance has been extended, not only because of changed circumstances and changed mood, but also technically by being isolated, brought into focus, and heralded. A nearly identical phrase has also slowed down, and in one sense all the following words to the end of the story visualize that one trite statement.

Yes, the newspapers were right: snow was general all over Ireland. (*D* 223)

The framing, the repetition, the pauses, the past tense, the lack of the article (no longer "*the* snow"[15]), contribute to a modulation in tune with the much more overt reversions of the story. Even "general" seems to have become something else, less of a weather forecast term: it moves towards the

[15] Such a minor difference may be felt when we learn that in French you cannot simply say "snow," because it takes the definite article, and so even as thoughtful a translator as Jacques Aubert is idiomatically forced to say: "La neige était générale sur toute l´Irlande" (*Dublinois*, in Joyce, *Œuvres I* [Paris: Bibliothèque de la Pléiade, 1982], p. 310), and a nuance of identity is lost.

generalization that spreads over the end of the story.[16] Gabriel's imagination, in so far as the story still stays with his increasingly dreamlike view, details the falling of the snow "all over Ireland." Some of this difference — our accumulated later associations — will be imparted to the previous casual mention of snow and newspaper with each new reading. We may forget that Gabriel cannot possibly know if the newspapers are right and if snow *is* indeed all over Ireland. It doesn't matter when the snow, truly general now, is transferred out of geographical reality.[17]

The evocation of the falling snow is expressed by the repetitions, the echoes, the chiasmic variations and by what almost inevitably has to be called a falling — the cadences of the final sentence: this is snowfall expressed — though by no means imitated — in words.[18] We may connect this falling snow with

---

[16] A minor symmetrical imbalance: in the last story a newspaper that called snow "general" was right; in "The Sisters" Eliza Flynn gets the name of a newspaper wrong - she calls it "*the Freeman's General*" (*D* 16).

[17] Or it matters only in the context of unreliability, as the relations between fact and report are thematically disturbing. Here, ironically, a report and, presumably, a forecast are verified by someone who is in no position to do so; and it may be significant of the power of mere words that many of us think the snow is actually falling into the Shannon waves and on the crosses and headstones, when all we have is Gabriel's imagination, as becomes clear when he hears it "falling through the universe" (*D* 224). The most puzzling item may well be the snow falling on "the spears of the little gate" (*D* 224). What little gate? Note its definite article, as though Gabriel who has never been to the west of Ireland, could have seen it. We have moved far beyond any point where newspapers or stories can be right or wrong.

[18] Western literature has a counterpart in its very beginnings. In the *Iliad*, the impact of the words of Odysseus are compared to snowflakes:

> *epea niphádessin eoikóta cheimeríesin*   (*Il*.3:222)
> (words like snowflakes of winter)

an earlier rain, from the song that resurrected the memory of her admirer of long ago: "O, *the rain falls on my heavy locks*" (*D* 210). These, too, are words of sorrow, and the singer's voice, we read, "faintly illuminated the cadence of the air with words expressing grief" (*D* 210), a cluster of rain falling, "faintly" and "cadence" and the general expressiveness of language.

The snow falling "faintly" and "softly" may even re-illuminate the carefully wrought initial paragraph of the first story, where a window is lighted "faintly" and a word said "softly." These are looks from outside at a window with a light within, not a glance out of the window and the lamplight outside; but it is all in relation with a death. Newspapers were "right" at the end of *Dubliners*; at the beginning "words" were felt to be "true": both views come about by implied reconsideration; in between we will find many reports whose veracity is doubtful. In our minds the beginning is modified — from behind, and the first paragraph links forwards, or is it backwards? These are links we could not suspect on a first reading of "The Sisters," nor could Joyce when he rewrote the opening cadences ("The Dead" was not even conceived until two years later), except perhaps by a whimsical sort of providence.

John Huston's movie version of "The Dead" may demonstrate

Pope creatively elaborated on this:

> But, when he speaks, what elocution flows!
> Soft as the fleeces of descending snows,
> The copious accents fall, with easy art;
> Melting they fall, and sink into the heart!

Pope generously added "fall, copious accents, soft descending." Joyce need never have known it or thought of the earliest introduction of his later hero by Homer. All that is indicated is that the cunning speech of Odysseus was likened to snow and that Joyce has turned his generalized snow into eloquence and a literary show piece.

what happens to a story (an event of language) when the cinematic medium requires time to be cut, when there is no past, hardly any memory, nor anticipation of the future, unless a character explicitly talks about it.

What Changes

Later stories reflect on the preceding ones. What happens to marriage in "A Little Cloud" and in "Counterparts" makes Mr Doran's matrimonial trap in "The Boarding House" seem worse. We can match Little Chandler's, Farrington's, and Maria's respective nights out, and then see the Conroys' as yet a final study in disillusion. Some minor matters are modified as well. We may wonder if anything has happened to Kathleen Kearney, who in "A Mother" seems an utterly submissive, and dutiful daughter, and is constantly chaperoned, but in "The Dead" Kathleen is listed as joining an excursion to the West of Ireland — "Mr Clancy is coming, and Mr Kilkelly and Kathleen Kearney" (*D* 189) — without any mention of her mother. Has she gained some freedom as a result of the disaster in the Antient Concert Rooms? Many stories contain narrative gaps, events of importance that are part of the plot, often a decisive part, and yet neither expressly nor too clearly told.[19] Such gaps are compensated for in "The Dead" where an occurrence of long

[19]   There are the gaps in Father Flynn's biography; some crucial events are obscure; the strange man in "An Encounter" does something mysterious, not seen by us ("Look what he's doing!"[*D* 26]); of Frank and his motives in "Eveline" we know relatively little; what happened between Corley and the girl when we were detained in the streets with Lenehan, and what happened in the house at the end of "Two Gallants"? Why exactly must Mr Doran make "reparation"? Most readers learn about the nature of the "Hallow Eve games" (*D* 104) and the reason behind the "pause" and the "whispering" from commentaries. We know very little of Mrs Sinico's last
four years and the inquest of her death is inconclusive. "Ivy Day in the Committee Room" depends largely on facts not stated about Parnell, etc.

ago, never suspected, emerges out of the blue. It is not only the disappointment of a husband but the reappointment of a lover.

"A Little Cloud" contains a reappraisal of the past. Within a few hours the past eight years take on a different meaning for Little Chandler. The comments given here will focus on nothing but the opening paragraph and guess at what happens to it in the course of our reading time:

Eight years before he had seen his friend off at the North Wall and wished him godspeed[1]. Gallaher had got on[2]. You could tell that at once by his travelled air, his well-cut tweed suit, and fearless accent[3]. Few fellows had talents like his and fewer still could remain unspoiled by such success[4]. Gallaher's heart was in the right place and he had deserved to win[5]. It was something to have a friend like that[6] (*D* 70).

Are these six statements, the portrait of a friend, a deserved winner, whose heart is in the right place? We find out in the next paragraph, that these are "Little Chandler's thoughts" at the outset; but not all of them will survive as his opinions. The first of the six is a factual memory and still probably right. Chandler may well have kept track of the years and once more gone over these events.

The thoughts in Chandler's mind are ordinary, but they all sound rehearsed (and in critical commentaries have been classified as clichés). The six sentences set the scene economically, and they also serve as an expository briefing. This is the kind of clarification that has to be pieced precariously together in "The Sisters." These opening sentences paint a successful and absent Gallaher, at the same time they characterize the thinker and his apparently conventional mind; he is concerned about his reputation and the possible reflected glory of such an association.

"A Little Cloud" could be seen as the gradual devaluation of these introductory statements. Before Gallaher is named in [2], he is "his friend," but "friend," the term generally used, means fairly little.[20] In the concluding sentence [6], it means someone useful for social prestige: "It was something to have a friend like that." In the sequence it amounts to an air of affability: "Gallaher was only patronizing by his friendliness" (D 80). A patronizing attitude is not quite synonymous with a heart "in the right place" [5]. Once we readers have met Gallaher in person, we can qualify the pre-announced "success": when "the equipoise" of Chandler's "sensitive nature" is "upset," his mind confused, he decides that "Gallaher was his inferior by birth and education. He was sure that he could do something better." The "fearless accent"[3], first used as evidence of "having got on" [2], will be observed differently: "Gallaher's accent and way of expressing himself did not please him" and become part of Chandler's disillusionment (D 77). Gallaher does not appear to have remained "unspoiled" either: there was "something vulgar … But perhaps it was only the result of living in London" (D 77). "Few fellows had talents like his" [4] is not quite the same judgement as a grudging concession later on: "But nobody denied him talent" (D 72). What further evidence we have of Gallaher shows that his undeniable talent is a brash exuberance, but never far away from what *talentum* originally was in the Bible, a sum of money to be well invested.[21]

A later denigration, extrinsic to "A Little Cloud," can be applied. Gallaher conforms to Lily's censure of men in "The Dead": he is "only all palaver," but, in fact, he has turned it into

---

[20]   Compare the weight given to it for example in *Exiles*, where Richard's question "You are my friend then?" is answered by Robert's protestation of "I will fight for you" and of "faith" (*E* 44).

[21]   See the Parable of the Talents in Matthew 25:14-30. A *talentum* was a sum of money, a Greek loan word, *talanton*, meaning something to be weighed on a balance. In the story Gallaher (and, of course, Chandler in self-evaluation) is being weighed and found wanting. Little Chandler "tried to weigh his soul to see if it was a poet's soul" (*D* 73), to discover, in other words, whether he had talent.

an asset and makes a professional living out of it. His boast, "I mean to marry money. She'll have a good fat account at the bank or she won't do for me ... See if I don't play my cards properly" (*D* 81), is summed up in Lily's "and what they can get out of you" (*D* 178). Chances are that Lily has recently run into someone like Gallaher or Corley.

Appearances are important. That Gallaher "had got on" is immediately confirmed by external evidence: "You could tell that at once by his travelled air, his well-cut tweed suit, and fearless accent[3]." Success can only be demonstrated by externals, and we tend to take them on trust. The air of having travelled for one moment turns "had got on" into mere getting around. Well-cut clothes may spell affluence, while a "fearless accent" looks more like a real characteristic, one that would naturally impress a person like Little Chandler who deplores his own "unfortunate timidity" (*D* 80). What really might give us pause is how the whole "You could tell that" sentence fits in at all. Chandler, we find out afterwards, has not seen Gallaher for eight years, so the well-travelled air is not part of his own experience as yet. It might well depend on report or hearsay. When Gallaher left, obviously in some disgrace ("some money transaction ... one version of his flight" [*D* 72]), he was hardly a nonchalant traveller. So the evidence remains questionable; in fact, later reflection may suggest that the success is protested a little too loudly too early. It seems as though the initial thoughts were mentally directed to someone who needed to be persuaded about Gallaher's sterling qualities. "You could tell" sounds both general and like a transcript of a colloquial assertion.

The more Chandler's opening thoughts are studied and read cross-referentially (which means changing a linear sequence into a spatial arrangement in which any two points can be connected), the more it emerges that, Chandler is turning over phrases in his mind he might use to explain or brag about his encounter while implying his own secondary importance. Some of the thoughts are colloquial ("You could tell that ... Few fellows"). In the end, most of the terms will be discredited. Perhaps it was very little "to have a friend like that," and there may be no one Chandler can talk to about him, when he reviews the recent past (*D* 72). In view of his wife's "bad humour," her cold eyes, and her dominance at his late return home, we may decide that Chandler's thoughts at the beginning have been prepared for Annie: he might explain himself to her in such terms if he could muster the courage. The visit of his great, well travelled, unspoiled friend Ignatius Gallaher would justify his late return home. Like Farrington but, by contrast, before the event, Chandler may be considering the terms, and in such a context "You could tell that by his travelled air ..." might simply be the imagined anticipation of something to report back home in expiation. It is one of the ironies and disappointments that the well-considered phrase is never to be spoken. The phantom characterization, a stock of handy phrases, would be quite in keeping with Little Chandler's habit of making up press reviews of unwritten poems.

The waste of so much well meant verbiage is even more pitiable beside the facile ease with which Gallaher, of "mere tawdry journalism" (*D* 80), seems to be able to talk himself out of a "tight corner" (*D* 73). Words, whether spoken, thought, or never fashioned into rhymes ("express the melancholy of his soul in verse," *D* 84), or even poetic words quickly read during his wife's brief absence, will not help Chandler out of his tight corner: "He was a prisoner for life" (*D* 84). Byron's words actually may have led to the association of such a prison: the next to last line Chandler read before the child's wailing used the phrase "this narrow cell" (*D* 84). It also used the word "clay," which we can later tie to a story that shows other facets of a life of unfulfillment.

In all of these remarks, the story itself has not really been touched, nor will it be. The mini-focus is on the initial paragraph and what it might mean. Its meaning will differ with the stage that our reading has reached. Some of the words are "true" and some will turn out to have been "idle," but none of them stay quite in place. Most are challenged and modified by those that will follow; a few are problematic in and of themselves. The point to be made here is substantiated not in any critical agreement to the views put forward, but in the discomfort some readers will have in following the above account. How do we put those six sentences in Little Chandler's mind? Few of us will be content with any diagnosis of them: they won't stay in place, they require categorization and defy it. Similarly, the title "A Little Cloud" is just now being plausibly explained.[22] The bright sky of the imminent meeting with Gallaher is immediately clouded by minor inconsistencies, but that, certainly, is not one of the title's main implications.

Joyce may well have been sincere when he wrote to Stanislaus that "A page of A Little Cloud gives me more pleasure than all my verses" (18 Oct 1906, LI, 182). The story itself was written earlier in the same year; it contains verses never written and some of Byron's that are abandoned. Joyce's creative self liked what he had done, the letter tells us, and generations of readers have agreed. The continuing pleasure has to do with the delicacy of judging, if we want to judge, the characters, motives, and natures of Gallaher and Little Chandler, or how far they "have got on," but it is also related to the fact that even to pin down some simple declarative statements and to explain how they fit into a mind or into a story, or into a life's work, is more than can be settled with complacent ease.

At the end of the dinner in "The Dead" the acclamation which follows one of the tritest phrases in a festive ritual, is taken up

---

[22]   The source was traced easily, 1 Kings 18:44, but no one seems to have known quite what to with it and its promise of rain. Earlier interpretations that ingeniously wove irrigation and fertilization into the story now point mainly to a phase of criticism where fertility was all the sterile rage. The little cloud still has to be spotted and explained.

by the guests and then "renewed time after time" (*D* 206).
Somehow this happens to apply to the stories, their
interrelations, their details, their individual moments and
phrases, and to our studying the lighted squares of our choice
passages.

Zurich

GNOMON AND TRIANGULATION: THE STORIES OF CHILDHOOD IN *DUBLINERS*

WOLFGANG KARRER

In this essay, I will focus attention on the context of "The Sisters," "An Encounter," and "Araby" and show how these three stories form a truly coherent grouping and share more than a common set of motifs and symbols. I will prioritize the wider relationships in the three stories above character analyses. I think all three titles point to social relations. While this is self-evident in "The Sisters" and "An Encounter," "Araby" shows the relationship of the Dubliners to orientalism — or to their desire for the exotic. I will then put the stories of childhood stories back into a framework of *Dubliners* suggested by Ulrich Schneider.[1] Each story deals with a new set of characters illustrating the general social and spiritual condition of Dublin. In this scheme the first grouping of stories deals with a partially paralyzed childhood, prefiguring adolescence and maturity and reflecting an absence of public life. Most importantly, these stories illustrate Joyce's transition from a naturalist-symbolist mode to the modernist technique of juxtaposition or montage. It is important to recognize that the stories reflect each other and the reader must reconstruct the parallels.[2]

Of the three stories that open the sequence of childhood in *Dubliners*, "The Sisters" has eclipsed the other two in critical attention. In 1984 Bremen, who lists sixteen articles on "The Sisters," could still find no definitive reading of the story. Time

---

[1]   Ulrich Schneider, *James Joyce: Dubliners* (Munich: Fink, 1982), pp. 25-47.

[2]   Wilhelm Fuger, *James Joyce: Epoche Werk-Wirkung* (Munich: Beck, 1994), pp. 140-147.

has added at least another ten readings to this list.[3]

The reasons for such unflagging critical attention are not hard to find. *Dubliners* is often read as a story cycle and "The Sisters" gains prominence as it prefigures and balance the final story and coda of the collection, "The Dead." There is another reason for the recalcitrance of "The Sisters." The story raises strong ideological issues in the figure of Father Flynn and his relation to the boy. Critics have offered contradictory readings. To some Flynn is a salivating and alcoholic pederast, or a sadomasochist, a Gnostic or agnostic; others read him as a man who followed the vows of silence too closely or as a spiritual, instructive and paternal mentor of the boy.[4] A parallel debate, summarized in Chadwick but still unresolved, asks if the boy shares the general paralysis of his surroundings or if he begins to overcome these obstacles. Two additional reasons for the unending critical debate about "The Sisters" are the prominent silences and the various revisions of the text.

I

There was no hope for him this time: it was the third stroke. Night after night I had passed the house (it was vacation time) and studied the lighted square of window: and night after night I had found it lighted in the same way,

---

[3] Brian Bremen, "'He Was Too Scrupulous Always': A Re-examination of Joyce's 'The Sisters'," *JJQ,* 22 (1984), 55. For additional interpretations see Wilhelm Fuger, *James Joyce: Epoche-Werk-Wirkung* (Munich: Beck, 1994), and Laurent Milesi's essay in this collection.

[4] See for example, Leonard Albert, "Gnomonology: Joyce's 'The Sisters'," *JJQ,* 27 (1990), 353-364; Edward Brandabur, "The Sisters," in *Dubliners* ed. Robert Scholes and A. W. Litz, Viking Critical Library, (New York: Viking, 1969), pp. 333-343; Eileen Kennedy, "Lying Still: Another Look at 'The Sisters'," *JJQ,* 12 (1975), 362-70; Joseph Chadwick, "Silence in 'The Sisters'," *JJQ,* 21 (1984), 245-55; A. James Wohlpart "Laughing in the Confession Box: Vows of Silence in Joyce's 'The Sisters'," *JJQ,* 30 (1993) 409-417; and Bremen, pp. 55-66.

faintly and evenly. If he was dead, I thought, I would see the reflection of candles on the darkened blind for I knew that two candles must be set at the head of a corpse. He had often said to me: *I am not long for this world,* and I had thought his words idle. Now I knew they were true. Every night as I gazed up at the window I said softly to myself the word *paralysis.* It had always sounded strangely in my ears, like the word *gnomon* in the Euclid and the word *simony* in the Catechism. But now it sounded to me like the name of some maleficent and sinful being. It filled me with fear, and yet I longed to be nearer to it and look upon its deadly work. (*D* 9)

"The Sisters" opens with this paragraph, which is often subjected to analysis.[5] It provides the reader with three key words for the story (*paralysis, simony, gnomon*) but it raises complex questions about the narrator's voice and the boy's consciousness. The "I" of "The Sisters" contains both.

The boy seems to accept social rituals unquestioningly; his insights are limited, and his vocabulary shows some "linguistic contagion" from the priest. The boy also uses many sophisticated terms. Such usage suggests that the narrator oscillates between the points of view of an adult and a child. This oscillation is a central source of the debate on the boy's status.[6]

Critics have shown by numerous elaborations of the term *paralysis* that to the adult reader there is more to the word than its sound or spectral interpretation. Such critics read the first paragraph as a thematic announcement of all the stories. Dublin, standing for Ireland, is paralyzed economically and intellectually because of the double hegemony of England and the Roman Catholic Church. Feminist critics have pointed out that both state and church use patriarchy to fortify hegemony and base it

[5]   Staley, pp. 533-550; John Paul Riquelme, *Teller and Tale in Joyce's Fiction: Oscillating Perspectives* (Baltimore and London: Johns Hopkins University Press, 1983).

[6]   Riquelme, *Teller and Tale.*

in the father.[7] Joyce, in fact, has encouraged such readings by declaring his rebellion against home, country, and church through Stephen Dedalus.[8]

Simony, the second mystifying word, has received less attention. The boy/narrator does not seem to understand the word; it may stand for sodomy, or it may or may not apply to Father Flynn.[9] Most critics, however, make it "fit" Father Flynn because he somehow betrayed his calling.[10] The term also "fits" "Grace,"[11] and, by extension it applies to Gabriel in "The Dead" and James Duffy in "A Painful Case." "Traffic in that which is sacred" is the failure of Irish intellectuals who — unlike Joyce — ignore the moral lethargy of their audiences and settle for security instead. And not the boy/narrator does not "betray the soul of that paralysis which many consider a city." Rather, he keeps silent.

The third and last word, *gnomon*, has been nearly ignored. Only Albert (1990) seems to have given it extended attention. *Gnomon* is a word from Euclid's geometry, well known to school boys. At first glance, it seems to do little beyond characterizing the narrator's fascination with unusual words. Brandabur (1971) reads it as "a figure" with something missing," and Albert as "a chip off the old block," signifying the boy and the priest.[12] I will try to show that *gnomon* is as

[7]   Frances L. Restuccia, *Joyce and the Law of the Father* (New Haven: Yale University Press, 1989).

[8]   See Chadwick, p. 245.

[9]   Chadwick, pp. 245 and 252; Albert, p. 360; Bremen, p. 61.

[10]   See Bremen, note 26.

[11]   Schneider, p. 54.

[12]   Brandabur, p. 388; Albert, p. 355.

important as *paralysis* and *simony* to an understanding of this first triad of stories and that it provides a structural key to the reinterpretation of "The Sisters," the stories of childhood and perhaps, *Dubliners* as a whole.

Before I do so, let me support my case for a structural reading of these three terms. The first paragraph of "An Encounter," again contains three elements in italics — this time three magazine titles point to the narrator's reading (*D* 19). The third story "Araby" also starts with three literary references in italics: *The Abbot*, by Walter Scott, *The Devout Communicant* and *The Memoirs of Vidocq* (*D* 29). I will argue that the titles of these works are emblematic in and of themselves. In fact, they serve as embedded epigraphs, and function contextually in *Dubliners*. They therefore have the same status as the three italicized terms from the first paragraph of "The Sisters." I will arrange words and titles in the following chart for future reference:

Chart #1

		A	B	C
1.	"The Sisters"	*paralysis*	*simony*	*gnomon*
2.	"An Encounter"	*The Union Jack*	*Pluck*	*The Halfpenny Marvel*
3.	"Araby"	*The Abbot*	*The Devout Communicant*	*The Memoirs of Vidocq*

All nine terms are relevant to an analysis of religion, money and politics, but their explanatory power only emerges if we extend our coverage to the whole group of stories instead of assigning them singly to each story in such a way that "The Sisters" = A1, "An Encounter" = B2 and "Araby" = C3. However illuminating such single identifications can be, a structural reading assumes that all three categories bear on each story individually, and — if the stories turn out to be related — all nine terms together bear on the three stories. By "bear on" I mean that the terms function as embedded epigraphs. And by "together" I mean it is useful to look at these groupings as triangulations.

In this context, it may be useful to recall the growth of the four sections of *Dubliners* as it was revised. Childhood, adolescence, maturity and public life grew from 3:3:3:3 to 3:4:4:3 to 3:4:4:3:1(the coda).[13] The original four triads were replaced by two matching groups, and the coda, "The Dead" added weight by balancing "The Sisters." In the first version, the childhood group mirrored all other groups; in the enlarged version it matched only the last group, in the final version it also reflected "The Dead," or at least "The Sisters" did — as first and last, and also it is thematically joined by sisters — the Misses Flynn and the Misses Morkan — and the looming reality of death. The childhood section is not enlarged, it remains a triad, and it shows the older conception clearly.

Titles and epigraphs are important metafictional devices to focus and superimpose meanings.[14] Titles in *Dubliners* carry multiple messages from the implied author, and they focus the reader's attention on social relations ("An Encounter"), themes ("Grace"), symbolic details ("Clay") or typological parallels ("A

---

[13]   See Fuger, pp. 126-32.

[14]   Wolfgang Karrer, "Titles and Mottoes as Intertextual Devices," in *Intertextuality* ed. Heinrich Plett (Berlin and New York: W. Gruyter, 1991), pp. 122-34.

Little Cloud").[15] Joyce has, for the most part, done away with the nineteenth century convention of complete epigraphs at the beginning of a literary work (a flourish abundantly used by Walter Scott), only to downgrade and embed them as allusions in the first paragraph. Joyce drops this convention after the stories of childhood and returns to it only once more. In "A Painful Case," the triad is *The Maynooth Catechism*, *Michael Kramer* and the Bile Beans ad. I use the verb "downgrade," because title, epigraph, and textually embodied allusion cover different ranges of enriched meanings in a given story. They work like highlights arranged in a hierarchical order. The title "The Sisters" overrules an epigraph, but both hold sway over an embedded allusion like gnomon. And characters would have priority over all three of them. Nannie and Eliza Flynn are Dubliners and they have something to do with gnomon.

If the allusions A to C in 1 to 3 serve as embedded epigraphs, they can be expected to work like the double motto in the first chapter of *The Abbot*, for instance.

> Domum mansit-lanam fecit
> Ancient Roman Epitaph
> She keepit close the hous, and birlit at the quele.
> GAWAIN DOUGLAS [16]

The two epigraphs interact in meaning: they focus the reader's attention on domesticity and women, and they set the antiquitarian tone of what is to follow. Lady of Avenel's domestic actions in the first chapter of *The Abbot* will be

---

[15]   Ulrich Schneider, "Titles in *Dubliners*," *Style*, 25 (1991), 405-415.

[16]   Walter Scott, *The Abbot*, rpt. (London: Nelson, 1910). "Domum mansit -lanam fecit" translates "she keeps house, she makes the cloth," and "She keepit..." in Modern English reads "she keeps the house snug and spins at the wheel" (my translation).

measured against this thematic focus and tone. Irony may be implied: she reprimands the preacher for his interference in her family arrangements — times have changed since Rome and Gawain Douglas. As the narrator points out in the first chapter, the continuity signaled by the epigraphs is always menaced by revolutions: the domestic role of women has changed over the centuries.

Now, if Joyce's allusions A, B, and C are weakened epigraphs, then they may well interact with each other, and measure out a semantic ground as in triangulation. It will not do to single out *paralysis* for instance, as a thematic focus for "The Sisters" or even *Dubliners*. If we take *paralysis* and *simony* to be the base line, then we need *gnomon* as a marker to complete the semantic field for the story. Only after the mapping has been done, can we determine whether this particular triangle extends further than the first story, and whether the second triangulation (A2 to C2) switches off the first one or is superimposed on it. The third triangulation might do the same to the first two. I shall assume superimposition and total extensions of the nine highlighted allusions and epigraphs in the stories of childhood.

"The Sisters" is not the story of Father Flynn alone. It tells of Nannie and Eliza Flynn and their relations to their brother. The relation would have to be covered by a semantic field established by *paralysis* (A1), *simony* (A2) and *gnomon* (A3). This assumption would mean not only the priest or his sisters would be affected by *paralysis* but their relationship as well. This relation (A1) would be due to *simony* (A2), and could be demonstrated by a *gnomon*.

In such a reading, it matters that Father Flynn fails to transmit to the boy/narrator any useful knowledge to improve his life in Dublin. Vestments, rituals, sins, and the mysteries of the Eucharist serve to impress the young boy with Father Flynn's unusual learning, but they do not help him to understand his situation or his relation with the priest. This failure comes out even more strongly with Nannie and Eliza who are helpless to do anything beyond simple domestic rituals. Nannie's silence, Eliza's pious superstitions about the chalice and confusions of scientific or technical terms such as "rheumatic" and "pneumatic," not only tell on them, but on Father Flynn as well. The sisters offer the empty sherry ritual to the boy and his aunt. It upholds the perfunctory civilities but demonstrates a total absence of love or understanding. This failure is mirrored in the absence of love, or the absence of *agape*, in the teachings Father Flynn gives to the boy.[17] The priest has failed them all as a teacher. As James Wohlpart explains "the sisters become the central figures of the story, deserving the title role, for just as they represent the enforcement of silence and the tradition of the Irish Catholic Church that has paralyzed Father Flynn, they also represent the Irish people, the people who are truly paralyzed."[18]

This brings in the *gnomon* (A3). *Gnomon,* "that part of a parallelogram which remains when a similar parallelogram is taken from one of its corners,"[19] suggests that the story comes in two parts: the incomplete parallelogram of the priest/boy story and the smaller parallelogram of the priest/sisters relationship. The two relations are similar: the smaller parallelogram mirrors the gnomon. We can match the elements of both stories, the shorter scene at the end recapitulates the earlier narration in a savage parody:

[17]   Schneider, *Dubliners,* p. 55.

[18]   Wohlpart, p. 415 f.

[19]   *Dubliners* ed. Robert Scholes and A. Walton Litz, Viking Critical Library (New York: Viking, 1969), p. 463.

Chart #2

```
GNOMON . . . . . . . . . . . . . . . . . . . . . . . . . . . . . . . . SCENE
Rome  . . . . . . . . . . . . . . . . . . . . . . . . . . . . . . . . Irishtown
pronounce Latin properly  . . . . . . . . . . . . . . . . . . . . rheumatic
the catacombs . . . . . . . . . . . . . . . . . . . papers for the cemetery
ceremonies of the church . . . . . . . . . . . . . . . . . . two candlesticks
vestments worn by the priest  . . . . . . . . . . . . . . . laying him out
sins mortal or venial . . . . . . . . . . . . . . . . laughing in the chapel
duties, the Eucharist . . . . . . . . . . . . . . . tea, the broken chalice
```

"The Sisters" has the structure of a *gnomon*. It inserts a short dialogical scene into a longer first person narrative in which each part reflects the other. The dialogue is Ibsenite — Joyce charges it to the utmost with connotations from the participants' pasts without having them verbalize these connotations. It has taken six pages to prepare the reader for the dialogue which begins when Eliza Flynn puts her handkerchief away and says "He was too scrupulous always," (*D* 17). This is the function of the *gnomon*. It charges the epiphany with haunting secondary meanings.

"The Sisters" is particularly clear about this function of the *gnomon*. Like Poe's "The Purloined Letter," it repeats a standard configuration with varying characters. The epiphany includes the boy, his aunt, Nannie and Eliza. An earlier conversation in the story includes the boy, his curious aunt, his uncle and old Cotter. While the first conversation contains the boy/narrator's interpretations and reactions, the final speeches withhold them. Readers come to the final epiphany with expectations from the *gnomon* — the entire earlier part of the story.

"The Sisters" then focuses on the interrelations of *paralysis, simony* and *gnomon*. The title points to Eliza and Nannie as the keys to understanding the narration. Joyce foreshadows the sisters' appearance in the two poor women in front of the drapery shop as well as with the uncle and old Cotter, and he may have even had the priest and the boy themselves in mind.[20] The boy's limited point of view is not the result of his age alone. His ritual visits, his mystification and enchantment with words, his Persian dream, and his attention to the handkerchief all stem from Father Flynn's recondite teachings. It is most important to see that his value judgements seem to come from religious, even biblical sources — words such as idle, sinful and simoniac suggest this. Indeed, the boy's momentary identification with his priest/teacher and role reversal is nearly explicit when he says, "I felt that I too was smiling feebly as if to absolve the simoniac of his sin"(*D* 11). Father Flynn's teachings color and limit the boy's perceptions. Even in 1904 when Joyce submitted the first version of the story to *The Irish Homestead*, he had begun a subtle attack on the Catholic Church.

II

I find the *gnomon* structure repeated in "Araby" and would like to look at it before discussing "An Encounter." A lengthy descriptive introduction sets up the narrator's tenuous relation to Mangan's sister followed by a short dramatized scene at the bazaar. "Araby," the title, refers specifically to the last scene of the story which is written in dialogue — and the same is true of the relationship of the title and the last scene in "The Sisters." Again the *gnomon* and the small corner parallelogram, the epiphany, are similar; they mirror each other. Through the short, banal dialogue of the young English woman and two young men at the bazaar, the boy recognizes his own desire. What is being said is unimportant; the phrases are part of a playful flirtation which the English woman seems to enjoy. Her glance at the boy/narrator makes him even more uncomfortable, and he suddenly detects the irony of the situation: he himself is

---

[20]   Bremen, p. 60; Albert, p. 362.

"a creature driven by desire and derided by vanity " in the form of the young woman. Her last remark also fits the narrator's oriental dreams — "O, there's a ... fib!" (*D* 35). Both are self-delusive fictions.

The boy/narrator's insight is limited. He fails to recognize his Eastern enchantment (*D* 32) as a preparation for maturity: his marriage and economic support of a woman. He fails to see himself in his uncle's role — yet the boy's actions often mirror his uncle's — they both arrive at their destinations late that evening - the uncle at home and the boy at Araby; both escape into another world by talking to themselves. The difference is, of course, the boy dreams of an event, while the uncle escapes through alcohol. Nor does the boy recognize Mangan's sister in Mrs. Mercer, who does not get "her used stamps for pious purposes" (*D* 33). The ironies multiply the closer the reader looks.[21]

Gnomon and scene in "Araby" form two related parts in the mind of the boy: illusion matches disillusion; immaturity and obtuseness counter intense self-awareness. These conflicts lead to his reaction of anguish at himself and anger at Mangan's sister, or possibly vice versa. The narrator's anger in "The Sisters" was directed at old Cotter who had called him a child. Here in "Araby" the narrator's final self-assessment is couched in biblical terms: "Vanity" carries all the connotations of a Catholic upbringing. Indeed, the aesthetic image the boy forms in his mind of Mangan's sister (bracelet, neck, hair, hem) owes something to the Pre-Raphaelites pictorially, and spiritually to other late nineteenth century conventions of idealizing women and representing them as exalted beings or even as angels. The narrator venerates Mangan's sister from afar; he is prepared to bring her offerings; he searches for opportunities to be near her.

---

[21]   Harry Stone, "'Araby' and the Writings of James Joyce," in *Dubliners* ed. Robert Scholes and A. Walton Litz, Viking Critical Library (New York: Viking, 1969), 344-367.

Romantic love for him becomes a form of religion as it did for many fervent Victorians. He is the devout communicant.

Indeed, in "Araby" Joyce makes the relation of the narrator to the books of the dead priest clear by setting the boy's prayer scene in the room where he found the books. The narrator confides:

> One evening I went into the back drawing-room in which the priest had died. It was a dark rainy evening and there was no sound in the house. Through one of the broken panes I heard the rain impinge upon the earth, the fine incessant needles of water playing in the sodden beds. Some distant lamp or lighted window glowed below me. I was thankful that I could see so little. All my senses seemed to desire to veil themselves and, feeling that I was about to slip from them, I pressed the palms of my hands together until they trembled, murmuring: *O Love! O Love!* many times. (*D* 31)

This is a remarkable passage. It supports the ironic references to books at the beginning (especially *The Devout Communicant* and *The Abbot*), and thus underlines the priest's legacy in this religion of love. The incantation *O Love!* as well as the window, the light, the evening, and the dead priest take readers back to a similar magic scene outside the window in "The Sisters"(*D* 9). (There is a similar scene in "The Dead"in the Gresham Hotel when Gabriel can be recognized as the young boy in love. It might be added that all three narrators talk to themselves.)

The quoted passage also raises the question of desire and the senses obliquely. "Desire" is a key word in this story. It also emerges in "The Sisters," in the boy's dream about the dying priest's face: "It murmured; and I understood that it desired to confess something" (*D* 11). By murmuring the boy/narrator of this story impersonates a dying priest, and the evaluation of his sexual fantasies with his soul receding into some pleasant vicious region (*D* 11) betokens a romantic but still orthodox Catholic imagination.

The boy's senses seem to desire to veil themselves, and he fights temptation by pressing his palms together as if to pray. "I was thankful I saw so little," he said (*D* 31). Desire blots out the perception of reality, and creates illusions. His soul luxuriates in Eastern enchantments, and the word Araby becomes magic. The scene in the back drawing room carefully sets up the final scene of self-recognition at the bazaar. *Gnomon* and scene mirror each other as they did in "The Sisters." The two stories share the same structure, but "Araby" narrows the field of interpretation because it gives the reader the boy's reaction to the epiphany. The discovery effectively ends childhood and the stories of childhood: the narrator must face himself as just another creature driven by sexual desires. Further, he discovers bazaars, no matter how exotic, do not answer his dreams — they are marketplaces where the young and impressionable are encouraged to spend money to negotiate their romantic desires. Hence, simony, for the boy in "Araby" has the specific and idiosyncratic meaning of violating his religion of love through buying trinkets or his acceptance by Mangan's sister or both.

III

"An Encounter" forms the middle piece in this unholy triptych of desire. Like the other two stories, it is built as a parallelogram with a *gnomon*. Again the *gnomon* leads to a short scene in dialogue, and the title points to that short ending scene. Here as well the reader can expect the scene to mirror the larger parallelogram ironically. This time the pervasive influence of the Catholic Church seems to recede; the boys take off for a day of truancy. A strange spirit of unruliness seems to pervade the story;[22] Father Butler can safely be derided as Father Bunsen, and an imaginary world of adventure, clearly modeled on the magazines provided by Joe Dillon begins. Gradually the adventure slips into familiar disappointments. The boys never reach the Pigeon House; the day grows sultry; they settle for musty biscuits and lemonade and content themselves with an empty field. The frustration is captured very well in the following paragraph:

We walked along the North Strand Road till we came to the Vitriol Works and then turned right along the Wharf Road. Mahony began to play the Indian as soon as we were out of the public sight. He chased a crowd of ragged girls, brandishing his unloaded catapult and when two ragged boys began, out of chivalry, to fling stones at us, he proposed that we should charge them. I objected that the boys were too small and so we walked on, the ragged troop screaming after us: *Swaddlers! Swaddlers!* thinking we were Protestants because Mahony who is dark-complexioned, wore the badge of a cricket club in his cap. When we came to the Smoothing Iron we arranged a siege; but it was a failure because you must have at least three. We revenged ourselves on Leo Dillon saying what a funk he was and guessing how many he would get at three o'clock from Mr. Ryan. (*D* 22)

Mahony and the narrator are alone. They lack both allies and enemies. The two overcome their frustration by verbalizing revengeful fantasies about Joe Dillon. The ragged children similarly vent their anger by chanting the insult *Swaddlers*. The paragraph leads to further frustrations at the harbor and Ringsend which the boys handle with similar transformations

---

[22]   Fritz Senn, "Joyce's 'An Encounter'" in *James Joyce's Dubliners: Critical Essays*, ed. Clive Hart (London: Faber and Faber, 1969).

into fantasy. Running away to sea or chasing a cat down the lane hardly make up for the loss of momentum. So far the paragraph is simply a stepping stone on the road to the tired disillusion in the field. But if we give it a gnomonic reading, that is, if we read it against the encounter scene, another layer of meaning emerges. The man who reveals his sexual fantasies to the boys — the old josser — is laying siege to them. His accent is good (*D* 26) — perhaps English or Anglo-Irish, if readers assume a parallel to the shopgirl in "Araby." The josser's fantasy of nice soft girls clashes with the reality of the ragged girls Mahony chases. (In Mahony's parallel fantasy, the girls were victims of an Indian assault.) Furthermore, the punishing fantasy the two boys develop for Joe Dillon can be compared to the fantasies of the josser. The imaginary pleasures of spanking boys may well originate in the schools, and Mr. Ryan may share a pleasure with the josser — or to stretch an idea to its furthest point — the josser may be a teacher or a former teacher himself. The text is silent on this point. His reading recommendations, however, parallel those of Father Butler, and Mahony's question about what would Father Butler be doing at the Pigeon House (*D* 21) may point in this direction. It is even more important that the josser vents his sexual frustration in incantatory repetitions of exciting words, perhaps in an effort to gain some understanding of his excitement. He thus mirrors the two boys and their fantasies of whipping Joe Dillon, and he joins the boy/narrators of the other two stories of childhood who excite themselves with words like *paralysis* and *Araby*.

The man is an adult version of the three boy/narrators in the stories of childhood and what takes place may be viewed as an encounter with a double. Joyce sufficiently underlines the affinities between the two and the resulting discomfort of the boy/narrator in "An Encounter" to make his point. The tables of the boy's fantasy have been turned on him, but he escapes because it takes three to make a siege. The narrator makes his escape to Mahony and returns to him as a penitent. There is no self-recognition as in "Araby," but the story ends with a religious evaluation: "idle," "penitent" and "vanity" form the concluding triangle of value judgements in "Araby" and the stories of childhood.

I would like to come back to the beginning of the story and the function of submerged epigraphs. *The Union Jack* emphasizes the Protestant-Catholic hegemony, also observed in the other two stories. *The Halfpenny Marvel* is a book of adventure stories, and the title emphasizes the precarious nature of schoolboy economics, which, incidentally, plays a role in all three stories. *Pluck* returns the reader to the narrator and his fantasies. The narrator, more reflective than his counterpart in "The Sisters"-- explains joining the adventurous gang fearfully, for he does not want to seem studious or lacking in robustness (*D* 20). He may have read *Pluck* and the other magazines to toughen himself. Scholes and Litz explain that boys' magazines like *The Union Jack, Pluck,* and *The Halfpenny Marvel* originated in the 1890's to counter the effects of the penny dreadfuls which were considered unwholesome for children.[23] There was nothing wrong with these magazines, the narrator hastens to assert in the face of Father Butler's criticism (*D* 20). Indeed, the priest's criticism is not directed at the "wholesomeness" of the magazines which is probably a euphemism for their lack of sexual content, but at the irrelevance of Apache history as compared to that of Rome (*D* 20). In fact, the reading of these magazines is perfectly compatible with the priesthood, as the narrator shows in two early asides on Joe Dillon and his parents (*D* 19). The "doors of escape" (D 20) these magazines seem to open to the narrator turn out to be trapdoors. This is the central irony of "An Encounter" on which the *gnomon* turns. When the 'Apache Chief' (*D* 20) finally encounters his enemy in Ringsend on the

---

[23]   Scholes and Litz, p. 465.

Dodder, he meets a possible presentiment of himself. The priest in the first, the old josser in the second, and the young men around the shopgirl's stall in the third story are, doubles — if that is not too strong a term — or projections of what the boys might become if they stay in Dublin. The encounters of older and younger men in all three stories are confrontations of romantic orphans with distorting mirrors.[24] While the boys grow older, their doubles grow younger, but unlike Dorian Gray's picture, they do not necessarily become more handsome.

In "An Encounter" both the narrator's and the man's fantasies come from reading, and the reader might see the possibility of Mahony and the narrator ending up as jossers — or becoming "Two Gallants." The josser's sexual fantasies and his verbal exhibitionism seem to stem from repressed sexuality and an education similar to that of the two boys. Fantasy and the ritual enchantment of words do not in themselves provide escape from Dublin, and if they are not followed by action or physical escape, they will trap the character even more firmly in Dublin under patriarchal control. The action in all three of the stories of childhood bogs down in empty rituals and frustrations. To overcome fear with pluck remains an illusion, if the underlying sexual motivation is not laid open. The narrator, in contrast to Mahony, prefers American detective stories for their "unkempt fierce and beautiful girls"(D 20). These fantasy girls not only offer a contrast to the ragged girls on the Liffey, they also rival the fantasy girls of the josser who recommends Bulwer-Lytton for exciting content. The pulp and best seller authors are true simonists who pander their wares to commercial interests.

Paralysis (D 9) whipped (D 27), and O Love (D 31) belong together as three forms of the same debilitating fantasy. And" idle" (D 18), "penitent," (D 28) "and "vanity" (D 35) as

<hr />

[24] Karl Miller, *Doubles: Studies in Literary History* (Oxford: Oxford University Press, 1987), pp. 21-55.

concluding evaluation are hardly remedies: they are religious cover terms for inertia, masochism and narcissism. The boy reaches an ambivalent self-recognition at the end of "Araby," but neither he or the other two narrators can free themselves from Dublin's hemoplegia.

IV

Triangulation has taken us far into the thematic network of the first three stories which map the territory of childhood. We have only touched on some of the strands tying the stories together. Let me try to make some generalizations, and then fill out some further gnomonic connections.

Chart #3

```
/ 1. Boy--Priest      /      "The Sisters"   /
/                   · /      "An Encounter" /
/ 2. Boy--Boy         /        "Araby"         /
/                   /_____/
/ 3. Boy--Girl                              /
/_____/
```

Each of the three stories uses the *gnomon* construction: there is a long narrative preparation, culminating in a dramatic scene that illuminated what has gone before by exactly mirroring it or presenting a symmetrical inversion: the Eucharist becomes crackers and sherry; an American Indian adventure, child molestation; an Eastern enchantment, a nearly deserted bazaar. The first gnomon ends with the words "the end of the dream" (*D* 14); the second with "our jaded thoughts and the crumbs of our provisions" (*D* 24), and the third with "the magical name" (*D* 34). The irony in each of the three stories consists in the boy/narrators' obliviousness to the inversion between *gnomon* and scene. The implied author directs the implied reader to the underlying layers of meaning by triangular allusions and by juxtaposition and montage. The triangular allusions function as embedded epigraphs for the stories. Both the Ibsenite scene and the montage are transformed if the reader follows these directions. The dialogues become epiphanies; the stories transubstantiate Dublin's everyday life like the Eucharist. Each set of three allusions introducing the three stories relates to the others like an intricate network that stretches over all the stories in various ranges and intensities.

Triads, however, can become hopeless and frustrating, and three, at times, does not seem to be a positive number. I have looked at the stories of childhood for references to the number three or multiples of three. The following were the only references I found, and all seem to be associated with hopelessness and failure:

> There was no hope for him this time: it was the third stroke (*D* 9).
> When we came to the Smoothing Iron we arranged a siege; but it was a failure because you must have at least three. (*D* 22)
> I allowed the two pennies to fall against the sixpence in my pocket. (D 35)(three coins)

Paralysis, *simony, gnomon,* the three allusions in "The Sisters" (A1 to A3) are loan words — abstract concepts covering themes and construction throughout *Dubliners*. "An Encounter" narrows the range of allusions to generic magazine titles. It is rewarding to read "The Apache Chief" and the magazines for additional ironies,[25] but the story reveals all that is necessary to understand the adventure fantasy and its erotic underpinnings. In "Araby" the allusions take us to single books, and here a careful scrutiny of the three books will also enhance our understanding of the narrator's dilemma. But the descending range of the allusions probably corresponds to their intensity in each story and their extension over the whole of *Dubliners*. *Paralysis* and *gnomon* will last to "The Dead." *The Union Jack* leads gently into adult and public life and opens political dimensions. But *The Abbot* and *Vidocq* will not survive the stories of childhood.

This triangulation becomes too complex semantically to work out completely, and I will caution the reader that I am not a semanticist, and a technical analysis would have to be undertaken by someone more qualified. I will, however, outline some of the semantic components implied in the allusions of the three epigraphs (A to C) in each of the three stories (1 to 3, Chart I).

The nine allusions share at least the following semantic components:

Religion	B1, A3, B3
Economics	B1, C2
Politics	A2, A3, C3

and if we add more abstract components to encompass the remaining allusions with the rest we get:

Union/Separation	C1, A2, A3
Lack /Fullness	C1, A1, B1, B2, B3.

---

[25] See R. B. Kershner, *Joyce, Bakhtin and Popular Literature: Chronicles of Disorder* (Durham: University of North Carolina Press, 1989).

Both oppositions are interconnected. Both apply to *gnomon* which lacks fullness due to its separation from the corner parallelogram. Lack of movement (A1), of honesty (A2) or of formal complement (C1)leads to desire to overcome the lack. It emerges in the boy's dreams about the priest and ends in the reader's desire to get beyond the meaninglessness of Dublin's everyday life. Joyce orchestrates all these desires circling the triple lack of "The Sisters" (A1 to C1). The secularization of religious yearnings to erotic and literary ones in the first three stories is certainly worth further study.

Each of the first three stories provides a variation on escape: it is religion in the first, adventure in the second, and romance in the third. In each the boy encounters a repressed part of himself in older people. The corruption of the josser in "An Encounter" implicitly stains Father Flynn and the young men at the bazaar stall. The nameless boy/narrators achieve limited insight into the irony of what they tell. Even if the incidents are taken from Joyce's childhood, the revisions and orchestrations detach them from any biographical identification. Joyce stands above the stories and the implied authors. The boys are at best ambivalent portraits of the artist as young men. On the other hand, they may become Lenehans, Duffys and Farringtons.

This does not exhaust the lack/fullness opposition. An important and expectable cluster of images from the first paragraph of *Dubliners* turns around light and darkness. It often intersects with windows, a second image group, separating inside from outside. *Gnomon* also introduces a set of images dealing with boxes and rectangles of all sorts. *Gnomon* also covers silence. Both *gnomon* and scene, word and void lose an important part of their meaning without the other.

V

I will conclude my reading with a closer look at the lack in economics and politics. The stories of childhood are the foundation of the scarcity economics that rules most of *Dubliners*. All three stories of childhood insist on dealing with poverty and an exact number of pennies — so crucial to a schoolboy's economic life. The poverty of old Cotter and the Flynns in "The Sisters," the sixpence investment in romance in "Araby," and the shilling spent on adventure in "An Encounter" define the limits of possible escapes in Dublin. Economy dictates both aspirations and limitations. Real poverty exposes the irony of pretensions in education. The reader might consider Father Flynn's useless erudition (*D* 13), the pretended superiority of National School boys (*D* 20,27) and the snobbishness of the narrator as he considers the inferiority of the Christian Brothers School and "the rough tribes from the cottages" (*D* 29,30). Beyond the perspective of the boy/narrators, a classist society emerges and it poises an impoverished Irish middle class against "the curses of the laborers"(*D* 31) and their ragged girls and boys (*D* 32). The Flynns, the josser, and the boy in "Araby" must rest their self-esteem on shabby gentility.

Beyond that social structure sketched into the early stories emerges the political dimension of English domination, which is already distorted by a child's perspective. Those adventurous boys — the narrator and Mahony in "An Encounter" — are mistaken for swaddlers, and the English accent of the young woman at the bazaar adds humiliation to the anguish and anger of the boy/narrator. The naive reference to O'Donovan Rossa and "the troubles in our native land" (*D* 31) add poignancy to what will become a major theme of the stories of public life. The lack alluded to in *paralysis*, *simony* and *gnomon* has a solid foundation in the social, political and economic conditions of Ireland around 1900.[26] Structuralist and Marxist readings of *Dubliners* do not necessarily contradict each other.

[26]   Schneider, *Dubliners*, pp. 25-47.

Indeed, if we assume that the social relations highlighted in the first three stories imply larger institutions, then Joyce's critique of home, country and church assumes familiar Marxist contours. In such a scheme, Father Flynn represents the church, Mahony the school, and Mangan's sister the family.

Church, school and family are the first three categories in Louis Althusser's critical list of ideological state apparatus.[27] The stories of childhood dramatize then what Althusser calls "*l'asujettissement ideologique*" of the individual, the boy's subjection to the dominant ideology by constituting him as "subject" or in other words as Catholic, Irish and male. Home and school permeate all three stories, and beyond them the church appears embodied by its "Fathers." The patriarchal ideology becomes material in the corresponding practices, rituals or everyday routines that reproduce and stabilize social relations,and subject men and women to gender roles. Rituals and ideology together constitute the paralysis of Dublin society.

The subjection happens by interpolation, and by singling out the individual as different from others. Significantly, Joyce's boy/narrators, remain nameless, and perhaps orphaned and they try to claim individuality by stealing away from home and school.[28] It may be more important that the escapes become subjective rituals reinforcing the dominant ideology as many end where they began. This and the oscillating narrator seem to form the political unconscious of Dubliners.

Dortmund

---

[27] Louis Althusser, "Ideologie et appareils ideologiques d'état," in *Positions (1964-1975)*, (Paris: Editions Sociales, 1976), p. 73 and 83.

[28] See Miller, pp. 23 and 39-55.

JOYCE'S MANY SISTERS AND THE
DEMODERNIZATION OF DUBLINERS

WILLIAM A. JOHNSEN

"...Here is the marvellous novel delivered upon you by my twenty-third sister..." (signed "Stephen Dædalus" in 1904, *SL* 22).

    The park trees were heavy with rain and rain fell still and ever in the lake, lying grey like a shield. A game of swans flew there and the water and the shore beneath were fouled with their greenwhite slime. They embraced softly impelled by the grey rainy light, the wet silent trees, the shieldlike witnessing lake, the swans. They embraced without joy or passion, his arm about his sister's neck. A grey woolen cloak was wrapped athwart her from the shoulder to her waist: and her fair head was bent in willing shame. He had loose redbrown hair and tender shapely strong freckled hands. Face. There was no face seen. The brother's face was bent upon her fair rainfragrant hair, the hand freckled and strong and shapely and caressing was Davin's hand. (*Portrait* 228)

---What are you doing here, Stephen?
 Dilly's high shoulders and shabby dress.
 Shut the book quick. Don't let see.
---What are you doing? Stephen said.
 A Stuart face of nonesuch Charles, lank locks falling at its sides. It glowed as she crouched feeding the fire with broken boots. I told her of Paris. Late lieabed under a quilt of old overcoats, fingering a pinchbeck bracelet, Dan Kelly's token. *Nebrakada femininum.*
---What have you there? Stephen asked.
---I bought it from the other cart for a penny, Dilly said, laughing nervously. Is it any good?
 My eyes they say she has. Do others see me so? Quick, far and daring. Shadow of my mind.
 He took the coverless book from her hand. Chardenal's French primer.
---What did you buy that for? he asked, To learn French?
 She nodded, reddening and closing tight her lips.
 Show no surprise. Quite natural.
---Here, Stephen said. It's all right. Mind Maggy doesn't pawn it on you. I suppose all my books are gone.
---Some, Dilly said. We had to.

She is drowning. Agenbite. Save her. Agenbite. All against us. She will
drown me with her, eyes and hair. Lank coils of seaweed hair around me, my
heart, my soul. Saltgreen death.
We.
Agenbite of inwit. Inwit's agenbite.
Misery! Misery! (*U* 10:199-200)

Meanwhile his extraordinarily gifted sister, let us suppose, remained at home.
She was as adventurous, as imaginative, as agog to see the world as he was.
But she was not sent to school. She had no chance of learning grammar and
logic, let alone of reading Horace and Virgil. She picked up a book now and
then, one of her brother's perhaps, and read a few pages. But then her parents
came in and told her to mend the stockings or mind the stew and not moon
about with books and papers (Virginia Woolf, *A Room Of One's Own* [New
York: Harcourt, Brace & World, 1957], p. 49).

"The Sisters" was the first work of fiction Joyce published. It is
quite properly seen as a beginning for *Dubliners* and, in some
ways, for all of Joyce's fiction,[1] and it has received as much
careful commentary as any other story. In particular, Hugh
Kenner and Marvin Magalaner, and later Therese Fischer and
Florence Walzl, recognized the significance of the evolution of
this story from *The Irish Homestead* to the Yale and Cornell
manuscripts, to the final version, as an act of increasingly
conscious self-criticism.[2] But where does "The Sisters" itself

[1]   Thomas F. Staley, "A Beginning: Signification, Story, and
Discourse in Joyce's 'The Sisters,'" *Genre,* XII (Winter 1979), 533-49.

[2]   Hugh Kenner, *Dublin's Joyce* (Bloomington: Indiana University
Press, 1956); Marvin Magalaner, *Time of Apprenticeship: The Fiction of
Young James Joyce* (New York: Abelard Schuman, 1959); Therese Fischer,
"From Reliable to Unreliable Narrator: Rhetorical Changes in Joyce's 'The
Sisters,'" *JJQ,* 9 (1971), 85-92, and *Bewusstseindarstellung im Werk von
James Joyce Von Dubliners zu Ulysses* (Frankfurt am Main: Athenäum
Verlag, 1973), 29-65; Florence Walzl, "Joyce's 'The Sisters': A
Development," *JJQ,* 10 (1973), 375-421. For an extensive elaboration of

begin, and where does it end? And *why* do its revisions become increasingly self-critical?

Revision makes "The Sisters" increasingly modern. But that is not all. If we develop the theoretical potential of Joyce's revisions, we will be on our way to considering Joyce in the light of René Girard's work, to suggest an alternative theory of modernism which one might call provocatively "demodernization." Further, we will understand how Joyce proposed to his country a non-violent alternative tradition to what Conor Cruise O'Brien has recently described as *Ancestral Voices*, voices of the dead (like Pearse) who ask for blood sacrifice, including self-sacrifice, voices that are more persuasive than the voices of the living who ask for peace.[3]

Against such ambitions we must mind Girard's own insistence on the theoretical power of literary texts to keep from simply transcoding Joyce into Girard at the beginning, a process that would teach us nothing more about either one of them. It will be time to introduce Girard once we have elaborated the theoretical potential of Joyce's many sisters.

Joyce first wrote "The Sisters" in July 1904. It was an invited submission to *The Irish Homestead* and its revision continued until July 1906, when it serves as an introduction to a fourteen-story *Dubliners*.[4] "The Dead" would be written more

---

the readings of Magalaner, Walzl, Scholes and Staley on the revision of "The Sisters," recoded into Roland Barthes's scriptible/lisible distinction, see L.J. Morrissey, "Joyce's Revision of 'The Sisters': From Epicleti to Modern Fiction," *JJQ*, 24 (1986), 33-54.

[3]   Conor Cruise O'Brien, *Ancestral Voices* (Dublin: Poolbeg, 1994).

[4]   According to Hans Walter Gabler's dating of the Cornell manuscript for the *James Joyce Archive* (*JJA* 4, xxix). Thus Gabler's dating requires the adjustment of all previous commentary relating "The Sisters" to "The Dead." "The Sisters" still magnificently anticipates "The Dead," but in the way it anticipates, as Fritz Senn has insisted, *Finnegans Wake*: as a portal of

than a year later.

To better understand the context of this compositional process for "The Sisters," we must begin with Stanislaus Joyce's invaluable commentaries, which explain that his brother had already tried out modes of short fiction entitled "Silhouettes," epiphanies of the sordidness of others, told by a first person narrator. Stanislaus remembered the first story, which gave the series its title, as a young boy walking along the mean streets of Dublin, suddenly observing in a window, a fight between husband and wife which the husband ends with a blow. The shade is drawn. After a while, the profile of two figures reappears, cast by candlelight, this time a mother and child. The mother figure cautions the smaller not to "waken Pa."[5]

Stanislaus has clearly in the back of his mind, as he remembers "Silhouettes," the progress of his brother's early work in prose. He consciously lines up "Silhouettes" as antecedent to *Dubliners* through the cruel dynamic of the intermediary "Epiphanies." As Stanislaus shrewdly explains them, the epiphanies expose precisely what the subject tries to conceal:[6] each draws the shade, each portrays itself in outline, revealed.

Stanislaus Joyce is our sole source for whatever we know of this material. Our gratitude to him should encourage us to study both the consequences of his associations, and his further analysis. He thinks of his brother's epiphanic method as explanation for these early short silhouettes/narratives because he has just been describing how he discovered that other Dublin

---

discovery. See Senn, "'He Was Too Scrupulous Always': Joyce's 'The Sisters,'" *JJQ*, 2 (1965), 66-72.

[5]   Stanislaus Joyce, *My Brother's Keeper* (New York: The Viking Press, 1958), p. 90.

[6]   *My Brother's Keeper*, p. 124.

families, apparently more respectable, hid the same sordid family lives as the Joyces. This leads him to consider, with understandable preference, that his brother's candor is superior to the more general hypocrisy.

We could simply concur with Stanislaus that candor transcends hypocrisy, but a much more interesting speculation opens up before us. If we remember that Stephen trumped the snobbism of Clongowes schoolboys by claiming one uncle a magistrate and another uncle a judge, we may see "Epiphanies" for the matriculated Joyce as a more advanced hand in the game of what René Girard calls "mimetic rivalry." (We will come to a more fully elaborated relation between Joyce and Girard's theories later.) Candor is not innocent of the pretensions which surround it; rather, it characterizes its fellows as hypocritical by comparison, unless they can outperform it with a greater audacity. Later, we will learn to ask, what identity does candor mask, when it mocks the hypocrisy of its rival? How do "Epiphanies" themselves "epiphanize" their author, revealing precisely what *he* would conceal?

The slender evidence of letters and manuscripts for whatever sequence Joyce intended for "Epiphanies" has made agreement difficult, but most critics accede to their division into two kinds:[7] confessions and observation — the confessed ecstasy of seraphic life, and the observed meanness of others. In any combination or sequence, one kind tends to serve and validate the other. The writer has the authority to unmask others, having unmasked himself. The resentment of Gogarty and other acquaintances of Joyce at being epiphanized is not answered by Stanislaus's disclaimer, pointed mainly toward Gogarty, that friends were rarely the subject of his brother's writings. In reality, they had reasons to feel put down.

---

[7]   See James Joyce, *Dubliners*, ed. Robert Scholes and A. Walton Litz (New York: The Viking Press, 1969), p. 254.

Eglinton's and Ryan's refusal of Joyce's submission to their new journal *Dana*, and Joyce's response to their refusal, suggest that rivalry is the dynamic of "A Portrait of the Artist" (January 1904) as well as its subject. In the language of the rejected essay, the young artist, "divining of intrigue," composes "an enigma of a manner." He presents himself as indifferent to rivalry in order to vanquish rivalry, to reunite the children of the spirit, jealous and long-divided by a competitive order employed against itself. "But he saw between camps his ground of vantage, opportunities for the mocking devil...."[8] The essay unmasks the artist in a manner too audacious for *Dana*, but what follows, in the covertly autobiographical *Stephen Hero*, (the exponential expansion of this essay) according to Stanislaus, is the mockery of others.

Stanislaus's contemporaneous *Dublin Diary* insists on the satirical direction of *Stephen Hero*'s evolution after "A Portrait of the Artist" was rejected by *Dana*. Further, he identifies satire, the mocking devil, as a family character-trait, representatively Irish. Their parents, even their young brother Charlie, are credited as being mimics. Finally, Stanislaus quotes Yeats to the effect that Swift, the Dean of Satire, made a soul for Dubliners by teaching them to hate others as they hate themselves. Stanislaus, then, fully approved of familial and national satire.

In the long run, *Dana*'s rejection of "A Portrait of the Artist" probably changed nothing. The common experience of Joyce's earlier editors, Longworth of *The Daily Express*, and Hugh Kennedy of *St. Stephen's*, or even Joyce's teachers, suggests that suffering, soliciting, or refusing Joyce's work could never blunt, could only sharpen "that little pen" "dipped in fermented ink".[9]

---

[8]   *JJA* 7, 83 and 84, 104.

[9]   Even two early examples of Joyce's schoolboy prose seem to bait their sponsors. Joyce must have derived ironic satisfaction by paying back the

Granting Joyce what he himself called an "all-too-Irish" habit of mind, a reader could hardly imagine a more provocative invitation for a contribution than George Russell's oft-quoted letter, especially if we consider it as issued sometime in July, after a certain discussion in the National Library which *Ulysses* dates as 16 June 1904.[10]

> Look at the story in this paper The Irish Homestead. Could you write anything simple, rural? livemaking?, pathos?, which could be inserted so as not to shock the readers. If you could furnish a short story about 1800 words suitable for insertion the editor will pay £1. It is easily earned money if you can write fluently and don't mind playing to the common understanding and liking once in a way. You can sign it any name you like as a pseudonym. (*SL* 76)

Stories in *The Irish Homestead* were regularly published over pseudonyms as "Our Weekly Story," so although Russell would have been reading the early chapters of the *Stephen Hero* manuscript at this time (*SL* 22), it is not certain that he is

---

pandybatting episode later described in *Portrait*, when in "Trust Not Appearances" he concluded that the eye betrays the character of a person ("See it in your eye"--*U* 15:3670). "Force (the futility of)" was perhaps the matriculation-essay assigned to Joyce, but by the evidence of the surviving fragment, its working title ought to be "Subjugation," by which Joyce subversively affiliates the common discipline and consequences of being "subject" to priest and king.

[10] Alan Denson, *Printed Writings by George W. Russell (A.E.): A Bibliography* (Evanston: Northwestern University Press, 1961), makes it clear that A. E.'s *New Songs*, the anthology "Stephen" is excluded from, was published in March 1904, and selections finalized perhaps as early as the date of Russell's preface, December 1903. Denson also notes that *New Songs* was reviewed by Gogarty in *Dana*'s first issue; a reading of Gogarty's review suggests an uncertain compromise between puffery and satire, the Yeats and the Joyce touch.

referring disparagingly to their subject "Stephen Dædalus."[11] But Joyce had already perceived slights in much less ambiguous offers of assistance. Ellmann tells us that Skeffington, for example, when he became Registrar of the College, offered Joyce, by letter, tutoring work in French. Joyce declined the offer, in person, going to the Dean of Studies himself, on the theory that the College authorities wished to silence him by putting him in their debt (*JJ* II 140).

Strangely enough, no one seems to have identified Russell's model story for submission. Because of a hiatus in story publishing at *The Irish Homestead*, the three published stories closest to hand (for the tone and construction of Russell's note suggest hastiness) would have been Louise Kenny's "Ryan Rascal" (11, 18 & 25 June 1904), Berkeley Campbell's "The Old Watchman" (2 July 1904) and Alice Milligan's "A Farmyard Tragedy" (16 & 30 July). The late date of the last story, and the serial publication of both Kenny and Milligan (Russell writes":Look at the story in *this* paper") make them less likely choices. Finally, H. F. Norman's letter of acceptance to Joyce for "The Sisters" is dated 23 July 1904 (*JJ* II, 164).

On the other hand, "The Sisters" bears a striking resemblance to Campbell's story.[12] A narrator describes his interest as a twelve-year old in an old watchman who took what he calls his "fancy. He was apparently about sixty-five, and his

---

[11] In any case, Declan Kiberd's note in his edition of *Ulysses*, that "The young Joyce was so ashamed of the fact that his first story was published in 'the pig's paper' *The Irish Homestead* that he adopted the pen-name 'Stephen Dædalus' to conceal the embarrassing connection" (London: Penguin Books, 1992), p. 956 cannot account for Joyce's insistence on associating himself in manuscript and letters with this pseudonym.

[12] Berkeley Campbell, "The Old Watchman," *The Irish Homestead*, X (July 2, 1904), 556. Frank Atkinson, *Dictionary of Literary Pseudonyms* (London: Clive Bingley, 1982), p. 173, lists "Berkeley Campbell" as the pseudonym of Charles Lionel Duddington.

clean-shaved, wrinkled face had a sad and lonely expression." The narrator adds that he was "surprised to hear that he [the old man] spoke with a very nice accent and a cultivated voice." The boy becomes familiar with the old watchman, "my old man," as he calls him, from the boy's father's practice of walking home from the theater, "as Dad said it was good for us to get a breath of fresh air after coming out of the stuffy theater." Finally, the father talks to the watchman, who admits to serious illness: "...sometimes my cough is too bad for me to go out, and James, that's the other workman, takes it for me. I have had a cough ever since I had pleurisy, and I'm afraid it won't leave me here much longer." On the way home, the narrator remembers "...the many different conjectures we came to ... as to what his story was. Then I got a very bad cold, and was not let out with Dad for about a fortnight."

Ultimately, the old man in Campbell's fiction confesses his story of opportunity ruined: he was the younger son of the Dean of St. Patrick's, who was to have gone through Trinity to study for the Bar. But "I only stayed up to the small hours of the morning drinking and gambling, and losing more money than I could ever hope to pay." He ran away to Australia after his father offered him a new start in Canada. When he finally returned, he knew no one, and now waits to die. The boy's father gets him into a hospital: "I used to go and see him very often, but he only lived a few weeks, and I was awfully sorry when he died. But now I always look at the watchmen on the tramline and wonder if they have a story like 'my old man's'!"

This first person attention of a young boy to the narrative of an old man gives a lot of material to Joyce's satirical mind for successive versions of "The Sisters" as well as later stories. Just as Father Flynn is opposed to Old Cotter, the old watchman is opposed to a fresh air advocate. Also like Father Flynn, his high education has come to nothing, and he is near death. Campbell's boy/narrator is, as well, a curiously patient observer of his old man's decline: his interest is, like the narrator's interest in

Father Flynn, a "fancy" ("The fancy came to me" *IH* 677; *D* 14). The boy develops a "sympathetic" respiratory illness, an aspect of contamination Joyce would certainly have enjoyed trumping in "The Sisters" with an etiology of paralysis or paresis as glossed by Walzl and Waisbren.[13]

The first version of "The Sisters" seems a pretty mean satire of unambiguous uplifting testimony characteristic of *The Irish Homestead*, and helps the reader believe that most improper readings of the story (like the recent suggestion that the "unassuming shop, registered under the vague name of *Drapery*" is meant to call up, to a Dublin cavalier, a locally known source for prophylactics)[14] just as later stories[15] have caught the spirit, if not always the letter, of *Dubliners*. Joyce has deviously violated every caution of Russell's, with stories that shock *The Homestead* readers, and later, Grant Richards's printer.

The early James Joyce, Dublin's Joyce, the Joyce of the university essays, reviews, and Dublin literary folklore, contentiously allied himself with the modern in drama and prose, suggesting everyone else was already too old to be modernized. "The Sisters" modernizes "Our Weekly Story" according to the futile discipline perfected by Flaubert: the fashion-dynamics of modernization require that any text which aspires to virtue by breaking new ground must deconstruct a rival text as obsolete, but such a procedure must ultimately lead to self-modernization, self-rivalry, self-destruction. Such

[13] "Paresis and the Priest," *Annals of Internal Medicine*, 80 (1974), 758-762.

[14] Zack Bowen, "Joyce's Prophylactic Paralysis: Exposure in *Dubliners, JJQ*, 19 (1982), 257-273. Also, James F. Carens, "Some Points on Poynts and Related Matters," *JJQ*, 16 (1979), 344-346.

[15] Edmund L. Epstein, "Hidden Imagery in James Joyce's 'Two Gallants'" *JJQ*, 7 (1970), 369-370.

modernism can only end by unwinding Yeats's wonderful observation, that spiritual resentment of others amounts to self-hatred. Having 'modernized' *The Irish Homestead*, "The Sisters" must modernize itself.

However, as the beginning of *Dubliners*, it must modernize itself, as Hans Walter Gabler suggests, in the context of successive moments of reflection on *Dubliners* as a whole: it happens in October 1905, just before writing out "Grace" as the end of a twelve-story collection, and in July 1906, when Richards sent the whole fourteen-story manuscript back to Joyce for major revision and recantation.

The Yale manuscript version of "The Sisters," which Gabler dates as October 1905 (*JJA* 4, xxviii), remains very similar to *The Irish Homestead* version. First, Joyce improves accuracy: Father Flynn is given a real church (undoing an editorial revision of H. F. Norman), and he is vested, not habited for burial, following Stanislaus's research (*L* II 114). But the narrator remains a stable, complacent agent of language and attitude: in the opening paragraphs, "providence" (*pro-videre*) guides his attempts to foresee Flynn's demise, and he is a "prophet" (προ) to himself by foretelling his disappointment. (In contrast, the opening paragraph of the 1906 version will emphasize the powers vested in language which control the narrator.) In 1905, he still speaks easily of how "people will blunder on what you have elaborately planned for" (*JJA* 4, 335), he lightly refers to "three women of the people," to his aunt, "what they call good-hearted," and supposes that Father Flynn prefers his own intelligence to the sisters' lack of it. It is unsurprising that he tolerates Father Flynn's "egoistic contempt for all women-folk" (*JJA* 4, 341). His precocious scorn for others remains uncontested.

Most interestingly, in revision, the narrator grammatically removes himself from Dublin. *The Irish Homestead* version read "Now I find … [Cotter] tedious," and his aunt "is a bit of a gossip." The present tense of 1904 makes "Stephen Dædalus," like "Berkeley Campbell" ("Now I always look at the watchmen...") a Dubliner still, probably at the same address. "Afterwards he became tedious" (*JJA* 4, 334), and "...she was a gossip..." (*JJA* 4, 345), like the signature to "The Boarding House" manuscript of 1 September 1905 ("Stephen Dædalus"/Via S. Nicolò, 30"/Trieste, Austria," *JJA* 4, 45), show how easy detachment and relocation seem in 1905, in Trieste, before Joyce's elaborate conflict with Richards began.

It is only later, in the July 1906 (Cornell manuscript) revision, that "The Sisters" will admit to the pros and cons of Dublin. The narrator will still recall Cotter as tedious, but he will also remember puzzling his head to extract meaning from his unfinished sentences, in a manner which suggests that he is *still* somewhat puzzled.

Critics have been drawn to elaborate the meanings of simony in the Catechism, gnomon in Euclid's *Elements,* and paralysis in *The Principles and Practice of Medicine,*[16] as important signs of revision of "The Sisters." These revisions first occur in the 1906 version; the 1905 version retains the original first paragraph from *The Irish Homestead.* We might add that these improvements of 1906 are at the boy's expense. "Stephen Dædalus" in 1905 deals confidently with a material and an audience he has mastered. This narrator of 1906 is no master of his own words; rather, he has heard an adult voice give an elliptic significance to simony and gnomon (probably in geometry or catechism class), and paralysis (whenever Father Flynn is discussed), without sufficient explanation. These adult voices are given more to denying than granting him competence. Further, he cannot conclude his own imaginative attempt to extract meaning from the sentences Cotter uses to puzzle him.

The series of notations of Cotter's tediousness, across

---

[16]   See Walzl and Weisbrun, "Paresis and the Priest."

successive versions of "The Sisters," mark nicely the narrator's "progress" of modernization as self-deconstruction. To *The Irish Homestead* version of 1904 ("He used to be very interesting when I knew him first, talking about 'faints' and 'worms.' Now I find him tedious") the 1905 version "draws the shade" ("...afterwards he became tedious" — [*JJA* 4, 333]). The narrator of 1905 removes himself in a double sense: grammatically, as we have already seen, he is no longer present, in time or place, to find Cotter tedious; secondly, Cotter *is* tedious, not found to be so by the narrator's subjectivity.

The 1906 version reads "When we knew him first he used to be rather interesting, talking of faints and worms; but I soon grew tired of him and his endless stories about the distillery" (*JJA* 4, 355). This sentence, by shifting pronouns, shows how the boy modernized himself, rendering Old Cotter, his aunt and uncle, obsolete. Further, it strengthens the parallelism of Cotter and Flynn as the boy's rival pedagogues.

Here we see the local dynamics of futile resentment affiliated to cultural modernization. Irony is the technique of modern rivalry, artistic as well as sexual, and a defeated rival is necessary to the ironist's sense of superior being. To be defeated, in turn, is to think of oneself as a vanquished rival, to be exposed as a mere imitator or follower. Joyce will name this ironic hero in 1907 the "loveless Irishman."

The new, comprehensive version of "The Sisters" in 1906 becomes the first story of *Dubliners* in a structural as well as a chronological sense. More than being the first story written, it introduces three narratives of self-defeat and self-hatred before going on, after "Araby," to the hatred of others. We might take up any of the subsequent stories, but perhaps "The Dead" is most important, because it ends the revisions of "The Sisters" and the writing of *Dubliners*. Joyce wrote two further stories during early 1906 before revising "The Sisters" — "A Little Cloud" and "Two Gallants," but put them inside a series which still ended with "Grace." Only "The Dead" could bring the revisions of "The Sisters" to a halt as it completed or capped *Dubliners*.

René Girard is required reading on the subject of modern rivalry; as I have argued elsewhere, his work implies a theory of the modern as well.[17] In the early *Deceit, Desire, and the Novel* (1965),[18] Girard analyses narcissism and coquetry as symptoms of the advances of modern emulation-as-rivalry. In the more advanced (modern) stages of mimetic or triangular desire, the *terzo incommodo* has become unnecessary, in fact outmoded. The coquette increases her self-esteem by inciting, then frustrating her lover's desire, produced by his imitating and unsuccessfully rivalling *her own self-love*. If Gretta seemed to hold herself away, however lightly, from Michael Furey, then he emulated her apparent self-sufficiency with the ultimate narcissism of self-sacrifice, which makes him, in turn, an unattainable model of metaphysical desire, an external mediator without rival. One could only follow him in self-sacrifice, but he would always be first.

But we cannot afford to make a scapegoat of Gretta, by making her the coquette responsible for instigating all this emulation. Like Isabel Archer, she was incapable at the time of resisting the interpretation put upon her by suitors representing an advanced system of disguised emulation which we ourselves still serve. Nor can we afford to completely exonerate her, to divinize her as the single being innocent of mimetic rivalry. We must not deny our identity to her, by exiling her below, or exalting her above our society. If Gretta's letter to Michael

---

[17]   "Myth, Ritual, and Literature After Girard," in *Literary Theory's Future* (Urbana: University of Illinois Press, 1989), p. 118-145; "René Girard and the Boundaries of Modern Literature," *boundary 2*, IX (1981), 277-290.

[18]   Translation of *Mensonge romantique et vérité romanesque* (Paris: Bernard Grasset, 1961).

Furey was written with design, similar in some way to the apparent coyness of Mangan's sister, or the practiced banter of the girl overheard at the Araby bazaar (although we must now, after Gabriel, warn ourselves that resentment perhaps makes our narrator a poor guide to what is on the mind of the women he meets), this woman we see is no coquette. It takes a snob to know one, to know the snobbism in others, as Girard argues, but it takes a revolutionary change of heart to renounce resentment and rivalry unilaterally.

--There were no words, said Gabriel moodily, only she wanted me to go for a trip to the west of Ireland and I said I wouldn't.

His wife clasped her hands excitedly and gave a little jump.

--O, do go, Gabriel, she cried. I'd love to see Galway again.

--You can go if you like, said Gabriel coldly.

She looked at him for a moment, then turned to Mrs. Malins and said:

--There's a nice husband for you, Mrs. Maiins. (*D* 191)

Unlike the narrator, and most readers, Gretta doesn't suspect Molly Ivors, and presents herself without guile as a companion. Gretta Conroy is our sister as well, and we feel, without needing to see, that she nursed Mrs. Conroy through her last illness *unresentful* towards her primary rival for Gabriel's love. Like Christopher Newman, Lona Hessel, and especially Nora Helmer, Gretta has learned how to break the cycle of mimetic rivalry, by refusing to imitate an attempt to incarnate divinity through self-sacrifice, the last modernization of violence-as-the-sacred. It is from models like Gretta that we can learn what the heart is and what it feels.

In short, we need as readers to care more for Gretta's reading of Michael and Gabriel than for the narrator's reading. He is

Gabriel's spiritual brother. She wants Gabriel to live, with her. She is regretful, not proud, that Michael Furey died for her. Gretta is right about her husband: Gabriel *is* generous, although he is crippled by irony and self-hatred. Gretta is greater than Gabriel's ironic reading, the narrator's, or the reader's, in such declarations as "I was great with him at the time" (*D* 220). In the earlier stories of *Dubliners*, narrator and discerning reader mock the ignorance of simple Dubliners to the irony of what their words might be taken for; here, in "The Dead," the skills of a scrupulously mean reading double back on themselves, shaming their practitioners. I cannot agree with critics who suspect Gretta of conceiving with Michael Furey. Gretta Conroy and Nora Barnacle are sisters, Joyce's sisters, incipient signs (but without mitigating the necessary recognition of Joyce's sexism, which resists the fuller development of sorority) of the potential for Virginia Woolf's enlightening *supposition* ("let us suppose...") of imagining the career of a great writer's sister. Virginia Woolf is herself Joyce's twin sister — they are the children of Eighty-Two, modernism's future, but that must be left for another time.

"The Dead" *supposes* the de-modernization of *Dubliners*, in part by a more generous portrayal of sisterhood than Mangan's, in "Araby," in "The Sisters," or in "Clay." There is no clear family bond between the boy and Father Flynn's sisters in the first story. The sisters address the boy's aunt respectfully as "ma'm," and the narrator has no compunction in pointing up their commonness. The narrator's complicity in "The Dead," however, does not make inevitable or unalterable Gabriel's "modern" view that he has been orating to vulgarians, and serving as a pennyboy for his aunts. Gabriel denigrates others whenever he enters the zone of self-hatred. When we read as Gretta reads, we can see that these sisters love their sister's children, especially Gabriel; he is their favorite. We can learn as well to hear Gabriel's love for these aunts underneath his after dinner speech (note also the narrator's love for Parnell, when he quotes Joe Hynes's poem, in "Ivy Day in the Committee Room"), now only partially muffled by the perverse devil of a literary conscience.

The perverse devil of satire which thwarts sympathy, only for it to return in a more sentimental, self-defeating form, like the suicidal narrative of *Madame Bovary*, continues to dominate Gabriel and the narrator. The failure of Gabriel's ironic treatment of Gretta (and himself) is exemplary of all Dubliners. When Gabriel, in his own mind, not Gretta's, fails to supersede the rival he perceives, Michael Furey, he sacrifices himself with his own irony: "better to pass boldly into that other region of superior influence, the dead; better to maintain his precedence by killing himself before that "impalpable and vindictive being" (*D* 220), his sacred model, gets him first. In short, he becomes Michael Furey's disciple, in metaphysical rivalry.

The narrator of *Dubliners* remains, for the most part, a rival-disciple of *The Irish Homestead*. "The Dead" is written "in another sense" than the unfinished "Christmas Eve" (*JJA* 4, 5-11), which was clearly intended to mock the "Celtic Christines" (Joyce's mocking phrase for regular contributors to the annual "Celtic Christmas" issue of *The Irish Homestead;* see *L* II 77). The failure of Gabriel's irony, and Gabriel's self-sacrificial response (to the self-sacrifice of Michael Furey), incites an emulation of self-sacrifice by the narrator so complete that many readers find a single narrator replaced by ghostly mediators who speak through him.

But what does it mean for us to prefer to read as Gretta does, rather than the way Gabriel and the narrator (or narrators) do? When Gretta says of Michael Furey, "I think he died for me" (*D* 220), we hear an echo of the Passion, but surely Gretta must mean that Michael Furey made a terrible mistake that she would never see repeated for her *sake*. This allusion is more properly the responsibility of its author, Michael Furey himself. The narrator, like Gabriel, abandons himself to the glamorous self-destruction of Michael Furey, garnishing the suicide with the imagery of Calvary: crosses, spears, headstones, thorns.

The choice between Gretta's reading and Gabriel's reading, (with which the narrator identifies), of Michael Furey's passion, is the choice between a sacrificial and postsacrificial unanimity of the living and the dead, fundamental to Joyce's analysis of what makes his country eat its young. "The most Catholic country in Europe" (Joyce's phrase) identifies with the Passion in Freud's hostile sense of *Identifizierung* — identification-as-appropriation, rivalry. Ireland mimics, satirizes the Passion by sacrificing itself, and observes communion by eating its own — that is, the Irish identify themselves with precisely the practices of collective violence the Passion exposes.

According to Girard's analysis, periodic human sacrifices in primitive culture are offered to totem, ancestor, the gods, to satisfy their insatiable appetite for blood victims, in the hope they will grant the peace they alone provide. In *Violence and the Sacred* (1977)[19] Girard deconstructs this mythical explanation to expose a cultural mechanism for generating unanimity. Girard argues further that such an analysis is now possible in the modern period because the mechanisms of violent unanimity are themselves deconstructing, revealing their secular dynamic of human violence, but, until his next book, Girard is mostly silent about what force is accelerating this dissolution of sacrificial practice which makes his analysis possible.

Beginning with *Things Hidden Since The Foundation of the World*,[20] Girard proposes the hypothesis that the dominant agent in Western culture for the desymbolization of sacrificial practice, including the violent practices of a sacrificial Christianity, are the Gospels. The Good News undermines, over

---

[19]   Translation of *La violence et le sacré* (Paris: Bernard Grasset, 1972).

[20]   Translated from *Des choses cacheés depuis la fondation du monde* (Paris: Bernard Grasset, 1978).

time, the covertly violent mythology of Christianity, even the sacrificial reading of the Passion itself, by means of the absolute singularity of its innocent victim. Jesus, according to Girard's postsacrificial reading, seized the historical opportunity to push forward the deconstruction of sacrificial unanimity already written into the history of the Hebrews as it developed in the Old Testament, away from neighboring sacrificial cults, towards an apocalyptic moment: the opportunity of unanimous peace without exclusions, the Kingdom of God now at hand. Jesus described the Father of this kingdom as one for whom sacrifice is an abomination, who loves all his children, hairy, smooth, dutiful, prodigal, and asks them to love their enemies, unilaterally if necessary, reconciling each to all through a common brother whose absolute commitment to peace shows him as a Son of God. Jesus does not masochistically seek self-sacrifice, divinity through violence, but he cannot moderate his commitment to the Kingdom of God when that commitment becomes personally dangerous.

The clarity of Jesus's analysis of violent unanimity, such as "let he who is without sin among you cast the first stone," provokes a crisis: the community of accusers is threatened with disintegration. If they are to remain a society, they must either follow his way of positive reciprocity, without any exclusion, or they must expel this threat to the unanimity-minus-one of sacrificial violence. The community chooses negative reciprocity, uniting in opposition to this victim who serves the usual ritual function of enemy twin. The Kingdom of God is delayed, but the crucifixion of an innocent victim introduces a destabilizing element into sacrificial societies that will mark every outcast with the sign of Christ.

It is important not to follow one modern misreading (brilliantly half-stated by Nietzsche), which would masochistically heroize and identify with victims. This sign of Christ represents Jesus's analysis of victimization, not the divine being of the victim. The victims of unanimous violence are not perfectly innocent; rather, their accusers are guilty as well of what they charge. Thus, in 1909, in "Oscar Wilde, il poeta di «Salomè»," Joyce, following Wilde's own argument, calls Wilde a scapegoat, and insists that only those who are themselves guilty know enough to accuse him.[21]

Michael Furey is so potent an influence on Gabriel and the narrator because he sums an all-too-Irish, all-too-susceptible motive to imitate self-immolation. To die for Gretta's sake is to make Gretta guilty for Michael's innocence. Self-sacrifice mimics, satirizes the singularity of Christ's innocence, his Passion, a negative discipleship of rivalry with divinity, a demonic *imitatio Christi*. In *Deceit, Desire, and the Novel* Girard calls this motive deviated transcendency.

What does Gabriel call it? "He had never felt like that himself towards any woman but he knew that such a feeling must be love" (*D* 223). Infinite are the resources of self-hatred: Gabriel knows that love is what he has never felt. All jealous rivals know that they alone are excluded from the true passion that others feel. Michael Furey, Gabriel, and the narrator are what Joyce identified for his Triestine audience on 27 April 1907, a few months before completing "The Dead," as "the loveless Irishmen": "quegli strani spiriti, entusiasti freddi, artisticamente e sessualmente ineducati, pieni di idealismi ed incapaci di aderirvi, spiriti fanciulleschi, infedeli, ingenui e satirici,..." (*Scritti Italiani*, 123). These Irishmen abort their enthusiasm with coldness, they are full of idealism but incapable of sticking to it (*aderire*/adhere), unfaithful, ingenuous, and satirical by turns.[22] This is the same self-defeating pattern Joyce admitted to

---

[21] James Joyce, "Oscar Wilde: Il poeta di «Salomè»," *Il Piccolo della Sera*, 24 marzo 1909; rpt. in *James Joyce. Scritti Italiani*, eds. Gianfranco Corsini e Girgio Melchiori (Milano: Arnoldo Mondadori, 1979), pp. 60-66.

[22] The translation of *scritti italiani* in *CW*, omits "infedeli" (unfaithful) and mistranslates "incapaci di aderirvi" as "unable to yield to it" (p. 173).

Stanislaus in his remorse over *Dubliners*.

Will Gabriel not despise Gretta and himself the next morning, as faithlessly as the "reluctant Indian" that narrates "An Encounter"? The narrator of "The Dead" is already breaking faith with generosity, by the callow, sly phallic humor of "one boot stood upright, its limp upper fallen down: the fellow of it lay upon its side" (*D* 222), and the possibility left open by cautious phrasing (unlike Gretta's forthrightness), that the generousness of Gabriel's tears describes their size more than their quality.

The possibility for choosing Gretta over the testimonies of Michael Furey, Gabriel, and the narrator makes the spiritual liberation of Ireland only a supposition for *Dubliners,* but the rewriting of *Stephen Hero* into *Portrait* calls forth a revolutionary change of heart, which constitutes Joyce's redefinition of modernism as a positive, postsacrificial tradition, adumbrated in "The Dead." The ironic counterpointing of ecstasy and manure in the Agricultural Fair scene in *Madame Bovary* allows only one conclusion. Disciples of modern fiction know they are to read ironically, from the point of view of excrement: to know Emma's desire for a better life is manure is to have the last word of satiric violence on romance. Before such a unanimous judgment, which no one dares to contravene, narrator and reader betray, in both senses of the word, their identity (*c'est moi*) with Emma Bovary, their sister. But the structurally similar juxtaposition of Stephen and his mocking school fellows at the end of Chapter IV, potentially ironic, urges rather a choice for what Tom Paulin has called "Ireland's future" instead of irony, which is no future at all. By refusing to sacrifice himself for Ireland, Stephen chooses, in the same spirit

---

The difference is, of course, that they yield often enough, but can't "stick it." *CW* elsewhere translates *aderire* literally as "adhere": "non aver potuto aderire scrupolosamente" (*SI* 132) is rendered "not having been able to adhere scrupulously..." (*CW* 180).

that Gretta chooses Gabriel's generosity, the "great wish" Ireland, living and dead, has for *all* its children, despite its bafflement by the historically compromised forms in which they must express it: to live, not die for them. Stephen must find, as he has not at the end of 16 June 1904, a companion very like Gretta, in order to be heartened to write a joyful novel like *Portrait*, for the spiritual liberation of his country.

East Lansing

JOYCE'S ANAMORPHIC MIRROR
IN "THE SISTERS"

LAURENT MILESI

In a letter to Grant Richards dated 23 June 1906, Joyce stated rather solemnly the moral vision that he had planned *Dubliners* to reflect:

> I seriously believe that you will retard the course of civilization in Ireland by preventing the Irish people from having one good look at themselves in my nicely polished looking-glass.   *(SL* 90)

Indeed, Joyce's collection of short stories is striking in its imagery. There is a recurrence of mirrors, and also windows and (barred) perspectives, as well as an insistence on gazing. Bearing in mind both the circular structure of the collection and the permutability of the titles of the first and last stories, one need only reread the *incipit* of "The Sisters" and the concluding scene of "The Dead" to appreciate how tightly knit by haunting lexical returns this cluster of motifs is.

John Paul Riquelme, in his stimulating essay, "Joyce's 'The Dead': The Dissolution of the Self and the Police," assumes that literary texts can provide an experience that is analogous to being looked at. He follows a Lacanian lead to argue for Gabriel Conroy's inevitable recognition of his own mortality after his self-representations have been shattered by Gretta's revelation.[1]

---

[1]   John Paul Riquelme, "Joyce's 'The Dead': The Dissolution of the Self and the Police," *Style,* 25 (1991), 504, n. 7. Although his study has different overall concerns and though I became aware of its existence only after the main lines of my argument had been developed, I wish to acknowledge Riquelme's priority in having first seen the relevance of anamorphosis to an allegorical reading of *Dubliners*.

While recalling the angered frustration nourished by several protagonists in previous stories, the figure of Michael Furey, whose name gives an ironic snub to Gabriel's earlier feelings of "rage" and "dull anger" and to "the dull fires of his lust [glowing] angrily" (*D* 217, 218 and 219), is raised from the dead by Gretta's acute anamnesis, and his resurrection from the past triggers the emptying out of the full image that Gabriel had previously glimpsed of himself.[2] Here is how Gabriel Conroy reverses the former perception of his own bespectacled reflection:

> As he passed in the way of the cheval-glass he caught sight of himself in full length, his broad, well-filled shirt-front, the face whose expression always puzzled him when he saw it in a mirror and his glimmering gilt-rimmed eye-glasses.
> (*D* 218)

> He saw himself as a ludicrous figure, acting as a pennyboy for his aunts, a nervous well-meaning sentimentalist, orating to vulgarians and idealizing his own clownish lusts, the pitiable fatuous fellow he had caught a glimpse of in the mirror. (*D* 220)

Riquelme's serviceable précis of Lacanian theories of the mirror stage and the gaze, and the way he brings them to bear on his analysis of the conjunction of the mirror scene with Gabriel Conroy's thoughts about death, must be quoted at some length as they open up possibilities of interpretation which we shall attempt to take further. Riquelme begins:

> At the conclusion of his essay on the mirror stage, Lacan implies that psychoanalysis can bring the patient to realize

[2]   Riquelme, p. 497.

that the self is nothing, that every self-representation is empty because it is always only a representation: that is, a construct rather than something full and present. That realization, which reverses the mirror stage by replacing an apparent fullness with a lack, would seem to involve a return to the prior stage of development, the body in pieces, not yet sufficiently aware of representations of itself to constitute an "I," or unified self. In fact, it is the beginning of a new stage, since the return need not and perhaps cannot be entirely regressive. Instead, it is an adult version of the body in pieces, like Gabriel's premonition of eventual death...

He continues:

At issue in the closing style of "The Dead" is something like the curiously double or multiple form of the anamorph, a figure that, as the word's etymology suggests is always forming anew ... [Joyce's free indirect speech] resembles the anamorph in Hans Hoblein's *The Ambassadors*, which Lacan uses to sketch his concept of the gaze ... The anamorph ... undoes temporarily the effect of the mirror stage by giving us the experience of being looked at and controlled rather than being the viewer that occupies the position of control. That experience is one version of what Lacan calls the gaze. Instead of controlling the vanishing point, we experience vanishing and dissolution in the conceptual space projected by the representation's seeming incoherence ... The radical shift and potential effect are captured in Gabriel's recognition of his connection to the dead....[3]

The anamorphic distortion that Gabriel's self-image undergoes in the allegorical ending of "The Dead" circuitously points back

[3]   Riquelme, pp. 498-500.

to an even more graphic instance in "The Sisters." Although this study will focus mainly on the programmatic opening story of Joyce's collection, it is my conviction that the issues which it implicitly raises about (self-)representation in writing offer a protocol of reading that can be implemented for the other stories. For the sake of progression and clarity in the argument and because such a division respects the internal structure of the story, the reading will be carried out in three stages.

1. The *incipit*

Often praised for its suggestive efficacy, the first paragraph *(D 9)* was one of the most heavily reworked sections of "The Sisters" (see *D* 243-52). The marked iterations and redistribution of its lexical items (including the boy's recollection of what the priest told him on several occasions) highlight the dominant theme of a scopic pulsion which the protagonist repeats with a degree of obsession equal to the perverse enjoyment he seems to be deriving from it. The boy recalls," It filled me with fear, and yet I longed to be nearer to it." The parenthetical precision "(it was vacation time)," under cover of verisimilitude, rather betrays self-justification. In this initial configuration, a young boy gazes upward towards a "lighted square of window" whose reflection holds the symbolic power to indicate whether the priest, unseen and as yet unidentified, is alive or dead. To sum up economically, the boy gazes but does not see (note the conditional in "I would see"). This fascination of an occulted gaze raised towards an unreachable," superior" subject is then inverted, as if by mirror reflection, in the following supper scene, when the boy, soon after evoking dismissively the former identificatory model of Old Cotter and in sharp contrast to the opening, doggedly refuses to raise his eyes to the self-righteous assembly: "I knew that I was under observation." A few lines later, the boy remembers, "I felt that his little black beady eyes were examining me but I would not satisfy him by looking up from my plate" (*D* 10). During the scene Old Cotter pours forth his insinuations and the uncle tries to get across to his nephew his conception of the real *stature* of a masculine subject: "And that's what *stands* to me now," possibly deflated by the offer to Old Cotter to "take a pick of that *leg* of mutton" (*D* 11; my italics). The cheap canon of virility shared by Old Cotter and the uncle does not stand up to the boy's initiation by Father Flynn into the loftier order of religion, with such occult mysteries and duties as the Eucharist and the secrecy of the confessional (here, a surreptitious debunking of the boy's naive admiration creeps into the narrative,[4] in the implied irony that "the fathers of the Church had written books as thick as the *Post Office Directory* and as closely printed as the law notices in the newspaper" [*D* 13]). This initiatory catechism also works as a performative ritual upon the boy by a kind of mimicry or mimesis, as the disturbing smiles of the priest during his instruction haunt the first occurrence of the dream, at the end of which "I felt that I too was smiling feebly" (*D* 11). We shall see later how this mimetic work of compulsive repetition, which extends to all the characters as if by contagion and suggests that the diseased

---

[4] In his book-length study, *Teller and Tale in Joyce's Fiction: Oscillating Perspectives* (Baltimore and London: Johns Hopkins University Press, 1983), Riquelme convincingly makes a case against collapsing the boy and the narrator on the grounds that "[t]hat assumption must overlook both the adult vocabulary and the use of the past perfect as well as the past tense" (p. 98; see also esp. pp. 101 and 103). The logical implication of this position is that whatever maturation process the young boy is shown to undergo must be conceived as a remembering and reenactment in writing *after the fact*. This corollary as well as Riquelme's minute analysis of the deictic expressions and especially the temporal coordinates will stand us in good stead later when we consider the narrative status of the dream.

priest images their inner unacknowledged malaise,[5] constitutes, in Joyce's scrupulously mean writing of an Irish symptomatology, a calculated strategy which contributes to setting the scene for the final "hallucinated vision."

2. The dream

As Lucia Boldrini has shown in her meticulous study of a Dantean intertext[6] in "The Sisters" and "The Dead," the dream episode picks up some of its themes from the first paragraph of "The Sisters." The boy's imagination seems to work in similar ways both at the beginning and in the dream itself, extracting words from their usual contexts and transforming them into beings by new associations (paralysis "sounded to me like the name of some maleficent and sinful being" [D 9]), or, in the

---

[5]   Like the priest, Nannie is "disappointed" (D 15) when at first the boy declines to partake of what is obviously meant as a secular Eucharist of sherry and cream *crackers* (as opposed to *breaking* the holy bread), while her pointing upwards and the "aunt's nodding" (D 14) curiously mimic the boy's gazing up and one of the priest's attitudes during his proselytizing. One may add the quasi-religious "secrecy" of orthodox Old Cotter who detects an element of perversity in the boy's relationship with Father Flynn but does not "confess" it (a reticence which was absent from the first version). Even the room itself, where the corpse is lying, becomes a "dead-room" (D 14), in an unobtrusive case of the rhetorical "transference" called "hypallage." The text seems to exploit perversely such "lexical contagion," as when the expectation for Eliza to ritually "break the silence" (D 17) is mocked by her subsequent mention of the chalice that the priest had broken and which had led to his breakdown.

[6]   "'The Sisters' and the *Inferno*: An Intertextual Network," *Style*, 25 (1991), 453-65. Through intertextual references to Canto 15 of the *Inferno* where Dante meets Brunetto Latini and the sodomites, Boldrini establishes a connection between sodomy and simony in both Joyce and Dante (pp. 457, 461), an interpretation which Jean-Michel Rabaté articulates further in his view that simony is caught between paralysis and sodomy in *James Joyce* (Paris: Hachette, 1993), 31-36.

dream, turning the priest into an object, a face severed from the body, which then becomes a neutral(ized) "it" that the dreamer invests with desire. In this regard, it is interesting to note the narrator never names Father Flynn directly but only refers to him as "he," "the paralytic," "the simoniac" or "the old priest." The dream sequence proper, which is conspicuously missing in the first published version of the story, is made up of two parts *(D* 11, 13-14), both signalled by a repeated allusion to old Cotter whose no doubt orthodox "theory" *(D* 10)[7] seems inextricably linked with the dreamlike vision of the priest. The first fragment, which occurs the night *before* the incredulous boy reads the death notice, appears to be the transcript of a dream in progress since the text skillfully avoids the trap of referring to itself explicitly. In other words, the dreamer cannot utter performatively "I am dreaming" unless it is a figure of speech). But what the reader witnesses here is by necessity an illusion of presentation since the dreamer, in trying to recollect in writing what he saw as a "spectator" of his dream, necessarily doubles as a distanced narrator[8] and the narration can only aim to be a *retrospective* re(-)presentation, despite the retroactive identification of this first scene as a dream in the second extract: "I ... tried to remember what had happened afterwards in the dream." In Samuel Weber's words," [t]he dream only comes-to-be *after the fact*, as it were, in the process of its repetition, recounting, and retelling,"[9] and its specificity, including as a writer's afterthought, lies in providing a specular

---

[7] Let us remember that the Greek words *theoria* and *theoros* called up "vision," "contemplation" or "speculation" but also referred to the consultation of divine oracles, the attendance of religious festivals or the observance of God's will *(theo-oros)*; see *Dictionnaire historique de la langue française* II, dir. Alain Rey (Paris: Le Robert, 1992), p. 2115.

[8] Cf. Samuel Weber, "It," *Glyph,* 4 (1978), p. 23.

[9] Weber, pp. 24-25.

representation of the conditions which preside over the story's narration (see note 3 *supra*). That the dream is intrinsically recollection, distortion and interpretation, already contaminating the event of its production and turning it into a re(-)production,[10] is sanctioned here by a blurring of temporal logic in the two sequences; the pluperfect in which the remembering process (second passage) refers back to the earlier event ("I remembered that I had noticed long velvet curtains.... I felt that I had been very far away...") is undermined as soon as one remembers that the earlier passage (had) featured one such instance, precisely introduced by an act of remembering *within* a dislocated "dream" which, since the boy both knows that the priest is deceased and yet has not seen written proof of it with his own eyes, oscillates between retrospection and anticipation. Its blurred temporality stands within an act of narration-as-remembering *(D* 11: "But *then* I remembered that it had died of paralysis"; my italics) reminds us that the dream has "no clearly defined beginning, middle, and end"[11] and creates the possibility of its congruence with other parts of the story. This lack of awareness in what the subject experiences manifests itself also in another "touch" of verisimilitude (the rendering of unclear vision in a dream), when the priest is reduced synecdochically to his "grey face" *(D* 11), then to the pronoun "it." This figural and linguistic disembodiment — what Freud would call the "dreamwork" — is performed on the already dead priest. The dreamer "remembers" his demise, and

---

[10] Cf. Freud's famous passage in *The Interpretation of Dreams*: "It is true that we distort dreams in attempting to reproduce them [...]. But this distortion is itself no more than a part of the revision to which the dream-thoughts are regularly subjected as a result of the dream-censorship," *The Standard Edition of the Complete Psychological Works of Sigmund Freud*, gen. ed. James Strachey, (London: Hogarth Press, 1958), V, p. 514.

[11] Weber, p. 24.

hardly disguises a wish to divest the cleric of his symbolic function as father. "The Sisters" remains strangely silent about, indeed never seems to remember, the boy's biological parents and one might argue that this curious omission holds the key to the boy's unconscious desire to repeat the death of this substitute father whom he never names as such.[12] The boy's need to wrench himself from his mentor's psychological hold is shown in a statement like," I felt even annoyed at discovering in myself a sensation of freedom as if I had been freed from something by his death"(*D* 12).[13] Such an acknowledgement would thus be the second dismissal of a father figure, perhaps more uncannily similar to the first one than old Cotter himself would have liked to admit,[14] if this ritual dismantling of sorts did not somehow

[12] See the connections between repression, the impossibility to remember and repetition as acting out in Freud's 1914 paper "Remembering, Repeating and Working Through." The "*altruicidal*" nature of the wishes that give rise to the dream is discussed in Mikkel Borch-Jacobsen, *The Freudian Subject*, trans. Catherine Porter. Foreword by François Roustang (Stanford: Stanford University Press, 1988), p. 20.

[13] That the boy cannot feel in mourning is perversely emphasized by the text's teasing juxtaposition of evening and mou*r*ning, its insistence on that "(yo)**u**" (in) which the alienated subject cannot be.

[14] After all, old Cotter and Father Flynn are both "distillers" of spirits, even if, as Donald T. Torchiana suggests ("The Openings of *Dubliners*: A Reconsideration," *Irish University Review* 1 [1971], 155), the priest's inculcation is a more refined, alchemical process. To understand how old Cotter's untold opinion of the priest's "uncanny" (*D* 10) behavior constitutes an enunciative symptom of the repression of an undesirable self-image, one must reread Freud's analysis and definition of "The Uncanny" (see esp. Freud's account of his failure to recognize his specular double; *The Standard Edition of the Complete Psychological Works of Sigmund Freud*, gen. ed. James Strachey, XVII [London: Hogarth Press, 1958], p. 248, n. 1). The essay's emphasis on "a doubling, dividing and
interchanging of the self" and "the constant recurrence of the same thing" (p. 234) encourages such an approach to the language of "The Sisters," with its

remain caught in the mirage of imaginary desires. Regardless of whatever effects the necessities of textual representation would have otherwise on the status of the scene, which hesitates between dreaming, waking and sleeping (the first extract is prefaced by "It was late when I fell asleep" but pictures the boy drawing the blankets over his head and making a seemingly conscious attempt at directing his thoughts),[15] one may question how much wishful thinking or how much fulfillment of the priest's "wish" (D 10; the uncle's word) for the boy goes into this dream of another's desire, introduced by "I imagined that I saw again" (D 11). One may equally read the persistence of the boy's perverse longing in "I felt my soul receding into some pleasant and vicious region" (ibid.), patterned on the syntax and carrying the context of the last sentence of the first paragraph, which is revised by daytime interpretation into the evocation of a faraway land with strange customs.[16] However well-founded a premonition this expression of a reversal (and perverse enjoyment of a ritual transmission) will be revealed to have been by the end of the story, it is also symptomatic of the blindness of the spectator-narrator-dreamer, who fails to see that, if one adheres to Freud's view that the dream always fulfills the desire or "wish" (Wunsch) of the other (or rather, for Lacan, the

---

haunting returns of "strange(ly)" and "uneasy," etc.

[15]   Even if one presupposes as settled the relation between the boy and the narrator (of himself as a boy), the question of narrative or authorial agency in this scene remains a vexing one, about whose internal complexities and contradictions there is unfortunately no space here to unravel in greater detail.

[16]   See Freud's remarks on the kinship between secondary revision in dreams and waking thought (The Interpretation of Dreams, especially p. 490).

Other[17]), this imagined understanding of the priest's eagerness to confess is inconceivable without the boy's own desire to understand it as such. One may read the boy's desire to take on the function of his mentor — the transference of the priest's smile to the boy noted above can now be seen as an oblique self-representation — as exhibiting the constraints within which the subject's status has been defined at the mirror stage, when the *statu(r)e* of the specular image is perceived by the child as an ideal narcissistic identification.[18] In the circuitous route that links desire and understanding in Freud's conception of the dream, the dream is a process that we "can never entirely *comprehend;* and yet which at the same time we cannot but *apprehend*,"[19] an overlap which adequately describes the

---

[17]   This, says Freud in *The Interpretation of Dreams*, is the real meaning behind the seemingly innocuous "I wouldn't dream of such a thing" (p. 67). Eveline's gaze at "those familiar objects from which she had never dreamed of being divided" *(D* 37), or the tell-tale double negation in "It was hard work - a hard life - but now that she was about to leave it she did not find it a wholly undesirable life" *(D* 38), may be read as similar outcroppings in the act of enunciation of a repressed, unconscious desire soon to be implemented.

[18]   In the words of Borch-Jacobsen, to whom I am indebted for his illuminating connections between the image, or the subject's representation (Freud's *Vorstellung*) of its own being, and statu(r)e in Lacan, the image is "'superior' (the prestige of standing erect, of the human 'statue' to which the infant *raises* its eyes)" (*Lacan: The Absolute Master*, trans. Douglas Brick [Stanford: Stanford University Press, 1991] p. 62). The following passage from Lacan's paper "Some Reflections on the Ego" is also worth reproducing: "The stability of the standing posture, the prestige of stature, the impressiveness of statues set the style for the identification in which the ego finds its starting-point and leave their imprint in it forever" (quoted in Borch-Jacobsen, p. 60). For Lacan's play on status (or state) and statue, see Jacques Lacan, *Écrits: A Selection*, trans. Alan Sheridan (London: Tavistock, 1977), p. 43.

[19]   Weber, p. 23.

centrality of the dream in the development of the young boy, if, like Weber, we consider that the ego "constitutes itself in and as the reactive movement of apprehension, suspended between recollection and anticipation."[20] For Lacan, the "in-sight" of the dream is that "*ça montre,*"[21] although the subject cannot see (himself). Unlike the supper scene in which the boy's "mastery" resides in seeing that he is the object of the others' gaze and in being able to adjust his visual stance accordingly - in short, he realizes the dichotomy of the eye and the gaze by which "things look at me, and yet I see them"[22] — the dream reveals as well as tries to hide from the subject (depending on which "point of view" precisely) the impossibility of "seeing oneself seeing" in the face of the other, which Borch-Jacobsen has connected with the work of blind mimetic identification.[23] Like the boy, but hopefully more critically than what his entrapped gaze of himself can achieve in the situation, the reader must try to piece together, re-collect or re-member the fragments of this *puzzle*, and by highlighting mismatched overlaps in the two part dream and how Joyce redistributes textual elements, it is possible to

[20]   Weber, p. 22.

[21]   *Le Séminaire de Jacques Lacan: Livre XI: Les quatre concepts fondamentaux de la psychanalyse*. Texte établi par Jacques-Alain Miller. Paris: Seuil, 1973, p. 72.

[22]   *The Four Fundamental Concepts of Psycho-Analysis*, ed. Jacques-Alain Miller, trans. Alan Sheridan (Harmondsworth: Penguin, 1977), p. 109.

[23]   Borch-Jacobsen's interesting interpretation of desire and identification as mimesis of the desire of the other is developed in a chapter called "Dreams Are Completely Egoistic" (*The Freudian Subject*, trans. Catherine Porter. Foreword by François Roustang. Stanford: Stanford University Press, 1988), pp. 10-52. On p. 42 he works through the different regimens of reflection in the dream and its interpretation according to Freud's theory, which may be implicitly contrasted with Lacan's views.

uncover the unstable narrative status of the episode. We shall see how such kaleidoscopic combinations and disjunctions, which prefigure in a nutshell the portmanteau technique of Joyce's night or dream book, are at work in the rearrangements of the final tableau and how the rewriting that the dream inevitably undergoes as a "traumscrapt" (*FW* 623). In that passage, scraps of a dream are trans-scribed, and translated on to the screen of the white page whose textuality prevents access to it, and, will become a dimension of the closing scene.[24] But before we move on to the concluding epiphany of the story, it is necessary to turn back (or move forward) to the end of "The Dead," when, after Gretta has finally fallen asleep, exhausted by the sorrowful evocation of her tragic romance, Gabriel is left brooding over the unexpected revelation. His eyes catch sight of one deserted boot which "stood upright, its limp upper fallen down" (*D* 222), and he then reflects on the mortality of his two aged aunts. The imagined scene of one of the two sisters' mourning cannot fail to take us back to the dead-room in "The Sisters," and soon after in the partial darkness he imagined he saw the form of a young man standing under a dripping tree. Other forms were near. His soul had approached that region where dwell the vast hosts of the dead. He was conscious of, but could not apprehend, their wayward and flickering existence. His own identity was fading out into a grey impalpable world... (*D* 223).

Gabriel's reverie in the near darkness may be read as a rewriting of the boy's dream vision of the dead priest in "The

___

[24]   This will become the central strategy in *Finnegans Wake*, where the "dream" is indissociable from the interpretations that the text already gives of it(self); or, in the words of Philippe Sollers: "Joyce dreams of a book that will be inseparably dream and interpretation, ceaseless crossing of boundaries - precisely a *waking*" in "Joyce & Co," *In the Wake of the "Wake*," eds. David Hayman and Elliott Anderson (Madison: University of Wisconsin Press, 1978), pp. 107-08.

Sisters." The phrase "he imagined he saw," is repeated; both stories mention a mysterious "region," which Gabriel's soul approaches and into which the boy's soul had receded. Both texts combine "grey" and "impalpable." In "The Sisters" "there is the insistent grey face of the priest and an echo of "some impalpable and vindictive being"*(D* 220), itself a rearrangement, detectable in the similarity of the syntactical structure, of "some maleficent and sinful being" and "some pleasant and vicious region" in "The Sisters."[25] If Gabriel's lack of apprehension may prolong his earlier puzzlement at his first full-length reflection *(D* 218) and takes us back to a similar frame of mind in the boy before the dream *(D* 11: "I puzzled my head"), his "vague terror" *(D* 220) equally echoes the boy's initial "fear" *(D* 9) and, within a circular conception of the collection, justifies Rabaté's interpretation of his refusal of the porter's candle as an unconscious fear "that their tête-à-tête would look like a mortuary vigil, a wake, watched from the outside by some unknown and wistful youth"[26] who would know the symbolic value of "the reflection of candles on the darkened blind" *(D* 9). The *dédoublement* of his self-reflection, which had doubly imaged his division, is succeeded by his evanescent "fading" or *aphanisis*. Gabriel's daydreaming by night raises Michael Furey from the dead in an epiphanic vision which promises a final atonement between the living and the dead; it also savagely punctures the vanity of the self-gratifying "picture" of Gretta absorbed in listening to the painful song from her past which had deceptively fanned his passion as he was gazing up at her: "what is a woman *standing* on the stairs in the shadow, listening to distant music, a symbol of?" *(D* 210; my italics).

[25] Cf. Boldrini, pp. 458, 461-62.

[26] Jean-Michel Rabaté, "Silence in *Dubliners*," in *James Joyce: New Perspectives*, ed. Colin MacCabe (Bloomington: Indiana University Press, 1982), p. 66.

3. The final tableau

In the course of his analysis of the gaze for his eleventh seminar, Lacan considers the significance of the anamorphic vision that awaits the puzzled and unsuspecting admirer of Holbein's *The Ambassadors* as he moves away to the left and, turning back to look down one last time, now sees the flattened, oblong figure that floated cryptically at the feet of the dignitaries erected or "rectified" into a skull, the *vanitas* of a death's head which all the while had been looking at him, reflecting an image of his own nothingness which he could not see face to face.[27] Later on, Lacan points out that Holbein's picture instances the condition of any painting: a trap for the gaze (p. 89) but also an invitation to "lay down our gaze" in the act of looking (p. 101), and one might equally argue that by calculating the place of the reader's inscription in his text, thus inviting him to look for interpretive clues, Joyce's strategies of writing similarly overpower our gaze and entrap us in his crafty designs so as to ensure our participation.

A literary transposition of the optical process of the anamorphosis can be seen to be at work near the end of "The Sisters" when, after the perfunctory civilities have been exchanged by the boy's aunt with the two elderly women, the conversation focuses on the last painful moments in the priest's disappointed life. Here is the enigmatic finale to which the text leads:

They looked high up and low down; and still they couldn't see

---

[27] *Four Fundamental Concepts*, pp. 85-89, and 92. Lacan also recalls the parallel developments of the science of perspective and the formation of the Cartesian subject as a geometrical point (p. 86), a connection which he probably first found in Jurgis Baltrusaitis, *Anamorphoses ou magie artificielle des effets merveilleux*. (Paris: Olivier Perrin, 1969), pp. 61-70. This book is dutifully acknowledged in the seminar (p. 85).

a sight of him anywhere.... So then they got the keys and opened the chapel and the clerk and Father O'Rourke and another priest that was there brought in a light for to look for him.... And what do you think but there he was, sitting up by himself in the dark in his confession-box, wide-awake and laughing-like softly to himself ?

She stopped suddenly as if to listen. I too listened; but there was no sound in the house: and I knew that the old priest was lying still in his coffin as we had seen him, solemn and truculent in death, an idle chalice on his breast.

Eliza resumed:

- Wide-awake and laughing-like to himself.... So then, of course, when they saw that, that made them think that there was something gone wrong with him....   (D 18)

What light shall we throw on this tableau if neither the torch which revealed the spectacle of madness to the benighted searchers, nor the symbolic reflection of the candles which the boy vainly tried to scrutinize, seems to be adequate for the task? The reader needs to detect the subtle nuances that attend this "wake" such as the almost hallucinated sensation of the priest's on-going laughter to appreciate this anamorphic vision fully. The vision operates in the disjunction between Eliza's insistence ("Eliza resumed") and the boy's persistence in stressing that the priest was lying in his coffin ("and I knew" echoes his symbolic knowledge at the beginning), one needs to detect the subtle nuances that attend this "wake," such as the almost hallucinated sensation that the priest's laughter may still be listened to, which has also been scrupulously prepared for by the narration's transit through various kinds of transformation seen above and through migrating   signifiers   which   one   might   call   "lexical anamorphoses,"[28] but also by the boy's earlier reminiscences and fancies (the second excerpt gives a more phantasmatic construction to Lacan's proposition that "the relation between the gaze and what one wishes to see involves a lure"[29]):

Had he not been dead I would have gone into the little dark room behind the shop to find him sitting in his arm-chair by the fire ... *(D* 12)

The fancy came to me that the old priest was smiling as he lay there in his coffin.
But no. When we rose and went up to the head of the bed I saw that he was not smiling. There he lay, solemn and copious, vested as for the altar, his large hands loosely retaining a chalice.   *(D* 14)

[28]   Thus the "box" metamorphoses from "box his corner" *(D* 11), of pugilistic origin but also co-opting the geometrical context defined by the "gnomon," to the confession-box, then to the coffin ("box" in slang; see Florence L. Walzl, "Joyce's 'The Sisters:' A Development," *JJQ*, 10 (1973), 400); "faints" (*ibid.*), a term for *impure* spirits in the distilling trade and associated with Old Cotter, are transcended by Father Flynn's spiritual essence before his *pneuma* or spiritual breath is debased by Eliza's parapraxis into a dying *rheuma*tic breath *(D* 17). Another possible instance of this intricate version of the punning technique, which operates in the interstices between literality and symbolicity or figurality, might be found at the junction of *si*mony and paralysis in "*s*yphilis," known at the turn of the century as the general paralysis of the insane; see Burton A.Waisbren and Florence L. Walzl, "Paresis and the Priest: James Joyce's Symbolic Use of Syphilis in 'The Sisters,'" *Annals of Internal Medicine*, 80 (1974), 8-62, for the suggestion that Father Flynn had central nervous system syphilis, now described as "paresis" but known then as GPI. Baltrusaitis points out (p. 70) that the deceptive mechanism of optical perspective has been linked with the way in which our senses are deceived in the mystery of Transubstantiation or in representations of Christ's transfiguration, an illusion which is thematically foregrounded in the mock communion of "The Sisters."

[29]   *Four Fundamental Concepts*, p. 104; see also p. 103.

The final "double vision" of the priest, raised from a "lying" to a "sitting" posture, also reworks Father Flynn's haunting smile, first transferentially "caught" by the narrator but now restored to the paralytic in the guise of an even more embarrassing laughter.[30] Although the delicate textual shifts could lend themselves to several conflicting but equally productive interpretations which would have to take into account the narrator's almost invisible *framing* of Eliza's account, Florence Walzl's comment is the most useful key for unlocking the asymmetry of the positions of the characters at the end of the story. She writes that, unlike the boy or Gabriel Conroy at the end," [t]he sisters cannot face the image in the 'nicely polished looking-glass' ... Joyce holds up."[31] For all those to whom the boy's initially occulted vision has been passed on as a blinding ("They looked high up and low down; and still they couldn't see a sight of him anywhere"), the priest's sitting works as an anamorphic erection insofar as it confronts them with the vanity and vacuity[32] of (religion in) their own lives which gazes at them/they gaze at but which they do not wish to see.[33] They are, as Lacan would say, (in)·the picture, framed by the boy's (adult) narration and mimicking the priest's mental confusion by their

[30]   See Walzl, p. 416.

[31]   Walzl, p. 417.

[32]   It would require a whole study to detail how, in this story "full" of silences and "unfinished sentences" (*D* 11), death and paralysis disseminate their many-faceted avatars and, right from the opening negation ("There was no hope"), infiltrate the very mechanics of speech and contaminate the characters' physical environment. Let us note for example the circular chain linking the priest's "idle" words with his "idle" chalice, broken when "it contained nothing" (*D*, 9, 18, 17), the emphasis of the gaze on the "empty fireplace" or "empty grate" (*D*, 15, 17), or the gnomon as the figure of "the lack of an expected lack" (Rabaté, "Silence in *Dubliners*," p. 52).

[33]   *Four Fundamental Concepts*, p. 103.

very bewilderment,[34] and, not merely by virtue of the interchangeability of the titles of Joyce's first and last stories noted earlier, *they* are the dead, as much as the uncomprehending sisters are.[35] On the contrary, the boy has already had his gnomonic vision[36] and been subjected to a corrective pedagogy since the priest's death loosened the hold of the illusory father he had constructed for himself. No need, therefore, to "bring home" the inaugural upward gaze in an enlightening vision, and this is how I choose to interpret the boy's stubborn and methodic reassertion ("I too listened; but there was no sound in the house: and I knew that the old priest was lying still in his coffin..."), missing in the first published version, of the priest's death by which the surrogate Father is

[34]   See *Four Fundamental Concepts*, pp. 96, 98-99, 106.

[35]   The imaginary relation according to Lacan bears some resemblance to the anamorphic *vanitas*. In the words of Borch-Jacobsen, who adduces examples from the first seminar and the *Écrits*, the specular image "presents to man his own unpresentable death, in the sense of his seeing himself in it as he will never see himself" (*Lacan*, p. 93).

[36]   The cut-out corner in the gnomon can be seen as a figural equivalent of the scotoma (from Greek *skotos*: darkness), that (partly) blind area in the field of vision, round in shape and grey or black in color which Lacan worked into his theorization of the gaze and which is here uncannily conjured up by the persecuting "grey face" of the priest (*D* 11; also 14: "His face was [...] *grey* and massive, with *black* cavernous nostrils and *circled* by a scanty white fur;" my emphases). In psychology and psychoanalysis, scotomization refers to the blotting out of an external reality which the subject does not want to see and on which, however, he projects desires. For Lacan, the gaze, like the voice, is to be added to the list of part objects (*objets a*) which, as in the mirror stage, the body casts forth from itself and through which the subject may apprehend himself in his division. For Lacan's remarks on "scotoma" and "scotomization," see *Four Fundamental Concepts*, pp. 83-84, and see Borch-Jacobsen, *Lacan*, p. 231, on the subject's being capable of engendering himself only on condition of separating himself from part objects.

finally laid to rest and denied the momentary resurrection afforded by the sisters' uncanny evocation. For the boy, the presumed orthodoxy of the priest's teachings has already given way to the "ortho-paedic" acknowledgement of the vanity of religion's trappings and human existence in the face of decrepitude and death, and in this "rectification" rather than the rectitudinous sermonizing of his entourage lies the possibility of his true "optical erection," the task that, for Lacan, psychoanalysis as "orthodramatisation de la subjectivité du sujet"[37] must equally assign itself. Within the economical confines of a short story, the boy has discovered the illusoriness of the search for a symbolic father, a quest which *Ulysses* will dramatize to much greater lengths.

Joyce's "nicely polished looking-glass" offers the writer's fellow citizens such an analytic opportunity to cross anew the mirror stage, where the subject experiences its radical alterity by way of the gaze, in order to realize the emptiness of imaginary desires and narcissistic identifications, and some of the short stories culminate with such a siiencing vision of horror, the epiphanic moment when the subject's nullity is apocalyptically revealed to him/her, thereby opening up a gap between his/her desire and what s/he actually is. This point of dissolution or aphanisis to which the subject is reluctantly brought can only be conceived in such a fugitive, self-abolishing trance,[38] in the silent performative recesses of the text or in the blank on which it closes, as in the curt final paragraph of "Araby" (the last of the three stories of childhood), which loops back to the boy's

---

[37]   Lacan, *Écrits*, p. 226.

[38]   If one follows Rabaté, for whom the epiphany "est elle-même une reconnaissance de la disparition plus que de la manifestation du sens dans l'expérience esthétique" (*James Joyce*, p. 14), and who sees the advent of such an aesthetics of the epiphany's disappearance with Joyce's reworking of *Stephen Hero* into *A Portrait*.

repeated, apprehensive gazing up at the window in the opening of "The Sisters": "*Gazing up* into the *darkness* I *saw myself* as a creature driven and derided by *vanity*; and my eyes burned with *anguish* and anger" *(D* 35; my italics). However, when the attempt to face oneself is too painful, perhaps only a sidelong glance at the mirror, like Gabriel's at the end of "The Dead," can be envisaged as an encouraging first step in this long journey towards the subject's psychological "redress." *Ulysses* will underscore how this optical side-stepping still obliquely reflects a priestly "paralysis," when Bloom, after seeing "POST NO BILLS" distorted into "POST 110 PILLS," muses on "parallax":

> Mr Bloom moved forward, raising his troubled eyes. ... Timeball on the ballastoffice is down.... Fascinating little book that is of sir Robert Ball's. Parallax. I never exactly understood. There's a priest. Could ask him. Par it's Greek: parallel, parallax. Met him pike hoses she called it till I told her about the transmigration. O rocks!
>
> Mr Bloom smiled O rocks at the two windows of the ballastoffice. She's right after all. Only big words for ordinary things on account of the sound. (*U* 8: 108-115)

As Bloom hesitantly parses the Greek "Polysyllabax" (*U* 15: 2335), the text weaves a "parallel" with the boy's fascination for the "sound" of paralysis *(D* 9). Its involuted punning is itself parallactic or anamorphic, as it projects themes and lexical motifs from an original context — Molly's exclamation "O, rocks!" *(U* 4:343) which punctuates her bafflement at metempsychosis (itself transmigrating into "Met him pike hoses"), and perhaps some elements from "The Sisters," like the smile, the raised eyes or the boy's perplexity — onto a different but intersecting plane where their meanings are deflected and redeployed ("Timeball" and "sir Robert Ball").

Joyce's text vacillates between the premonition of a possible escape from delusive identifications and the performative impossibility of presenting this choice, for his characters remain mired in a circular structure, full of iterative dead ends. If it wants to reach its effect, the epiphanic writing must "condemn" itself to a silent gesture of monstration, like Corley's epiphanic exhibition of the small gold coin on which the end of "Two Gallants" is suspended.[39] Its gaps, overlaps, repetitions, occulted vistas and imaginary visions call for an articulation as well as, at the same time, frustrate it," bear out yet partly mock these theories,"[40] as they expose the lures of (self-)representations that invite, trap, seduce and lead astray the (critical) eye. Riquelme's contention that literary texts can provide an experience that is analogous to being looked at may be reread in the Lacanian light seen above as "*what I look at is never what I wish to see,*"[41] and it is this gaping disjunction, in all its parallactic instability, which can arguably be seen as the "ultimate" problematic of *Dubliners,*[42] from the first person of its childhood stories to an "other" third person narration, provided that, as reader-critics, we avoid the stultifying effects of an unchanging point of view and learn to resist our blind, uncalculated desire to see in a text what we are looking for rather than what is looking at us or concerns us (to recycle Lacan's French pun on *regarder*).

[39] This strategy of reticence might also explain Joyce's lack of answer to Roberts's "narrow" questions concerning sodomy, simony and the reasons for the priest's suspension in "The Sisters;" see *L* II, 305-06 (letter to Stanislaus Joyce, dated 20 August 1912).

[40] Torchiana, p. 149.

[41] Cf. *Four Fundamental Concepts*, p. 103.

[42] Or, again in the words of Rabaté, *Dubliners* "constantly hesitates between the status of a cure, a diagnosis, and that of a symptom, produced by the same causes it attempts to heal" ("Silence in *Dubliners*," p. 47).

Insofar as it comes full circle, *Dubliners* is a reflective text, working like the surface of a mirror which returns light to its point of origin, but insofar as its writing inscribes us in a hermeneutic process which we share with its actors, its texture does not so much reflect as, like the tain of the mirror, enable and encourage reflection.

"EVELINE" AND/AS "A PAINFUL CASE": PARALYSIS, DESIRE, SIGNIFIERS

WOLFGANG WICHT

Readings of *Dubliners* have stressed the motif of paralysis, and with good reason. Joyce himself explained, in a letter to Grant Richards of 5 May 1906, that he had chosen "Dublin for the scene because that city seemed to me the centre of paralysis" (*SL* 83).[1] He also privileged the word paralysis by placing it at the beginning of the first story, "The Sisters."[2] Postwar criticism, with its tendency to see an aesthetic object as a special form of ontological argument, has developed Joyce's metaphoric notion into a symbolic one, and to a lesser degree psychological, autobiographical, and epiphanic, interpretations have emerged. In an exemplary way, Florence Walzl, one of the influential earlier critics of *Dubliners*, points out: "Analyses of the individual stories have shown that the paralysis motif tends to be developed by a number or related images, all variations on a basic death-life symbolism. They are stasis versus action, darkness versus light, cold versus warmth, and blindness versus perception."[3] Twenty years later, Torchiana still amends and modifies the older paradigm: "The timelessness of Irish paralysis reinforces what I might call mythic, religious and

---

[1] See also Joyce's letter to Constance Curran, July 1904 (*SL* 22).

[2] In the unpublished essay "A Portrait of the Artist," Joyce had characterized the state of things as "the general paralysis of an insane society;" cf. Hans Walter Gabler, ed. *A Portrait of the Artist as a Young Man: a Facsimile of Epiphanies, Notes, Manuscripts and Typescripts* (New York: Garland, 1978), 84-85. The phrase recurs in *Ulysses* 1:128-129.

[3] Florence Walzl, "Gabriel and Michael: The Conclusion of 'The Dead'," *JJQ*, 8 (1966), 18.

legendary patterns that Joyce seems to place so frequently at the very center of each story or picture."[4] Symbolic or ideational criticism has greatly illuminated the individual stories and the collection as a whole. At the same time, it has given *paralysis* a kind of metaphysical identity, bringing criticism itself to a moment of stasis. It has, on the whole, occluded what, in Margot Norris's words, might be called the artistic text's "'back answers' or protests"[5] which constitute the *politics* of Joyce's aesthetics.

The dominance of symbolic interpretations has been subverted by the political and theoretical paradigm shift in Joyce criticism based on poststructuralist, feminist, and Lacanian psychoanalytical theories. Jennifer Levine has pointed out, "two images of Joyce" have come "face to face in public"[6] since the seventies. As Norris, Williams, Leonard, Herring, Henke, or — very early — McCormack[7] have shown from different

---

[4] Donald T. Torchiana, *Backgrounds for Joyce's "Dubliners"* (Boston: Allen & Unwin, 1986), p. 9. See also the surveys of secondary literature in Craig Hansen Werner, *Dubliners: A Pluralistic World* (Boston: Twayne, 1988), pp. 14-23; Warren Beck, *Joyce's "Dubliners": Substance, Vision and Art* (Durham, N.C.: Duke University Press, 1969).

[5] Margot Norris, "Stifled Back Answers: The Gender Politics of Art in Joyce's 'The Dead'," *MFS*, 35 (1989), 502.

[6] Jennifer Levine, "Rejoycings in *Tel Quel*," in *JJQ*, 16 (1978/1979), 17. - Evidence of the change is given by the special theme of this issue of *JJQ* as "Structuralist/Reader Response Issue."

[7] Gary M. Leonard, "The Question and the Quest: The Story of Mangan's Sister," in *MFS*, 35 (1989), 459-477; Trevor L. Williams, "Resistance to Paralysis in *Dubliners*, in *MFS*, 35 (1989), 437-457; Philip F. Herring, *Joyce's Uncertainty Principle* (Princeton University Press, 1987); Suzette A. Henke, *James Joyce and the Politics of Desire* (New York and London: Routledge, 1990); William J. McCormack, "James Joyce's 'Eveline' and a Problem in Modernism," in Dorothea Siegmund-Schultze, ed. *Irland: Gesellschaft und Kultur III* (Halle: Martin-Luther-Universität: Wiss. Beiträge

theoretical points of departure, the state of paralysis is not confined to its representational and symbolic quality but must be taken as a moment of artistic presentation that immediately sets free aspects of the Other (dreams, visions, desires), and is to be related to the politics of gender and to processes of deconstruction and to the *différance* of meaning, which the Joycean texts perform.

The present essay will follow the latter critical direction and argue that the juxtaposition of paralysis and desire/dream/vision is an important aspect of signification in several, if not in most, of the stories. "Eveline" and "A Painful Case" appear to be exemplary cases; for this reason, they have been chosen as the objects of my investigation. Compared to *Ulysses*, where the dimension of visions, prospective and retrospective utopias, Bloomusalems, Pisgah sights, Mosaic promises, and religious redemption becomes strategically important, the importance of this Other *seems* to be less conspicuous in *Dubliners*. However, the various antitheses to paralysis and the susceptibility of paralysis to being interpreted metaphorically create textual openness and deferences of meaning in the stories, which negate the illusory closure, the narrator's pretended omniscience, and the privileged discourse in realistic and naturalistic fiction.

"Eveline" and "A Painful Case" also reveal, in a paradigmatic way, that the apparently mimetic representation of social, and individual, paralysis, which on the surface level replicates what it criticizes, is sabotaged by strategically ordered signifiers, or tropes, which are marked by semantic polyvalency and disrupt the linearity of the narration, and of reading. Lia Guerra has aptly spoken of "a special case of fragmentation," which she defines as "a break in semantic continuity involving the paradigmatic level only, since the linear structure is broken only in an embryonic way... The reader is suddenly faced with single

1982/8, 1982), pp. 252-264.

words or clusters of words or even descriptions that a linear reading takes as being empty or devoid of consequentiality."[8] This is an important extension of MacCabe's observation that, in Joyce, "interpretation is perpetually deferred as each segment of meaning is defined by what follows."[9] In the texts, signifiers occur whose meaning is not only redefined by the narrative flux but also by extradiegetic semantic possibilities, i.e. by segments of meaning which cannot be explained by narrative continuity. Thus, any homogeneity of meaning is disseminated. Strategic words of this kind, which vertically cut the horizontal story-telling, shall be named *vertical signifiers*. They can be compared to those textual marks that Derrida called "*by analogy* (I emphasize this) undecidables, i.e. simulative units, 'false' verbal, nominal or semantic properties."[10] The deconstructive function of these floating signifiers defines the representation of the paralytic state *in* fiction *as* fiction. Paralysis appears as a reality *and* a deceit. It is a moment of social practice and equally an aspect of desire, subjective self-legitimation, and ideological containment. The undoing of the representational "lie" of paralysis allows the formation of meaning which is not any longer aligned with what is represented. "Paralysis" itself is a vertical signifier. Its referential indeterminacy is illuminated by

---

[8]   Lia Guerra, "Fragmentation in *Dubliners* and the Reader's Epiphany," in Rosa Maria Bosinelli, Paola Pugliatti, and Romana Zacchi, eds. *Myriadminded Man: Jottings on Joyce* (Bologna: CLUEB, 1986), pp. 42-43.

[9]   Colin MacCabe, *James Joyce and the Revolution of the Word* (London and Basingstoke: Macmillan, 1978), p. 15. Jean-Michel Rabaté has investigated some striking "ambiguous signifiers" in his fine essay "Silence in Dubliners," in Colin MacCabe, Shoshona Feldman, eds. *James Joyce: New Perspectives*, (Bloomington: Indiana University Press, 1982), pp. 52-64.

[10]   Jacques Derrida, "Interview: Positions," conducted by J.-L Houdenine and Guy Scarpetta, first part, in *diacritics*, 2 (1972), 36.

the exegetic range of secondary literature which runs the gamut from socially representational assumptions to daring or foolhardy interpretations such as identifying it with the general paralysis of the insane, or *paresis*.

By selecting Dublin(ers) as the place of paralysis, Joyce intended "to write a chapter of the moral history of[his] country." Secondary literature has largely disregarded the following reflection "that he is a very bold man who dares to alter in the presentment, still more to deform, whatever he has seen and heard." The stress is clearly not on representation, but on presentation, deformation, composition, and textual performance. This allows Joyce to state, in the second instance, that in "the way I have composed it I have taken the first step towards the spiritual liberation of my country."[11] Still in the tradition of Shelley, he foregrounded the creative force of the "poetic" text, which was thought to be able to construct the alternative metaphysics of axiological systems, moral commitment, or social and political reform. It is the practical interference of the text that counts rather than the simplistic mimesis of a social situation characterized as paralytic by the biographical author. If meaning were restricted to the mimetic reflection of the work of paralysis in Dublin's Irish space, where characters are immobilized and caught within the confines of their narrow places, the stories could only be viewed as naturalistic. If, on the other hand, paralysis is considered to be the negative form from which positive moral messages can be deduced — the symbolic fallacy, — they would be reduced to religious, moralistic, or mythological allegories.

In *Dubliners*, paralysis, besides being an image of particular social and political conditions, may be defined as the absence of an essential emancipatory text in a situation that is socially

---

[11]   Letters to Grant Richards of 5 May and 20 May 1906 (*SL* 83 and 88).

hopeless. Related to the individual being, this would mean that there is no alternative text for those subjected to Dublin's/Ireland's social and religious systems. Within the paralytic circle, however, the characters in the stories develop a desire for the Other, which is inevitably thwarted. This Other can be recognized as the point of reference from which identity may tendentially be created. It is reified, in a figurative sense, in Frank for Eveline, the books of Nietzsche and Hauptmann for Mr Duffy, and Mr Duffy for Mrs Sinico. The Other can also appear as romance, as dream, hope, and promise of an altered situation, which either cannot be embraced because of the interiorized victim ideology (Eveline) or must be acknowledged as a compensating absence (Mr Duffy), and an unattainable idea (Mrs Sinico). Hope, to use a phrase coined by Geoffrey Hartman, is "unmasked as only catastrophe: as an illusion or unsatisfied movement of desire that wrecks everything."[12]

The interrelationship between paralysis in the socio-geographical space and paralysis expressed by the characters' attitudes, actions, and desires undercuts the classical philosophical (materialist and idealistic) polarities of subject and object. The subject, who by means of her/his visions, dreams, and desires centers her/his subjectivity, is decentered in the space beyond narcissistic self-identification. The self's knowledge of her or himself is unreliable. On the level of narrative presentation, the polarities are finally located in the object. Paralysis governs the self.

According to Lacan, the subject constructs her/his self by adapting oneself to the linguistic codes, or "symbolic register,"[13]

---

[12]   Geoffrey Hartman, *Criticism in the Wilderness: A Study of Literature Today* (New Haven and London: Yale University Press, 1980), p. 78.

[13]   Jaques Lacan, *The Four Fundamental Concepts of Psychoanalysis*, ed. Jacques-Alain Miller (New York: Norton, 1977), pp. 38.

of her/his world. Joyce's stories consistently demonstrate that self-identification is, in the given social space, an act of construction. The self is determined by the discourses, norms, and authorities that surround it. Her/his visions prove futile because the impact of social, cultural, and ideological determination is absolute, and because the visions themselves are fictive representations of the general discursive practice, which the subject calls into being as the "narrative" of her or his desire. Thus, *paralysis* is reified in a circular movement: paralytic situation — desire of something else — affirmation of the paralytic situation. Lacan's notion seems appropriate: "The very structure at the basis of desire always lends a note of impossibility to the object of human desire. What characterizes the obsessional neurotic in particular is that he emphasizes the confrontation with its impossibility. In other words, he sets everything up so that the object of his desire becomes the signifier of this impossibility."[14] Seen in this way, Eveline, Mrs Sinico, and Mr Duffy can all be defined as neurotic. But far from focussing on character, the literary texts decode the social and ideological determinations of subjectivity and counteract the narration by the unwieldy vertical signifiers. The "Benstock Principle" states that a narrative "is contextually (not narrator-) governed" makes contexts operative, and provokes the reader to "supply for himself the principles that govern the contextual setting of action in the text."[15] It is as effective in *Dubliners* as

[14]   Jaques Lacan, "Desire and the Interpretation of Desire in *Hamlet*," in Shoshona Feldman, ed. *Literature and Psychanalysis: The Question of Reading Otherwise* (Baltimore:Johns Hopkins University Press, 1982), p. 36. The interrelation between subject and desire, and the "Other" and subjectivity, as Lacan has illuminated it, can be disregarded in the present essay, which does not aim at a proper Lacanian reading of Joyce's stories.

[15]   Shari Benstock and Bernard Benstock, "The Benstock Principle," in Bernard Benstock, ed. *The Seventh of Joyce* (Bloomington: Indiana University Press, 1982), p. 19.

in *Ulysses*. The stories have meanings derived from representation as well as meanings derived from their linguistic articulation. Both meanings face each other in a position of difference.

Eveline

Eveline is arguably the most passive and most submissive major character in *Dubliners*. She has, however, a vision of escape. As Hart has noted, she is "the only one who is offered a positive opportunity to leave."[16] Both aspects, the objective state of her repression and her subjective dream, which proves to be futile, make her the very image of paralysis. Refuting psychological or metaphysical interpretations, William McCormack and Trevor Williams have emphasized that patriarchal norms, violence, and ideological indoctrination determine Eveline in such a way that "she cannot construct her own history"[17] and embrace the alternative of "Buenos Ayres." Nevertheless, Eveline's imaginings are highly relevant for making the story meaningful. She opposes Miss Gavan, who "had always an edge on her," (*D* 37) and her father, whose violence "had begun to threaten her" (*D* 38), as well as the gloominess of her life by evoking her happier childhood in a retrospective view. The fairy tale language of the free indirect discourse — "One time there used to be a field..."(*D* 36) — betrays her escape into a dreamworld, which actually is a representation of absence. The lack of happiness calls her desires into being — the "escape" (*D* 40) to a place where "people would treat her with respect" (*D* 37). The repeated use

[16]   Clive Hart, "Eveline," in Clive Hart, ed. *James Joyce's Dubliners: Critical Essays* (New York: Viking Press, 1969), p. 48.

[17]   Williams, "Resistance to Paralysis," p. 443. See also MacCormack, "Joyce's Eveline," pp. 255-260.

of the word "would," which denotes and marks her interior discourse, also exposes the illusory character of her desire for the Other, for "another life with Frank" (*D* 38). She is not able to establish her identity through the object of her desire. Quite the reverse, confronted with the possibility of escape she does not find her "hard life ... a wholly undesirable life" (*D* 38). The promise of Buenos Aires is effaced by the other promise she had given to her mother, "her promise to keep the home together as long as she could" (*D* 40). In her final confusion, "she prayed to God to direct her, to show her what was her duty" (*D* 40). The discursive regulation inherent in the word "duty," as she understands it, uncovers the ideological connotation of the signifier and tacitly changes the logic of her prayer. "Duty," the disposition encoded within her by father, mother, Church, and social norms, will direct her. As a consequence, she becomes voiceless; not even her eyes can speak: "She set her white face to him, passive, like a helpless animal. Her eyes gave him no sign of love or farewell or recognition" (*D* 41). Suppressed subjectivity has bred desires, which cannot be turned into reality because the subject is overdetermined by the greater force of this suppression.

Eveline is the victim of social, political, and ideological conditions. The victimization of subjects and individual manifestations of paralysis, have, on the level of representation, the double function that Julia Kristeva ascribed to sacrificial offerings: to practice violence and to be a means of control.[18] Violence becomes a symbol and a method of creating order. For example, Eveline's father is the individual symbol of general social and ideological mechanisms. As a victim, Eveline at least tries to protest, by keeping up her relationship with Frank against the authority of the father, and by nourishing the *idea* of

---

[18] Cf. Julia Kristeva, *La révolution du langage poétique* (Paris: Editions du Seuil, 1974), pp. 72-73.

leaving. But the law of the Father dominates, and she is reabsorbed into the system. What is not explained by the narrative voice in its act of telling but is instigated by the textual gaps, repetitions and ambiguities ("duty," "Buenos Ayres," "home," "life of commonplace sacrifices," "escape," "nausea," etc.), is that Dublin paralysis functions, from the point of view of hegemonic authority, as a practice of control.

Margot Norris notes in her reading of "Clay" that "the reader is obliged to reconstruct through elaborate inference both a scenario of what happens in the plot and an interpretation of what the events mean."[19] Moreover, the reader is provoked not to reconstruct but to construct meanings, which are not implanted by the authority of the narrator, but by the text and in particular its vertical signifiers. Even before the poststructuralist turn in Joyce studies, Clive Hart pointed to "words which will function at a further level of significance," such as "invade," "passed," "dreamed," "house," and "home" which occurs eighteen times.[20] Since then, several critics have enlarged on the icon of Blessed Margaret Mary Alacoque, or on the mother's crazy cry "Derevaun Seraun,"[21] and Robert Scholes has dwelled on the semiotics of "black mass" and "lying in."[22]

---

[19]   Margot Norris, "Narration under a Blindfold: Reading Joyce's 'Clay'," *PMLA*, 102 (1987), 211.

[20]   Hart, "Eveline," pp. 51-52.

[21]   The most revealing reading is given by McCormack, "Joyce's 'Eveline'," pp. 257-261. He does not insist on additions to the "teasingly wide" possibilities of speculative translation but argues that "the reader has no access to the formal alternative of further information retrieved from the past" (p. 260).

[22]   Robert Scholes, "Semiotic Approaches to a Fictional Text: Joyce's 'Eveline'," in *JJQ*, 16 (1978/79), 79-80. His definition of the signifiers as "symbolic code" is somewhat misleading, since obviously they are not symbols (of something).

The title of the story can be cited as the first vertical signifier of the text. "Eveline" is the only story out of the fifteen in *Dubliners* that has the name of the main character as its title. Ulrich Schneider has pointed out that Eveline Hill is then given four names in four different situations (Miss Hill, Eveline, Poppens, Evvy), "as if names could not warrant a fixed identity any more, but only different roles of the individual in society."[23] In other words, various names denote her lack of self-identity. In this context, the title of the story turns into an ironic device, which incidentally dismantles the protagonist-oriented story-telling of realistic fiction. When the name occurs for the first time, it is classified by the text as a synonym for the desire of being a subject: "Then she would be married, she, Eveline. People would treat her with respect then" (*D* 37). But the text immediately clarifies that *Eveline* is a signifier of the subjunctive. Eveline *would* be Eveline only when and *if* married. Thus, the signifier has no signified. It is a name without the identity imagined. It is the sign for an absence. It indicates a meaning that is not fulfilled. To this extent, "Eveline" is an ironic reversal of Frances Burney's famous eighteenth century novel of social initiation, *Evelina*, with the intertextually relevant sub-title *Or the History of a Young Lady's Entrance into the World* (1778). It is exactly what Joyce's Eveline is unable to do. In a different mode, the name is mocked by the intertextuality with a popular pornographic novel called *Eveline*. In it the heroine enjoys numerous sexual adventures and the most notorious are incestuous .

Torchiana and others have confirmed the referential validity of the name with respect to Eve, the first woman, and mother of humankind, cut from the rib of Adam. The Hebrew basis of the word, *Hawwàh*, which literally means "a living being,"

[23] Ulrich Schneider, "Titles in *Dubliners*," *Style*, 25 (Fall 1991), 407-408.

identifies Eve as "the mother of all the living."[24] Curiously, a substantial relationship between the biblical Eve and Joyce's Eveline can hardly be established, though the sarcastic implication is evident that Eveline probably will never be a mother and not even a fully alive being. Eve, however, is, when read in a deconstructive way, a symbol for the institution of patriarchal gender privilege in the Christian, and particularly Catholic, belief system. Thus, the reader can legitimately deduce the line from Eve to Eveline in a history of patriarchal authority. Eveline has been placed in a very low position within its constraints. Her story epitomizes the paralysis of Dublin/ers *and* of Irish women. The title contradicts the fictional centering of the subject, expected in the traditional canon. Instead, it centers the ambiguity and destabilization of the signifier itself, which in consequence turns into a questioning of the Christian tradition, and of discourses presenting emancipatory and upwardly mobile heroes or heroines.

Reproductions of Blessed Margaret Mary Alacoque were popular in Dublin households. The one in the Hills' home perfectly echoes the commonplace: "And yet during all those years she had never found out the name of the priest whose yellowing photograph hung on the wall above the broken harmonium beside the colored print of the promises made to Blessed Margaret Mary Alacoque"(*D* 37). The indeterminate variety of potential meanings is underlined by the possibility of reading the picture of Margaret Mary as a metonym of the given socio-ideological climate and as a metaphor of the theme of paralysis. *The Catholic Encyclopedia* states that Margaret Mary was a sickly child, but "after her first communion, at the age of nine...practiced in secret severe corporal mortifications, until paralysis confined her to bed for four years. At the end of this

---

[24]   Ernest Klein, *A Comprehensive Etymological Dictionary of the English Language* (Amsterdam, London and New York: Elsevier Publ., 1966), I, 133 and 552.

period, having made a vow to the Blessed Virgin to consecrate herself to the religious life, she was instantly restored to health." Later, when she was seventeen, "her mother besought her to establish herself in the world," but reproved by Christ for her infidelity, retired to a convent.[25] The moralistic religious message is overdetermined: Dedication to God, and obedience, overcome physical paralysis. Belief has wondrous results. With regard to Eveline, the picture of Margaret Mary is a symbol of her inability to escape *and* a textual sign that exposes the extent of her ideological manipulation. It contains the message that if Eveline suffers enough, God will somehow bless her. I disagree with Scholes's idea that this is ironic.[26] It seriously balances the ideologically positive valorization implicit in the story of Blessed Margaret Mary and in Eveline's unconsciousness with the intervening negative valorization which the text performs. In a parallel way, the photograph of the priest, who has *escaped* from Dublin, is balanced with the *broken* harmonium. As a result, the religious discourse and Catholic piety are, in de Man's terminology, disfigured.[27] They are exposed as the means of disseminating false consciousness.

Eveline's situation, which is tragic rather than ironic, is illuminated by the word "promise." Its foregrounded position — not the colored picture of Margaret Mary but the list of the promises made to her — affirms its function as a vertical signifier in its own right. Gifford's annotation, which states "the promises made through St. Margaret-Mary," is highly illuminating in this context: "The 'colored print' would illustrate the Sacred Heart and would list the promises made through St.

---

[25] Quoted in Hart, ed. *"Dubliners": Critical Essays*, p. 172.

[26] Scholes, "Semiotic Approaches," p. 79.

[27] Cf. Paul de Man, "Shelley Disfigured," in Harold Bloom et al., *Deconstruction and Criticism* (London: Routledge, 1979), p. 65.

Margaret-Mary to those faithful who display in their homes a representation of the Sacred Heart and who receive the Eucharist on the first Friday of each month: (1) I will give them all the graces necessary in their state of life; (2) I will establish peace in their homes; (3) I will comfort them in all afflictions; ... (5) I will bestow abundant blessings on all their undertakings; (6) Sinners shall find in My Heart the source and infinite ocean of mercy...."[28] The promises create a symbolic order. Eveline cannot escape from their imperative. They conquer her desires. With a different meaning, "promise" is used twice for the vow Eveline has given to her mother to stay at home. In these cases, it is the verbalization of the gender role she is expected to play. In his brilliant Lacanian reading of the story, Leonard has convincingly argued that "Eveline has been well instructed by her mother on the importance of actively participating in her own oppression."[29]

But "promise" is also the verbal gap that is the very agent of the plot: It is the offer of escape and a happier life that gives Eveline the initial impetus for dissent. This triangle of "promise" has no common denominator. The promise given to Blessed Margaret Mary by Christ, which is manifested in her redemption from paralysis, depends on her obedience. Eveline's promise of escape from paralysis would be an act of disobedience. The promise given to her mother is part of the paralyzing forces forming her. The text clarifies that promises can be stifling and liberating. The liberating function is thwarted as a potential *in* the story; it becomes, however, a dimension *of* the story.

---

[28]   Don Gifford, *Joyce Annotated: Notes to "Dubliners" and "A Portrait of the Artist as a Young Man"* (Berkeley: University of California Press, 1982), pp. 49-50.

[29]   Garry M. Leonard, "Wondering Where All the Dust Comes From: *Jouissance* in 'Eveline'," *JJQ*, 29 (Fall 1991), 27.

The end of "Eveline" plays with two obvious vertical signifiers. Eveline is intimidated by her indecision and scruples. The objective correlative of this disposition is the view of the ship: "Through the wide doors of the sheds she caught a glimpse of the black mass of the boat, lying in beside the quay wall" (*D* 40). Scholes has drawn attention to the two "innocent descriptive phrase(s)" that connote the black mass of the ship and the sacrilege of the Black Mass, and the boat's lying in and being delivered of child.[30] Since the narration oscillates between the "voice" of the narrator and the "mood" of Eveline,[31] the ship's body and its position are, from the point of view of the subject, a reification of the Other, which she rejects because she cannot embrace it as the positive promise. As a result, she is forced back into a state of passivity where she seems to lose her identity. Semiotically, "black mass" and "lying in" force, by their overt indeterminacy of reference, referential decisions upon the reader, who has to discriminate between the narration of the story and the association of different meanings. Unanswerable questions emerge: What has the Black Mass performed on the belly of a naked woman to do with the black mass of the ship? How can the childless and probably virginal Eveline be related to a woman in labor? Any semiotic closure is excluded. The text performs "the undoing of the representational and iconic function of figuration by the play of the signifier."[32] The difference of nominal concretions inherent in the textual signifiers cannot any longer be aligned to the "innocence" of the voice of narration and, even less, to Eveline's mood. The text is rife with all kinds of meaning, while the paralyzed subject

[30] Scholes, "Semiotic Approaches," p. 79.

[31] The terminology relies on Gérard Genette, *Narrative Discourse* (Oxford: Oxford University Press, 1980), p. 10, and passim.

[32] de Man, "Shelley Disfigured," p. 61.

cannot find her own language.

Mr Duffy and Mrs Sinico: Quest for Identity

Secondary literature on "A Painful Case" focuses on Mr Duffy and "explains" him according to psychoanalytic, temperamental, Nietzschean, literary, autobiographical, or symbolic pretexts.[33] Conspicuously, criticism has focussed attention on the male protagonist. The wholeness of "the story of a man with a divided character"[34] has been taken for granted by the majority of critics. A rare exception is Corrington's analysis of the story that points out that Duffy "is an emptiness," and "a kind of stand-in for what Joyce considered the end-product of modern urban, industrialized, godless, amoral and fragmented society."[35] This early essay suggests Duffy is a figure who functions as a means of dismantling the notion of the centered subject. Perhaps, he may be even regarded as the less important partner of that female Other in the text that is more of a void than a presence in the plot, Mrs Sinico.

The title ambiguously denotes the cases of both Mr Duffy and Mrs Sinico.[36] This semantic effect was intensified by Joyce who

[33]   Cf., for instance, Thomas E. Connolly, "A Painful Case," in Hart, ed. *Joyce's "Dubliners,"* p.108; Marvin Magalaner, *Time of Apprenticeship: The Fiction of Young James Joyce* (London, New York and Toronto: Abelard-Schuman, 1959), p. 88; Joseph C. Voelker, "'He Lumped the Emancipates Together': More Analogues for Joyce's Mr. Duffy," in *JJQ* 18 (1980) 1, 31; Bettina L. Knapp, "Joyce's 'A Painful Case': The Train and an Epiphanic Experience," in *Études irlandaises*, 13 (1988), 45.

[34]   Connolly, "A Painful Case," p. 109.

[35]   John William Corrington, "Isolation as Motif in 'A Painful Case',"
JJQ, 3 (Spring 1966), 182, 186.

[36]   Bernard Benstock even emphasized that the title is "eventually directed toward Mr. Duffy; see "The Gnomonics of *Dubliners*," *MFS*, 34

changed the title of his first draft of the story, "A Painful Incident." Mrs Sinico's deadly accident is Mr Duffy's paralytic (deadly in the figurative sense) case. Mr Duffy's story only constitutes the plot superficially. Mrs Sinico defines Duffy's character and determines the meaning of the story. In this way, structure becomes dominant, that is, the juxtaposition and conflict of different kinds of desires, hopes, dreams, and satisfaction. Even relating to the narrated plot, it can no longer be maintained, as Voelker did, against his own argumentation, that "in 1906, (Joyce) was still a sufficiently traditional writer to give Mr. Duffy exclusive rights to the primary level of narration."[37] Rather, the "story" represents a person who constructs himself as subject of his ego, whereas the "text" deconstructs this self-reflective construct of the "I." This was a paradigmatic innovation in fiction. By 1906, Joyce was far from being a traditional short story writer.

"A Painful Case" is framed by textual configurations that stress Duffy's self-willed isolation. The beginning reads: "Mr James Duffy lived in Chapelizod because he wished to live as far as possible from the city of which he was a citizen..." (*D* 107). It continues: "...and because he found all the other suburbs of Dublin mean, modern and pretentious" (*D* 107). The inclusive "all" and the pejoratively validated adjectives betray the subjectivity of *his* perspective. His dismissal of the rest of Dublin is idiosyncratic, and his choice of accommodation may imply more about his character, and even his politics. He sees himself as a decent, conservative (the Unionist *Dublin Evening Mail* is in his side-pocket), and as a modest person, whereas the reader is being prepared for a very different reading by this typical case of textual heteroglossia, in the Bakhtinean sense.

At the end of the story, Duffy waits for some minutes in the

(1988), 534.

[37] Voelker, "'He Lumped...'," pp. 31-32.

darkness of Phoenix Park, "listening. He could hear nothing: the night was perfectly silent. He listened again: perfectly silent. He felt he was alone" (*D* 117). The adverb "perfectly," and the intensification of "hear" to "listened" signal the end of the Emily Sinico nightmare. He is himself again. Each of the eight sentences of the final paragraph begins with the pronoun "he" as the grammatical subject of the unit. At last, he is at the very beginning, happy in his aloneness. The final indulgence in self-willed isolation represses his moments of worry about his possible failure, and of concern about Mrs Sinico, which Corrington has called "a kind of morbid empathy."[38] However, indeterminacy prevails at the end. It is open to the reader to decide to what extent Duffy's feeling that "his moral nature (was) falling to pieces" will continue to haunt him. Whether the question, "Why had he sentenced her to death?" (*D* 117), will be stifled permanently. The very inconclusiveness of the text affirms that Duffy is a "painful" psychological case. On one hand, his personal integrity, which makes him an outsider, who is excluded from Dublin's ordinary social life (what actually attracts Mrs Sinico), must be respected. On the other hand, by his careless rejection of Mrs Sinico, he acts like a male chauvinist. Though he has, for the most part, separated himself from the paralytic state of Dublin's social activity, he is, nevertheless, an example of the general paralysis. This may at first seem paradoxical, but let me explain. His mental physiognomy is partly blurred by narrative technique and the frequent use it makes of his mood. Duffy is telescoped towards the reader and thus becomes a kind of common case. In a cunning way, he is presented as the familiar neighbor on the tram or in the eating-house in Georges Street; he is a recognizable species of Dubliner.

Duffy is a man who fosters the notion of his stable ego: "He

[38]   Corrington, "Isolation," p. 189.

had neither companions nor friends, church nor creed. He lived his spiritual life without any communion with others, visiting his relatives at Christmas and escorting them to the cemetery when they died. He performed these two social duties for old dignity's sake but conceded nothing further to the conventions which regulate civic life" (*D* 109). The earlier juxtaposition of subject and civic life, or social duties, is repeated. Between *his* spiritual life and *others*, there is no "communion," in other words, if the reader interprets the semantic polyvalency of this vertical signifier, there is no exchange of thoughts and emotions, no sharing, no strong spiritual feelings, no membership in a group with common beliefs. Since Duffy has neither church or creed, the semantic layer of the spiritual union with Christ, or the participation in the Eucharist, does not apply. Activity only occurs in daydreams, which are exposed by the narrator with faked seriousness: "He allowed himself to think that in certain circumstances he would rob his bank but, as these circumstances never arose, his life rolled out evenly — an adventureless tale" (*D* 109). The tale about a man who does not communicate is a tale about the ineffectiveness of isolation.

The text discloses, in a marvellous anticipation of a deconstructionist reading, that Mr Duffy's subjectivity is a fiction: "He lived at a little distance from his body, regarding his own acts with doubtful side-glances. He had an odd autobiographical habit which led him to compose in his mind from time to time a short sentence about himself containing a subject in the third person and a predicate in the past tense" (*D* 108). He constantly constructs his auto-biography; he writes him-self. Standing besides himself, Duffy conceives of himself as the Other. He mirrors himself, and "things" in relation to himself. He delivers "discourses" (*D* 111) on politics and "the soul's incurable loneliness" (*D* 111), and in doing so, "he heard the strange impersonal voice which he recognized as his own" (*D* 104). In other words, addressing Mrs Sinico, he himself is the addressee of his narration, and he cannot but consider his viewpoints as privileged. He marginalizes his former flirtatious association with the Irish Socialist Party. The idea that "no social revolution ... would be likely to strike Dublin for some centuries" (D 111) is the excuse that stabilizes his ego. In 1905, James Connolly, even in America, would have vigorously protested against such a notion. Although Mr Duffy insists that he does not need the I.S.P, it is the I.S.P. which does not need Mr Duffy.

Neither is Mr Duffy Joyce's mouthpiece. But as a sentence in the text, which can be severed from its speaker, Mr Duffy's sense of the unlikeliness of revolution invites the reader to ponder its implications. A similar ambiguity is inscribed into the next passage: "She (Mrs Sinico) asked him why did he not write out his thoughts. For what, he asked her, with careful scorn. To compete with phrasemongers, incapable of thinking consecutively for sixty seconds? To submit himself to the criticism of an obtuse middle class which entrusted its morality to policemen and its fine arts to impresarios?" (D 111). The reflection of Ireland's paralysis in Duffy's cracked looking-glass is, by textual implication, an objective correlative of the social condition but equally, as subjective opinion, nothing but a self-defense, because he is incapable of social, or political, commitment. His narcissistic pleasure in himself, which he mistakes as an expression of his identity, actually shows his loss of identity. Unlike Mrs Sinico, and even unlike Eveline, he has no need for, and no dream of escape.

Narcissism protects Duffy from practical activity and from emotional and erotic involvement. Compensation is found, as happens in such instances, in the aestheticizing of himself. Literature, music, and after Emily Sinico — the Nietzshean hypostatization of the ego replace reality. Ironically, he calls up Hauptmann and Nietzsche, whose criticism of society had been a form of social interference, to support and justify his detachment, and to construct a subjective image of himself.

Mrs Sinico introduces him to another, previously unknown,

possibility for affirming his subjectivity. She rouses his desire which is directed toward another subject in order to be desired, recognized and identified. Always demanding the anticipated consent of Mrs. Sinico, he stages a scene in which "she becomes his confessor" (*D* 110). The religious terminology which is in his, rather than in the narrator's, consciousness utilizes a somewhat strange register, and is, at the same time, an adequate metaphor of his pompousness. The text covertly says that sacramental terminology and biographical impulse create an incongruity. It overtly foregrounds the inner contradiction which the text establishes by the nearly Lacanian rendering of Duffy's desire:" He thought that in her eyes he would ascend to an angelic stature" (*D* 111). To confess, in order to become a saint, implies the identity of the confessing and the confessor. Again, the text ironically comments on his self-centeredness, which neither the narrator nor the protagonist seems to notice.

Mrs Sinico, in revealing her sexuality, threatens his complacent egocentrism. At this moment, she is transformed from Duffy's desired Other to an Other desiring her own dreams and wishes. Suddenly, she appears as the potential creator of different meanings. She might even become a signifier that would define him differently from his self-construction and free him from his isolation. Questioning the male subject's given identity, she could initiate the renewal of his self-awareness. Vice versa, as the object of her desire, he could initiate her redefinition. In a reversal of accepted male and female role playing, she shyly takes the initiative. Her first gesture (and it is only a gesture), reveals that she is a subject as well. Immediately he rejects her. In the language of the text, there can be no mediation between (the vertical signifiers) "intercourse" and "sexual intercourse" (*D* 112). He commits himself to celibacy which here seems synonymous with paralysis.

Mr Duffy and the narrator share the perspective of male gender ideology, which naturally allows them to treat Mrs

Sinico as passive, as an object, who or which, has no voice of her own. The following exemplary passage combines the narrator's voice and mood: "Little by little *he* entangled *his* thoughts with *hers*. *H*e lent *her* books, provided *her* with ideas, shared *his* intellectual life with *her*. *She* listened to all" (*D* 110 — emphasis mine). It is *he* and the possessive *his* that occupy the grammatical and functional subject position. When *she* becomes the subject, she is described as utterly dependent on him. As feminist scholarship emphasizes, man defines himself against the(negative) female other. Referring to Freud's failure to see the two sexes, Luce Irigaray states, "The feminine is always described in terms of deficiency or atrophy, as the other side of the sex that alone holds the monopoly on value: the male sex."[39] An ideological stance of this kind excludes the feminine from the author's story, which, in this respect, apes the culturally dominant male discourse. But the very foregrounding of the male view in the quoted passage should make the reader suspicious. The text again works against the narrator's control. Questions may be asked: Does Mrs Sinico only listen? What are her thoughts compared to his ? What does she learn from his books ? Does she share her emotional life with him? Isn't it her tacit strategy to win him over when she admits his influence? Her double attempt to "cross the line" morally and physically, which "knocks her down" and brings about her "fall" cannot be understood in the way it is represented either by the narrator's rendering of Duffy's reflections or by the reporter of *The Mail*. From both their points of view, her emotions and sufferings do not count. Female subjectivity is occluded from the narrative. But since its absence from the male-dominated and conventional newspaper report and from Duffy's dismissive perspective is made conspicuously present by the text, the reader is urged to

[39]   Luce Irigaray, *This Sex Which Is Not One* (Ithaca: Cornell University Press, 1985), p. 69.

criticize these reactions.

The story conceals and the text reveals that the locus of the Other, as Mr Duffy and Mrs Sinico have separately internalized it, is contradictory. Whereas Duffy affirms his isolated ego by merely renewing his wish to be desired by her, Mrs Sinico desires to constitute herself as a subject by raising his desire to love her. She is denied this subject status by Duffy and the narrator. The intervening reader, however, can grasp the unconventional and daring attempt she makes to liberate herself — an attempt which is viewed as socially and religiously dissident. Joyce criticism has perhaps not noticed that the triangle involving Mrs. Sinico, Mr Duffy and Captain Sinico parallels the situation of Kitty O'Shea, Parnell, and Captain O'Shea. Like Captain Sinico, Captain O'Shea "took to spending longer and longer periods abroad"[40] following business interests. Like Kitty O'Shea, Mrs Sinico may eventually want, though the reader can only speculate, to break up her unfortunate marriage against moral norms. Unlike Parnell, who went ahead and married at the cost of his career, Mr Duffy is a coward, an egocentric neurotic, a nothing.

The subversion of the male-dominated story is intensified by the vertical signifiers, which the text presents in abundance. The most important are "Chapelizod" and " Phoenix Park" (with their evocation of the legend of Tristan and Iseult, which would parallel the Parnell-Kitty O'Shea alliance, and negatively acknowledge Mr Duffy's case). Some of the other vertical signifiers are "Bile Beans,"[41] "communion," "saturnine," "exotic," "life's feast," and" laborious." They may be called feminine since they defy authoritative strictures of meaning and the narrator's arrogance. The difference and the deferral of

[40]   F. S. L. Lyons, *Charles Stewart Parnell* (London: Fontana, 1991), pp. 126-7.

[41]   For an explanation, see Connolly, "A Painful Case," p. 107.

meaning can be shown more clearly with some specific examples.

The narrator's description of Duffy's character features a curious statement: "A medieval doctor would have called him saturnine" (*D* 108). The primary meaning of *saturnine* is "melancholy," or being of" gloomy temperament," which has traditionally been associated being born under the influence of the planet Saturn.[42] It also means, "relating to lead," or "symptomatic of lead poisoning." Medieval astrologers called Saturn the planet of misfortune; children born under its sign were regarded as the outcasts of society. According to Robert Graves, "the medieval alchemists,following ancient tradition, reckoned silver to the Moon as presiding over birth, and lead to Saturn as presiding over death."[43] Does this clue suggest that Duffy will preside over the death of Mrs Sinico? Speculations are possible, but nothing is determined. Another example of hypoglossia would lead the reader to the Roman god of agriculture and vegetation, and with him to the festival of the *Saturnalia* "renowned for its general merry-making," or (sometimes, not cap.) a period of wild revelry"[44] which would

---

[42]   Charles D. Wright, "Melancholy Duffy and Sanguine Sinico: Humors in 'A Painful Case'" *JJQ*, 3 (1966), 171-181. Wright quotes Alchabitius, from Walter Clyde Curry, Chaucer and the Medieval Sciences (New York,1926), p. 129: "He controls a certain heaviness of cold and dry, and from a combination of these qualities under his influence is produced and fostered the wise man of melancholic complexion. He signifies darkness of counsel, profound silence, and ancient and precious things pertaining to judgements. He is deserving of mistrust and suspicion, moving men to complaints and mutterings" (quoted p. 171). Whether this can be related to the story or to Joyce's knowledge of the Saturnian implication, is indeterminate and undecidable.

[43]   Robert Graves, *The White Goddess* (London: Faber, 1975), p. 194.

[44]   *Collins English Dictionary: Major New Edition* (Glasgow: Harper Collins, 1991), p. 1377.

be the very opposite of "melancholy." The signifier gives Duffy a character and alludes to what is, could be, or is not in the narrated story.

Introducing Mr Duffy, the narrator lists among the objects on Duffy's desk, "an over-ripe apple which might have been left there and forgotten" (*D* 108). The apple is a random object. Its presence on Mr. Duffy's desk, however, runs counter to the character already described by the sentence: "Mr Duffy abhorred anything which betokened physical and mental disorder" (*D* 108). The over-ripe apple signifies what he abhors. It alludes to Eve's apple and to original sin and man's fall: the temptation Mr Duffy/Adam will resist. In *A Portrait*, Dante Riordan misquotes the angel in Zechariah 2:8, "for whoever touches you, touches the apple of his (God's) eye" (*P* 37). Do the angel's words apply to the untouchable Mr Duffy? For a German, apples such as this bring to mind Goethe's friend Friedrich Schiller who used to keep half-rotten apples in his desk because he believed their fragrance intensified his imagination. Whether Joyce knew this, is not verifiable, and it does not particularly matter, but it is as typical of the false semantic properties established by the text as the intertextual reference to *Macbeth* evoked by Duffy's twice-told self-dramatization: that he was "Outcast from life's feast" (*D* 117). Macbeth's esteem of sleep as "Chief nourisher in life's feast" (*Macbeth* II: 2, 36) can by no means be made to coincide with, nor even to refer to, Duffy's covert quotation. The disruptions in meaning in terms of the vertical signifiers can become extreme and result in deliberate incoherence.

Subjectivity and Meaning

The illusions and desires of subjects, who are scripted by the social conditions and the linguistic texts surrounding them, determine the value of their reflection of the empirical world and the ideational and psychological solidity of perception itself. Distorted and distorting perceptions inevitably collide with reality. Disillusion leads to breakdowns, silences and relapses. Eveline and Mrs Sinico suffer from the loss of their self-legitimization to break with oppressive circumstances to which they are confined. Mr Duffy withdraws into the isolation of his ego. Though these three characters are very different, their cases all reify states of confinement. Since desires cannot be fulfilled, each subject is reconstituted in his or her own nothingness.

Representing the objective and subjective situation of paralysis, Joyce's stories are, at the same time, the paradigm of Derrida's "dissemination," which resists "the effects of subjectivity, subjectivation, appropriation (sublation, sublimation, idealization, reinteriorization, Errinerung, signification, semantization, autonomy, law, etc.)."[45] Whereas the plot depicts the passivity of the subjects, the disfigurative act of artistic representation demands the intervention of the reader who is asked to face the challenges of the texts and of the reality beyond them. The detailed renderings of geographical, social and individual places and their relation to linguistic performance produce a paradoxical effect. The foregrounding of strategic signifiers installs, to use a phrase of Helene Cixous's, "the

---

[45] Jacques Derrida, "Interview: Positions," second part, *diacritics*, 3 (1973), 42.

disquieting work of the word. "[46]

The vertical signifiers disorganize the logocentric quasi-natural relationship between signifier and signified and "organize a structure of resistance to the philosophical conceptuality which might have claimed to dominate, to understand them. "[47] They neither support the theme of paralysis nor the desire for alternative states of being; they represent neither praxis nor vision. Designating meanings beyond the narration, they arrest the "realistic" progress of understanding, and oblige the reader to construct an independent discourse. The vertical signifiers produce "an asemantic 'drift' of differance"[48] which qualifies the narrative representation of paralysis and effaces the naive assumption that the meaning of the text can be generalized in monadic statements or metaphysical essences. Epistemologically, the text becomes unreliable. Its "undecidables" deconstruct referential explicitness, "but *without ever* constituting a third term, without ever occasioning a solution in the form of speculative dialectics," rather "producing a non-finite number of semantic effects."[49] They unmask ideology. The conjunction of horizontal and vertical signification appears as the artistic strategy of the criticism of ideology, of Catholicism, patriarchal norms, public discourses, narcissistic subjectivity, or Irishness. This is a per-form-ance that characterizes Joyce's early stories as non-realistic forms of fiction. The absence of definite messages negates the

[46] Helene Cixous, "Joyce: The (r)use of writing," in Derek Attridge and Daniel Ferrer, eds. *Post-Structuralist Joyce: Essays from the French* (Cambridge: Cambridge University Press, 1984), p. 27.

[47] Robert Young, ed. *Untying the Text: A Post-Structuralist Reader* (London: Routledge, 1981), p. 18.

[48] Young, p. 18.

[49] Jacques Derrida, "Interview: Positions," first part, pp. 36-37.

dependence of art on the hierarchy of power structures, doctrines, and dogmas.

Krauthausen

NARRATIVE BREAD PUDDING: JOYCE'S "THE BOARDING HOUSE"

MARGOT NORRIS

"She made Mary collect the crusts and pieces of broken bread to help make Tuesday's bread pudding" (*D* 64), we learn of Mrs. Mooney, the butcher's daughter, in Joyce's "The Boarding House." The passage goes on to enact the servant's gesture of boarding house thrift by serving us the twice baked crusts, as it were, of the previous evening's events: the redaction of a trimmed and hard account of Mrs. Mooney's and Polly's confrontation the night before, from which the interesting substance or "meat" — the juicy sexual and transgressive content — has already been extracted and consumed in advance. Why would Joyce at the advent of his career in 1905, leave the opulent and dramatic possibilities of nineteenth century literature behind, and feed us this bland and tasteless bread pudding of a story? The austerity of the narration makes it clear that Joyce is here "modernising himself," as William Johnsen puts it.[1] But the story of this story is not over, as we are surprised to discover in *Ulysses*, where the continuing scandal of the Mooneys and the Dorans is served up again in "Cyclops" — this time in an unsavory glut of succulent detail. The stylistic disparity between the two accounts — one cold and spare, the other hot and excessive — draws attention to the rhetoric and makes it clear that Joyce, who declared himself "uncommonly well pleased" (*SL* 63) with "The Boarding House" when it was finished, knew exactly what he was doing with this experiment in styles of

---

[1] William A. Johnsen," Joyce's 'Dubliners' and the Futility of Modernism,"in W. J. McCormack and Alistair Stead, editors, *James Joyce and Modern Literature* (London: Routledge and Kegan Paul, 1982), p. 6.

narration.[2] His retrospective revisitation of this family in
Ulysses does more than sate our narrative hunger by giving us
the story's ending and moral: that young people united in
shotgun weddings tend not to live happily ever after. By
supplementing with prurient gossip the insubstantial bread
pudding of the *Dubliners* story, a point about narrative language
and composition seems added as well. Joyce uses *Ulysses*, I
would suggest, to critique the modernistic prose of "The
Boarding House" as a replication of and collusion with the
hypocritical moralism that is the story's donnée.[3]

In offering an anatomy of a shotgun wedding, Joyce has "The
Boarding House" implicitly critique Christian morality's
vulnerability to serve immoral purposes, following a modern
philosophical tradition inaugurated by Nietzsche's *Genealogy of
Morals*. This double transgression of sexual despoilation
"remedied" by union enforced with threats of social, economic,
and physical violence exposes the hypocrisies of bourgeois
morality that is sanctioned and buttressed by the institution of
the Church. Bob Doran is made vulnerable to Mrs. Mooney's
coercions by his sacramental confession prior to their

---

[2]   Warren Beck, *Joyce's 'Dubliners' Substance, Vision and Art*
(Durham N. C.: Duke University Press, 1969). This treatment of "The
Boarding House" is one of the subtlest and most interesting pieces of
criticism on the text. But I disagree with Beck's admonition (p.148) against
letting the *Ulysses* sequel of the story modify a reading of the *Dubliners* text.
A noting of the characters' recurrence from one book to the next may
sometimes be illustrative and even supplementary, but the considerations
should never eclipse the substantive autonomy and uniquely fit mode in each
work." My argument is that the inverted style of the revisitation of the story
is intended to draw attention to certain limitations and poverties of the
original that can be used to interrogate the exoneration of Bob Doran as the
product of a certain implicated narrative rhetoric.

[3]   Margot Norris, *Joyce's Web: The Social Unravelling of Modernism*
(Austin: University of Texas Press, 1992).

confrontation — "the priest had drawn out every ridiculous detail of the affair and in the end so magnified his sin that he was almost thankful at being afforded a loophole of reparation" (*D* 65). The weight of force in the story resides in the institution, and although they are never represented as such in the story, this force is tacitly vested in forms of language and communication — the confession, the legal case, the threat, blackmail, the negotiation, the bargain, the marriage proposal. Joyce anticipates in "The Boarding House" Michel Foucault's elucidation of institutional discourse's role in the service of social domination — an argument that is overt and accessible to a reading of the story.[4] What is less accessible to the reader is the prospect that art or fiction might itself represent one of these institutional discourses bent one social domination, and that the narration of "The Boarding House" is itself suspect and must be interrogated for misdirection[5] and provocation to misprision.

What initially exempts "The Boarding House" from skepticism by a readership accustomed (since the eighteenth century, at least) to unreliable narration is precisely the Flaubertian purity of its modernistic style. The story's narrator has the impersonality and objectivity promoted in Stephen Dedalus's aesthetic theory, and therefore invites no resistance to judgements that appear to emerge from facts that seem to be speaking for themselves. Yet there are two possible explanations why the composition of this story (as well as others in the collection) was so significant to Joyce that he fought for it with great urgency. In defending the integrity of the stories' language

---

[4]   See Michel Foucault, *History of Sexuality,* Vol 1: *An Introduction.* Trans. Robert Hurley (New York: Vintage Books, 1980). Foucault stresses particularly the institutional deployment of the confession in the ecclesiastical and medical control of sexuality.

[5]   Fritz Senn, "'The Boarding House' Seen as a Tale of Misdirection," *JJQ,* 23 (1986), 405-413.

to Grant Richards in 1906, Joyce pleaded that the "points on which I have not yielded are the "points which rivet the book together ... I fight to retain them because I believe that in composing my chapter of moral history in exactly the way I have composed it I have taken the first step toward the spiritual liberation of my country" (*SL* 88). In the absence of narrational commentary and opinion, the "composition" of the story would bear the burden of providing the informational wherewithal for interpretation and readerly judgement. But beyond that, the "composition" — presumably encompassing the selection and arrangement of scenes as well as the rhetoric and epistemology of the narration — would make it possible to see the extent to which the seemingly formalistic and disinterested narration nonetheless manipulates the material in ways that create opportunities for misguided interpretation. Modernistic prose, with its spare and lean language and seemingly narcissistic self-reflection that appears to give it purely formalistic and aesthetic self-interest, is revealed, in Joyce's stories, to be by no means innocent.

The exposure of the ideological complicity of the narration in the very hypocrisies and coercions it purports to critique depends precisely on those elements of composition that make the text behave performatively. The narrative voice that begins by telling us of Mrs. Mooney — "She was a woman who was quite able to keep things to herself" (*D* 61) — quickly demonstrates that it, too, no less than Mrs. Mooney, Bob Doran or Polly Mooney — knows how to keep things to itself. The narration frequently gives us only redactions — synopses or summaries — of characters' thoughts and memories that are themselves already redacted, already edited and trimmed for a leaner and harder presentation. These redactions can aptly be troped as narrative crusts or rinds because they are rational and literary forms for thoughts whose content is omitted. The story is structured according to virtually classical unities: a double set of confessions on Saturday night (Polly confessing to Mrs. Mooney and Bob Doran confessing to the priest) followed by a double meditation (Mrs. Mooney'a calculation of her strategy and Bob Doran's terrified anticipation of its consequences) on Sunday morning precisely between 11:17 and 11:30. The story's climax is an implicit pairing of double sacrificial rites: the "short twelve" Mrs. Mooney will attend at the pro-cathedral on Marlborough Street after the off-stage slaughter of Bob Doran as her sacrificial lamb ("She dealt with moral problems as a cleaver deals with meat"[*D* 63]). But the confessions, the actual affair of Bob and Polly, the painful confrontation between Mrs. Mooney and Bob Doran and the farcical marriage proposal it produces, are all unrepresented except through the cold redactions Joyce referred to, in a letter to Stanislaus, as "the frigidities of 'The Boarding House' " (*SL* 69). Joyce — whose titles in *Dubliners* often serve as rhetorical euphemisms for the text — deliberately makes of the story a textual boarding house in which the reader is served narrative bread pudding.

As a story composed of the rhetorical crusts of redactions, "The Boarding House" raises the issue of authority that the impersonality of modernistic writing simultaneously affirms and subverts. The narrative redaction gives us fragments of information that imply that the narrative voice knows more than it tells. This allows the narration to project or adumbrate a totalized understanding of the whole affair, of which it tells us little and shows us less. At the same time, the fragmentariness of the redactions renders the narrative account incomplete and singular enough to admit the possibility of other versions and other accounts. The product of this double-sided hermeneutical effect is not only the misprision of the story's moral issues, but also the misjudgment of the moral neutrality of modernism's style of "scrupulous meanness." The most troublesome of the narration's hermeneutically misleading fragments occurs at the end of the story, when Polly Mooney's thoughts are indicated but not represented — "She rested the nape of her neck against the cool iron bed-rail and fell into a reverie. There was no longer any perturbation visible on her face" (*D* 68). We are told the occurrence and the effect of the reverie — that is, its form or crust — but not its content or substance. While producing a stylistic effect of simplicity and affect of peace and calm, the narrator has promoted an interpretation of Polly Mooney's role in her lover's institutional predation without having ventured an opinion or made a statement. But the implicit interpretation produced by the narrative — that Polly is a cool player in her mother's game — preempts alternative and different interpretations that could make the story far more heteroglossic than it seems, and that suggest a story fraught with silent discourses that together constitute "phrases in dispute" that must be adjudicated.[6] Insofar as the story eventually obliges us to take sides in a moral case, and to choose between the prosecution arguments of Mrs. Mooney ("He had simply taken advantage of Polly's youth and inexperience: that was evident. The question was: What reparation would he make?" [*D* 64]) and Bob Doran's statement of defense (He had a notion that he was being had ... It was not altogether his fault that it had happened" [*D* 66]), the narration leads or misleads the reader into positions from which an objective adjudication becomes virtually impossible. The text of "The Boarding House" produces undecidability of phrases in

[6]   R. B. Kershner, *Joyce, Bakhtin, and Popular Culture: Chronicles of Disorder* (Chapel Hill: University of North Carolina Press,1989). Kershner describes "The Boarding House" as written in the rhetoric of oxymoron, and gives the function of this rhetoric a different emphasis — namely, the de-essentializing of the characters and situations in the story. "There is no 'essence' to these people. All are afloat in a sea of conflicting ideological currents and opposed rhetorical systems, all of which are socially affirmed" (p. 92).

dispute that Jean-Francois Lyotard names *the differend*.[7]

This *differend* relates not only to meaning, but to problems aesthetic form and class as well, for by the end of the story (and its sequel in *Ulysses*) the reader is obliged to adjudicate forms of art and their moral and social responsibilities as well. Joyce's language, in his defense of his stories to Grant Richards, points resolutely toward their ideological, if not directly didactic, aims. Calling *Dubliners* "my chapter of moral history," and promising with it to make progress toward "the spiritual liberation in my country" (*JJ* 221), Joyce claims for his fiction extra-aesthetic functions motivated by his need to defend "The Boarding House,"among others. against charges of vulgarity. We see in this maneuver the ironic tensions of a Modernism driven by anxiety about its own Arnoldian cultural *Deklassierung* to embed idiomatic slang and obscenity in its formal discourse in order to target it for critique, only to be indicted for the impropriety of these very citations. The narration of "The Boarding House" works overtime to ally itself with the proper diction of a Bob Doran against the "soldiers' obscenities" (*D* 62) of a Jack Mooney, only to have the word "bloody" nearly cost Joyce its publication. Joyce held firm to the fidelity of Jack Mooney's speech — "Jack kept shouting at him that if any fellow tried that sort of a game on with *his* sister he'd bloody well put his teeth down his throat" (*D* 68) — telling Grant Richards "I shall delete the word 'bloody' wherever it occurs except in one passage in 'The Boarding House'" (*SL* 89). The 'bloody' does not even belong to the "style of scrupulous meanness" (*SL* 83) that makes the story's narration the rhetorical antonym of the cultural texts cited within the story itself — the bawdy music hall song (*"I'm a ... naughty girl"*) Polly Mooney sings and *Reynolds'*

---

[7]   Joseph Valente, "Joyce's Sexual Differend: An Example from *Dubliners*," *JJQ*, 28 (1991), 427-443.

Newspaper, Bob Doran's favorite tabloid. Indeed, the irony of Joyce's publishing problems is that the narration of "The Boarding House" — like that of many *Dubliners* stories — makes an effort to maintain itself as high art, as disciplined and formal discourse of high seriousness in resistance to the low art that it fears pressing against it from within the story.

The narration of "The Boarding House" can be construed as attempting to resist, more successfully than Bob Doran, both the moral and cultural degradations of the boarding house's denizens. The narrative rhetoric clearly aims to set itself in sober and credible opposition to alternative versions of the affair of which it is aware — for example the scandalmongering of the boarders of whom it tells us by means of Mrs. Mooney's free indirect discourse, "All the lodgers in the house knew something of the affair; details had been invented by some" (*D* 65). But the narrative version fails as badly as Bob Doran does, and the malicious defamations it holds at bay and crowds out in "The Boarding House" triumph as the sole surviving account of the Mooney-Doran marriage in "Cyclops." There, in *Ulysses*, the calumnies of Bantam Lyons and Paddy Leonard and the unnamed narrator are permitted to flourish unchallenged, we detect at least one discrepancy: the implied threat Bob Doran senses in Jack Mooney's truculent glance on the boarding house stair is literalized in "Cyclops" into a verbal brutality — "Gob, Jack made him toe the line. Told him if he didn't patch up the pot, Jesus, he'd kick the shite out of him" (*U* 12:815). It is impossible for the reader to adjudicate the reliability of the competing versions, or to extricate oneself from the embarrassment of enjoying *Ulysses*'s vulgar, scandalmongering account — with its juicy substance — more than the frigid redactions of "The Boarding House" narrator. The two versions put high and low art, modernism and the tabloid mentality of *Reynolds' Newspaper,* into conflict as Lyotardian "phrases in dispute." Our choice between them, as readers, also becomes a

moral choice with a twist, because it mirrors the hypocrisies of
a Bob Doran who speaks like a monk and acts like a libertine.

In taking sides with high art against the slander of "Cyclops"
as the morally correct version of the Mooney-Doran affair, the
reader sanctions a mode of narration and discourse that, in its
modernistic disinterestedness and probity, sets itself against
"Cyclops'" discourse of aggression. Indeed, the commitment to
form over content in "The Boarding House" expresses itself as
an attitude toward violence that itself becomes part of the moral
stance of this narration about violence. Joyce lets the narration
of "The Boarding House" draw attention to the metaphorical
uses of its content. When the text tells us that Mrs. Mooney
"dealt with moral problems as a cleaver deals with meat" (*D*
63), the reader is invited to interpret the text through a
tropology of social practices that — like the butcher's trade —
provide a civilized concealment to hidden violence and brutality.
The figure of the butcher's trade thus sets up the problem of the
story's rhetoric as one of maintaining a concept of violence as
having a separable outside and inside — a clean, sanitary public
shop on the outside, and a hidden bloody *abattoir* where animals
are slaughtered on the inside. But the violence in this story
refuses to let either narrative or rhetoric demarcate it into clean
and dirty, external and internal, language and meaning. Mrs.
Mooney's metaphorical meat cleaver is also her husband's literal
weapon of choice for domestic violence — "One night he went
for his wife with the cleaver (*D* 61) — and "The Boarding
House" cannot contain its thematic violence with its trimmed,
swabbed, and packaged redactions. "Why do you not object to
the theme of 'The Boarding House'?" Joyce asked Grant
Richards, baffled at the objection to the expletive 'bloody' in the
text. Joyce asks why violent language is more troubling than the
story's content. It is an excellent question, given that the
common intensifier (Is it not ridiculous that my book cannot be
published because it contains this one word which is neither

indecent nor blasphemous?" [*SL* 85] is literalized by its context because Jack Mooney is capable of making his rhetorical threat to "bloody well put his teeth down his throat" come true for the young English *artiste*. In Mooney's mouth, "bloody" signifies blood thirstiness. Yet Jack Mooney's vulgarity and violence are twice removed in the narration — embedded as citations in the redaction of Bob Doran's memory. Through such multiple indirections *Dubliners* attempts to hold at bay a violence that "Cyclops" — that most violent of *Ulysses* chapters — happily releases. The flat, hard, dry crustiness of the narration of "The Boarding House" attempts to conceal and contain a violent tale of threatened murder, assault, tacit prostitution and blackmail, culminating in the social and sexual coercions of the shotgun wedding. The story is a bread pudding with a nasty center of blood pudding.

The narrator's opening account of the Mooney marriage is riddled with gaps and contradictions that foreground the incomplete and impoverished information produced by the exercise of redaction:

She had married her father's foreman and opened a butcher's shop near Spring Gardens. But as soon as his father-in-law was dead Mr. Mooney began to go to the devil. He drank, plundered the till, ran headlong into debt. It was no use making him take the pledge: he was sure to break out again a few days after. By fighting his wife in the presence of customers and by buying bad meat he ruined his business. One night he went for his wife with the cleaver and she had to sleep in a neighbor's house. (*D* 61)

Ostensibly, this is an explanatory preface to the events about to be narrated, an illuminating prehistory that will (retrospectively) help us understand Mrs. Mooney's behavior in the moral travesty that will transpire in her boarding house. But the redacted form makes this information ambiguous, if not deliberately misleading. The substance that is missing from the account is causal explanation. Is Mrs. Mooney the victim of a bad marriage and a bad husband, as the trimmed and cleaned account implies, or is there another version implicit in the timing and the events of the plot? Did Mooney go to the devil after his father-in-law's death because some constraint or coercion — governing both his work as a foreman in his trade and as husband to the butcher's daughter — was lifted by the event? What constraint? Was it a physical threat by the butcher whose physiognomy can be reconstructed genetically from that of daughter and grandson, the "big, imposing woman" (*D* 62) and her son with a thick bulldog face and short thick arms (He was also handy with the mits" [*D* 62])? Or was it the moral force of a "reparation" and a forced wedding? If so, then the shotgun wedding about to transpire in the story belongs to a family genealogy that gives it an even more significant and disturbing historical dimension. Is "The Boarding House" the story of an isolated scandal, a social anomaly and a moral transgression, or does it imply that entrapment was a conventionalized and regularized way for parents "who could not get their daughters off their hands" (*D* 65) to arrange marriages in the social climate of an Irish historical period in which celibacy and delayed families were crucial forms of population control? Florence Walzl writes, "for over a century following 1841, Ireland had the lowest marriage and birth rates in the civilized world. As a natural concomitant, it also had the highest rate of unmarried men and women in the world."[8] The scepticisms and cynicisms that are invited by making the reader speculate on what the redaction leaves out inevitably turn on the redaction itself — and its seeming collusion in concealing a

---

[8] Florence Walzl, "*Dubliners* : Women in Irish Society" in *Women in Joyce,* ed. Suzette Henke and Elaine Unkless, (Urbana: University of Illinois Press, 1982), p. 33.

wider moral and historical problem. Like Mr. Mooney, the narration may have packaged bad meat as good meat, as it were, and thereby produced a story that itself becomes a ruined (fictional) business.

The synoptic, incomplete, and edited family history lacks the explanatory "meat" it implicitly promises because it gives no precise etiology for the failure of the Mooney marriage. What did Mooney fight his wife about in front of their shop customers? Why did he go after her with the meat cleaver one day? What enraged and perturbed this shabby little man (who is himself described as looking like bad pork[9]) with his "pink-veined and raw" little eyes into assaulting the large, imposing, determined woman he had married? The question is undecidable, although it seems to have to do with one or the other side of the issue of providence. Either Mooney — unlike Bob Doran — was simply improvident, in which case his double retention by the butcher is curious. Or he fought Mrs. Mooney because his labor earned him the right to none of the family resources, and he was forced to pilfer his own business — or rather her business, since he seems to have had no claim on the shop — for his own needs. Once separated from his wife, he appears to have absolutely nothing, and the reader is informed that "she would give him neither money, nor food, nor house-room; and he was obliged to enlist himself as a sheriff's man" (*D* 61). The marriage compact, whatever its initial terms, clearly failed Mooney sufficiently that he ruined both aspects of his business, the butcher shop, and the marriage itself. Both the marriage and the narration seem to have reduced Mr. Mooney to a cipher or a signifier of lack — that is, a human crust or rind. The narration — by giving us Mooney's violent and worthless outside, without giving us his inside, his motives or subjective feelings — formally replicates his thematic emptying

[9]   See Barbara McLean, pp. 520-1.

and negation. The marital separation extrudes Mr. Mooney from the family as well as from the narration; the only subsequent reference to him treats him as a mock-stranger — "a disreputable sheriff's man" (D 63) — whose last access to his daughter is severed by Mrs. Mooney's extreme measure of withdrawing her from the work force and confining her to the imbricated business and home of the boarding house. Mr. Mooney is cut off from the family and from the story as though by a rhetorical cleaver.

The story's narration changes with the marital separation of the Mooneys and assumes forms that are disturbingly replicative of the management of the boarding house. Once the narrator begins telling us about Mrs. Mooney's new business, the rigid, synoptic redaction of the pre-history is replaced by a line of narrative license — a far more relaxed and liberal story-telling whose gratuitous details and needless indulgences are a welcome relief from the earlier informational dearth. The narrator gives us enough innuendo about the rowdy clientele from Liverpool and the Isle of Man[10] and the music hall *artistes* who lodge there, to corroborate Bob Doran's concern about the "certain fame" (D 66) Mrs. Mooney's boarding house is acquiring. Further, the narrative voice is voluble and indiscreet about the second generation of Mooneys as it was terse and buttoned about the first. We learn the specific vices (swearing, gambling,womanizing and lewd gossip) that make Jack Mooney a "hard case" (D 62), and are given an unconvincing description of Polly's putative combination of a naughty outside and an innocent inside. The narrator's chatty gossip with the reader in this section seems to betray the determined reserve of the opening. This contradiction raises the possibility that the narrator manages us as Mrs. Mooney manages her lodgers —

[10]   Gifford, p. 63.

"She governed her house cunningly and firmly, knew when to give credit, when to be stern, and when to let things pass" (*D* 62). The narrator, having begun sternly, gives us a few passages of readerly credit or indulgence, for which (like Bob Doran) we shall have to pay later. The textual boarding house of the story subjects us to certain moral economies and discursive disciplines that — like Mrs. Mooney's practice with her lodgers — are calculated to make unwilling victims of the story's thematic and narrative hypocrisies. By subjecting us at story's end to the laconic deprivation of narrative crusts — telling us little and showing us less — the text seems to take revenge on the reader for having desired (like Bob Doran) a sweeter, tastier, more entertaining fictional or poetic fare than that offered by Modernism's scrupulous meanness. Readerly desire — for the moral liberties and discursive delights of, say, the adultery novel — are punished in "The Boarding House" by the thematic and narrative hypocrisies of the story's crusts: tales of "reparation," justice, and the outside appearance of stern action, masking the sinister calculations and cynical subornings of pleasure on the inside.

Mrs. Mooney's nickname *The Madam* makes explicit the continuities of her various businesses. The boarding house is analogous to the bordello and the butcher shop because in each a profit is made out of the body and its necessities: the home is turned into a business, the sexual body is turned into a business; the animal body is turned into a business; and shelter, sex, and food are transformed from basic necessities into commodities. But Mrs. Mooney clearly carries on more than one business at a time, and if her boarding house is a *prix fixe* affair ("fifteen shillings a week — [beer or stout at dinner excluded]"[*D* 62]), she carries on, like her son, a little gambling on the side. Even her endgame on Sunday morning — which the narration explicitly tropes as a game of chance: "She counted all her cards before sending Polly up to Mr. Doran's room" (*D* 65) — Mrs. Mooney has been moving Polly about like a pawn in a game of chess. Polly is clearly her ante, her stake or investment, in a venture with a possible jackpot. Her son acts as her enforcer or muscle, the narrator of "Cyclops" seems to imply — "Gob, Jack made him toe the line. Told him if he didn't patch up the pot, Jesus, he'd kick the shite out of him" (U 12:815). Mrs. Mooney's ambiguous intentions with her daughter are betrayed around the nice pivot of the word "business." When the narrator tells us, "Polly, of course, flirted with the young men but Mrs. Mooney, who was a shrewd judge, knew that the young men were only passing the time away: none of them meant business" (D 63), we are led to think that Mrs. Mooney is reassured and relieved. But the very next sentence betrays her disappointment — "Things went on so for a long time and Mrs. Mooney began to think of sending Polly back to typewriting when she noticed that something was going on between Polly and one of the young men" (D 63). Clearly Mrs. Mooney wanted a young man to mean "business." Polly as ante conflates with the more violent function of bait for prey.

But the overt allusions to prostitution made by the narrator of "Cyclops" ("And the old prostitute of a mother procuring rooms to street couples" [U 12:814]) fail to register the complex and bogus role respectability and morality play in Mrs. Mooney's game. As the narrator shows us Mrs. Mooney rehearsing her case on Sunday morning, it becomes clear that her transaction with Mr. Doran will suppress all reference to money except as a disavowal. Mrs. Mooney tries out a rhetoric of self-righteousness in her mind by claiming a disinterest in money — "Some mothers would be content to patch up such an affair for a sum of money; she had known cases of it. But she would not do so"(D 65). She further elides the commercial character of her boarding house in order to be able to pose as a despoiled hostess when she thinks, "She had allowed him to live under her roof, assuming he was a man of honour and he had simply abused her hospitality" (D 64). Doran's fifteen shillings per week are simply suppressed. Her open refusal to patch up the affair for a sum of money lets her disavow her secret fiscal calculations, whose vulgarity the normally circumspect narrator cannot disavow. Mrs. Mooney's financial predation is figured in extremely coarse commercial slang — "She knew he had a good screw for one thing and she suspected he had a bit of stuff put by" (*D* 65) — an uncommon descent into low idiom that makes the respectable front of the narrative language conspicuously visible. Mrs. Mooney may be a metaphoric type of "Circe" as Barbara McLean suggests cleverly,[11] but she is, simultaneously, a butcher's daughter for whom (unlike Circe) swine are a source of profit. But her cleaver, it must be remembered, is respectability and its power of blackmail — the very same sword Bloom raises against Bella Cohen when he intimates that a scandal could hurt her son at Oxford.

When the narrator of "The Boarding House" switches to Bob Doran upstairs, the return to a prim and formal diction ("Mr. Doran was very anxious indeed this Sunday morning" [*D* 65]) seems to corroborate Mrs. Mooney's judgement that she would win because "He was a serious young man, not rakish or loud-voiced like the others" [*D* 65]). The substance of his thought further seems to confirm the shrewdness of her strategy in exploiting the young man's bourgeois respectability by cloaking her own vulgarity in it ("But his family would look down on her ... She *was* a little vulgar" [*D* 66]). But there are troublesome inconsistencies and gaps in the narration whose significance become clear only retroactively as jokers in the deck — the mistake in Mrs. Mooney's calculations. The first symptom is the curious discrepancy between the putative control and rationality of Bob Doran's thoughts and the extraordinary physical agitation exhibited by his body. His hand trembles too much for him to shave, and the continual misting and fogging of

---

[11] Barbara McLean, "'The (Boar)ding House': Mrs.Mooney as Circe and Sow," *JJQ*, 28 (1991), 520-522.

his glasses suggest he is either in a hot sweat or weeping. There are clearly two Bob Dorans here — the sober and respectable bachelor clerk and the highly unstable weakling — prone, we later learn, to periodic collapses. The two are recognized and reconciled neither in Mrs. Mooney's nor in the narrator's conceptualization of him. The joke on Mrs. Mooney is that Bob Doran,too, knows how to keep things to himself, and what he has kept to himself is that he is neither as good a catch as he appears to be, nor immune to moral hypocrisy. Mrs. Mooney has been fooled by the separation of outer and inner, an extreme contradiction in Bob Doran's case, which he sustains by a temporal compartmentalization that confines his periods of drunkenness, lewdness, and blasphemy to a monthly bender — "for nine-tenths of the year he lived a regular life" (*D* 66). Mrs. Mooney wins only because of Doran's weakness and instability. His public character so embarrassingly in evidence in "Cyclops" will rob her daughter both of the respectability and of the money the forced marriage was meant to provide. By the time of *Ulysses* the "Cyclops" narrator retells Paddy Leonard's story of saving Bob Doran from arrest for "fornicating with two shawls and a bully on guard, drinking porter out of teacups" (*U* 12:803) in an after-hours "shebeen" — "And the two shawls killed with the laughing, picking his pockets, the bloody fool. And he spilling porter all over the bed and the two shawls screeching laughing at one another" (*U* 12:807). Since he is frankly described as being "rolled" by two prostitutes, "The Boarding House" is clearly not the only incident of Bob Doran's being "had" by unscrupulous women.

The *Ulysses* story about Bob Doran and the two "shawls" in bed — which may or may not be true — nonetheless fills a discursive gap in Bob Doran's self-justification in "The Boarding House." "As a young man he had sown his wild oats, of course; he had boasted of his free-thinking and denied the existence of God to his companions in public-houses. But that was all passed and done with ... nearly"(*D* 64). The ellipsis amends and qualifies the rehabilitation, and the story of the two shawls dramatizes the wild oats that the narrative syntax suggests were chiefly of a heretical rather than a sexual nature. Clearly the narrator presenting to us Bob Doran's thoughts in free indirect discourse is giving him the sort of "credit" denied him by Mrs. Mooney, when she rehearses her case: "He was thirty-four or thirty-five years of age, so that youth could not be pleaded as his excuse; nor could ignorance be his excuse since he was a man who had seen something of the world"(D 64). The "nearly" which corrects a near lie and retracts the abstention from wild oats is never elaborated by the narrator, who goes to some pains to reinforce the monkish image of Bob Doran by referring to him twice as a "celibate." The narrative "credit" takes the form of giving Doran credibility in spite of qualifications, gaps and discrepancies in his account. As a result we are vulnerable to being moved by Doran's rather synecdochic memory of his romantic seduction — a memory produced for the specific purpose of exoneration: "It was not altogether his fault that it had happened"(D 66). The evidence conjured for this purpose gives a domestic and *light* version of a delicate and metonymic eroticism. It is invested in fragmentariness (the first casual caresses her dress, her breath, her fingers had given him"[D 67]), in displacements ("From her hands and wrists too as she lit and steadied her candle a faint perfume arose" [D 67], and in highlighted details whose fetishistic features such as foot and fur ("Her white instep shone in the opening of her furry slippers," [D 67]) and is nearly unrecognizable as the site of the raucous "reunions" in which Polly sang naughty songs, men made free allusions to her, and she exhibited the flirtation produced by her job of looking after the young men ("As Polly was very lively the intention was to give her the run of the young men"[D 63]). Bob Doran's memory totally extracts Polly from the marginally respectable boarding house and its rather rough clientele, and gives her a tender wifely role ("And her thoughtfulness! If the night was anyway cold or wet or windy there was sure to be a little tumbler of punch ready for him"[*D* 67]). This account implies that Bob Doran was seduced by the domestic solace sorely missed in his bachelor living, rather than by the free and racy gaiety of Polly's entertainment and coquetry in the house. Without the later correction of the story of Bob Doran and the two shawls in bed — which reminds us of the putatively abandoned wild oats — the decent narrative account of Bob's sweet romantic memory might well seduce us into exonerating him altogether.

Once it begins to represent Bob Doran's thoughts, the narrative voice of "The Boarding House" shifts sympathy and takes sides with him against the Mooneys. It thereby implicates itself in the moral hypocrisies of the story. The narrational sympathy with Doran seems to take as its moral premise that the Mooney entrapment and implied violence is more transgressive than Doran's lust. But a stronger interpretive inference is that the narrative prejudice in abandoning Mrs. Mooney and shifting to Doran's side is motivated by class and philology. Against the discursive transgressions of the Mooneys — Jack's obscenities, Mrs. Mooney's slang and Polly's solecisms — Bob Doran upholds critical standards of proper usage and grammar, "Sometimes she said *I seen* and *If I had've known* " (*D* 66). His rhetorical question — "But what would grammar matter if he really loved her?" — answers itself in the posing with an imbricated set of functions. The questions establishes Doran's superiority twice over: confirming taste and distinction precisely by having grammar matter, and heart and sentiment by offering that it may not. But the credit Doran accrues through his defense of linguistic correctness — a credit both extended and retracted by its extension to matters of biblical philology in the "shawls" incident in *Ulysses* — must be clarified and questioned, like his putative romanticism, for self-serving disingenuity. "The Boarding House" tells us only that his rehabilitation notwithstanding, he "still bought a copy of *Reynolds' Newspaper* every week but attended to his religious duties and for nine-tenths of the year lived a regular life" (*D* 66). *Reynolds Weekly Newspaper*, Gifford tells us, was a fourpenny record of social and political scandals"[12] (a forerunner of modern tabloid journalism. Doran's skepticism toward religion — "he had boasted of his free-thinking and denied the existence of God" (*D* 66) — does not seem to extend to the tabloid press, suggesting that his own prurient curiosities and credulities give him good reason to fear scandal. Doran's heresies take a peculiarly philological form in "Cyclops," when he questions biblical authority on the ground of historical authorship — "talking against the Catholic religion, and he serving mass in Adam and Eve's when he was young with his eyes shut, who wrote the new testament and the old testament, and hugging and smugging" (*U* 12:805). Doran's scholarly interests are discredited by his forum, the two prostitutes who transform his question into a dirty joke, "How is your testament? Have you got an old testament?" (*U* 12:810), that Gifford and Seidman suggest, puns on "fundament." The curious narrative concatenation of wild oats and heresy in the moral account of Doran is dramatized in this scenario. The "Cyclops" version of Bob Doran's transgressions is *The Reynolds' Newspaper* reportage of his doings — that is, the version that would most interest himself if he were reading about someone else — while the *Dubliners* version is the sober, self-justifying account that would be cloaked in his own genteel idiom and shaped by the gaps and omissions of his own hypocrisies.

The story ends by describing Polly Mooney sitting on the bed in Bob Doran's room waiting for a marriage proposal. Yet curiously, this closure to the story's donée — namely the intricate history of this proposal — takes the form of a virtual blank, or — to return to my earlier metaphor — the thinnest of

---

[12]   Don Gifford, *Joyce Annotated: Notes for 'Dubliners' and 'A Portrait of the Artist as a Young Man,'* second edition (Berkeley: University of California Press, 1988) p. 66.

crusts. Not only is the dramatic meat of the upcoming proposal with its ghastly pretenses and ironies withheld from us, but the tight-lipped narrative style tells us nothing of Polly's version of the affair, and very little of what she is feeling. Either Polly resists narrative penetration, giving her simile of "a little perverse Madonna" new meaning, or the narrator, like Bob Doran, is not interested in Polly's subjectivity and makes no attempt to see or represent what goes on in her mind or in her heart. The narrator tells us that the sight of the pillows "awakened in her mind secret amiable memories" (D 68), but doesn't tell us what they are. We are told that her memories give place to hopes and visions of the future — "Her hopes and visions were so intricate that she no longer saw the white pillows" (D 68) — but they are not shared with us. The narrator makes it clear that Polly Mooney has not only an inner life of the body ("the blood glowed warmly behind her perfumed skin" [D 67]) but also an inner emotional and mental life; but either the narrator has no access to it, or chooses not to give the reader access to it. The third possibility is that the narrator sees Polly Mooney precisely as Bob Doran does, entirely as configured by a surrounding texture of metonymies (flannel,fur, perfume, candle, punch, pillows and, later, in the "Cyclops" narrator's account, patent leather boots and violets) that please the senses. Bob Doran's account, in retrospect, gives indication only of the comfort Polly provided for him, without evidence that he "knows" her at all.

Furthermore, all of the narrative information about Polly — and particularly her own words, leave open the question whether she is always acting and performing, as in the little song she sings when she is introduced into the story — "*I'm a ... naughty girl./ you needn't sham: You know I am*" (D 62). Do her signs or gestures — such as "the agitation of her bosom" Bob Doran feels through his shirt — represent "her" own feelings or nature, or do they belong to a calculated performance? Polly's words, when they are strung together — "I'm a naughty girl..."; "What am I to do?"; "O my God!"; "Yes, mama?" — constitute a little melodrama whose most dramatic moment — "She would put an end to herself, she said" (*D* 66) — sounds patently false. Her actions,too, are inconclusive. She weeps a little, alone, after Bob leaves. But her restorative gestures, "refreshing" her eyes and adjusting her hairpin in profile, appear to have all the calculation that would make her her mother's daughter. The relationship of her outer and inner self that the question of performance raises, remains undecidable — although not to the scandalmongering Dubliners. The "Cyclops" narrator firmly resolves the inconsistencies of Polly's public appearances against her — citing as evidence her self-display when she attends church with her husband — "Then see him of a Sunday with his little concubine of a wife wagging her tail up the aisle of the chapel with her patent boots on her, no less, and her violets, nice as pie, doing the little lady" (*U* 12:811). If Polly looks proper, she is "doing the little lady," whereas if she looks improper, she is thought to be genuine — "Bantam Lyons told me that was stopping there at two in the morning without a stitch on her, exposing her person to all comers, fair field and no favor" (*U* 12:44).

Polly is more absolutely bared and publicly exposed than any other Joycean female, but without being narratively "penetrated," as though, indeed like a little perverse Madonna, she remains inviolate. But the resolute exteriorization of Polly Mooney raises disturbing possibilities of misprision. By making Polly an enigma, a mystery, she continues to invite narrative penetration at the same time that clues persist that there may be something "wrong" with this young girl who has "the habit of glancing upwards when she spoke with anyone" (*D* 62). The "Cyclops" narrator's description of her as a "little sleepwalking bitch" (*U* 12:398) urges us to consider that Polly might be mentally and emotionally impaired in some way, and that her promiscuity is less a vice than either the pathology of a disturbed adolescent or the abused innocence of a mentally deficient girl. Then, again, perhaps she is a young Molly Bloom, taking charge of her sexual life as she pleases even in the face of scandal. These possibilities,too, are undecidable, but they remind us that all interpretations of this enigmatic young woman will function as narrative violations and predations, and put us as readers on the side of the more unsavory clients of the boarding house and Barney Kiernan's pub. We are left with the possibility that Polly Mooney's exteriorization makes her a narrative crust or rind with an inviolable center that may be an absent or missing center, no center at all, an unlocatable — a "sleepwalking" — subject. That may be too why her subjectivity remains irretrievable in the later texts — unlike such other mysterious women as the bird girl of *Portrait*, who is interiorized in Gerty MacDowell. Any attempt at exonerating Polly Mooney, however, crosses sharply with "The Boarding House"'s narrative agenda of making clear that, unlike the weak, scrupulous, Bob Doran ("But the sin was there; even his sense of honour told him that reparation must be made for such a sin" [*D* 67]), the Mooneys have "crust" — that is, a bold and vulgar audacity in the way they play their games, and in the way they use bourgeois morality for their own purposes and designs.

Among *Dubliners* stories, "The Boarding House" arouses relatively little critical interest, perhaps for two reasons. The "case" we are asked to decide seems pretty open-and-shut, and the mode of narration is dull and uninteresting. The result, I have tried to suggest, is narration as bread pudding — that is, a story in which there is little for readers or critics to get their teeth into, by way of interpretation. Unlike "The Sisters," "Araby," and "The Dead," where the narrative language draws a great deal of attention to itself, "The Boarding House" narration is so unobtrusive and impartial that it needs the contrasting wedge of the "Cyclops" sequel to dilate its seemingly homogeneous mass and restore a sense of heteroglossia and internal contradiction to its bland discursive texture. But once considered as tacitly self-interrogating and self-incriminating, "The Boarding House" can be restored to its historical moment in modern literature as an example of modernistic writing problematizing itself in its genesis. The story complicates the overturn of Victorian pieties blind to the violence of social control by problematizing this very progressivism for possible misogyny. The predations of the lower-class Mooneys may not, after all, exonerate the less blatant predations of bourgeois self-righteousness and class superiority. And the formalistic control of language may silence less disciplined discourses that may complicate the truth, and thereby have Joyce's style of "scrupulous meanness" contribute its own measure of violence to its censure of violence. "The Boarding House" may indict its own frigidities as clearly as "A Painful Case" indicts celibacy — turning the adultery novel on its head by making abstention from adultery the equivalent of murder. Narrative bread pudding — as lean and economical as modernism itself — may (Joyce seems to have been telling us all along) not be blameless.

Irvine

"A LITTLE CLOUD" AS A LITTLE CLOUD

JOHN GORDON

About the enigmatic title of "A Little Cloud," two observations are generally entertained. The first is that the title in some way refers to the main character, whose repeated nickname "Little Chandler," applied to someone who sees himself as remarkably diminutive and insubstantial, certainly sounds meant to signal some such connection. The second is that it is an allusion, of the sort that Chandler imagines putting in his poetry (*D* 74), to the "little cloud out of the sea, like a man's hand" summoned by Elijah in I Kings 18:44. Here again, the nature of the connection seems vague, but in general one can observe that many have found an Elijah-like spirit of denunciation running through *Dubliners* in general, and that "A Little Cloud" in particular does end with a noisy, if domestic, cataclysm. Perhaps because Elijah and Little Chandler are so utterly dissimilar,[1] no one has yet made a sustained effort at reconciling these two interpretations of the title. Here goes.

---

[1] Jackson I. Cope, *Joyce's Cities: Archaeologies of the Soul* (Baltimore: The Johns Hopkins University Press, 1981), pp. 18-19. Cope has been prompted by the biblical reference to equate the two; "Chandler envisions himself as an Ur-Eliot, poet of *The Waste Land*" thus like Elijah "Righteous" prophet against the modern waste land surveyed in Dublin and embodied in Chandler; his prediction that Gallaher will get married some day is actually a "prophecy" of the sort Elijah delivered against Ahab. I find this reading surreal. One, Elijah's prophecies are not primarily fortune-telling predictions, but dire warnings about the consequences of Israeli apostasy, and his main complaint is not about anyone's marriage, but, if anything, about the nation's divorce from its God. Two, neither Elijah nor Eliot can be imagined without heavy irony calling a sunset "a shower of kindly golden dust" (*D* 73), or using any of Chandler's other poetic prettifications of this sort. Three, both are about as temperamentally far as it is possible to get from Chandler's brand of benignity. Four, the kind of poetry to which Chandler aspires epitomizes what Eliot loathed most.

To begin with the first, let us take the hint and consider the possibility that Little Chandler might actually *be* a little cloud, on something close to a literal level. That may sound far-fetched, but the story is after all the work of the same author who took his only epigraph from Ovid's *Metamorphoses*, and who in *Finnegans Wake* will have Issy double as the "little cloud" (*FW* 256.33) Nuvoletta:

Nuvoletta in her lightdress, spunn of sisteen shimmers, was looking down on them, leaning over the bannistars and listening all she childishly could. How she was brightened when Shouldrups in his glaubering hochskied his welkinstuck and how she was overclused when Kneesknobs on his zwivvel was makeacting such a paulse of himshelp! She was alone. All her nubied companions were asleeping with the squirrels.

* * *

Then Nuvoletta reflected for the last time in her little long life and she made up all her myriads of drifting minds in one. She cancelled all her engauzements. She climbed over the bannistars; she gave a childy cloudy cry: *Nuee! Nuee!* A lightdress fluttered. She was gone. (*FW* 157.8 and 159.10)

Keeping her in mind, consider Little Chandler's introduction on the first page of his story:

His hands were white and small, his frame was fragile, his voice was quiet and his manners were refined. He took the greatest care of his fair silken hair and moustache and used perfume discreetly on his handkerchief. The half-moons of his nails were perfect and when he smiled you caught a glimpse of a row of childish white teeth.

The "white small hands" here may well be meant to recall Elijah's cloud the size of a man's hand, and in any case much of

the rest is distinctively like a little cloud: white, fragile, quiet —
there is no thunder yet — and "refined": a cloud is, literally,
refined sea-water. There is the fair hair of the wispiest texture,
the glimpse of a doubtless white handkerchief wafting its cloud
of scent, yet another "glimpse" of white in the teeth, even the
white half-moons, up there in the sky. Thus nebulized, Chandler
throughout his story proceeds to behave like a cloudlet being
blown over the Dublin landscape. Like Issy he is seen to "gaze"
(*D* 71) panoramically down on those - at least in one sense -
beneath him, whether the Dubliners outside and quite possibly
below his office window[2] or the urchins to whom he finds
himself feeling "superior" as he looks "down the river" (*D* 73).
At the outset he espouses a philosophy of drift, of not
"struggl[ing] against fortune" (*D* 71), and envisions himself a
poet whose "wistful" verse would identify him with the
famously misty "Celtic school." On his eastward passage to
Corliss's, as night is falling and the winds therefore likely
blowing east, toward the sea,[3] he wanders lonely as a cloud and,
head in the clouds, in "revery" (*D* 74), initially drifts past the
entrance.[4] Once inside he meets his old friend, a man who
complains of having gotten "a little gray" in the hair atop what

---

[2]   See Donald T. Torchiana, *Backgrounds for Joyce's Dubliners*
(Boston: Allen and Unwin, 1986), p. 126. The breadth of Chandler's prospect
from his office window, encompassing as it does the actions of various
parties amid "grass plots and walks," seems to suggest an elevated vantage.
According to Donald T. Torchiana's source, Chandler's building has two
stories.

[3]   "Meteorology," *Encyclopedia Britannica*, 15, 1946, p. 346. The
entry under "Meteorology" states, "At places on a coast there is usually a
pronounced tendency for a wind to blow from the sea to the land in the
morning, and from the land to the sea in the evening."

[4]   See Warren Beck, *Joyce's Dubliners: Substance, Vision, and Art*
(Durham, N.C.: Duke University Press, 1969), pp. 163-4. Beck has
remarked on Chandler's cloud-like drift and sense of elevation.

Chandler perceives as his "heavy, pale" face (*D* 74-75), who then proceeds to fill him up with liquid, with water mixed with larger and larger amounts of whiskey, which as *Finnegans Wake* readers know takes its name from the Gaelic for "water of life." In fact it is at about the point that Gallaher is filling his old friend's glass with water and asking "Water? Say when" (*D* 75) that "A Little Cloud" starts becoming, against heavy competition, among the wettest of *Dubliners* stories. Taking up about $11^1/_2\%$ of the book's word count, "A Little Cloud" contains ten of its 31 occurrences of the words "drink," "drinks," or "drinking," two of its eight "water"s, eight of its 17 "whisky" or "whiskies," one of its three "boose"s, and one of its two "liquor"s, along with its only "liqueur." The main points of its course are the bridge over a river, a watering-spot in which the main topic of conversation is what transpires at other watering-spots such as the "cafes" of Paris, and a room in which Chandler stands accused of having missed the consumption of one beverage, tea, of having forgotten another, coffee, and of letting the baby break out, liquidly, into tears, soon matched by the tears in his own eyes.

While in Corliss's Gallaher shares another pleasure with Chandler, thus occasioning the one passage in "A Little Cloud" where the story seems most aware of its title: "- I'll tell you my opinion, said Ignatius Gallaher, emerging after some time from the clouds of smoke in which he had taken refuge..." (*D* 78). This tells us that Chandler, also smoking a cigar, is similarly enveloped, in clouds of a darker and heavier cast than have attended him up to now. And he himself, under influence of cigar and drink, has become, literally, darker and heavier in the face: "warm and excited" (*D* 80), blushing repeatedly until he feels the "blush ... establishing itself" (*D* 80), his "color ... heightened" (*D* 81), the white which was so marked a feature of his early presence now obliterated by congestion of blood. The encounter, he tells himself, has "upset the equipoise of his sensitive nature" (*D* 80).

"Equipoise" is not a bad word to describe the nature of that diffused suspension of water droplets in process of condensing from gas to liquid that we call a cloud. When a cloud's equipoise is "upset," when its droplets become too heavy, it darkens and produces rain. Particulate "nuclei of condensation" - from cigar smoke, say - will help facilitate the process.[5] Sometimes, in a parallel process of disrupted equipoise, the rain is accompanied with lightning and thunder, which perhaps explains why "A Little Cloud" becomes so noisy in its last pages, from the loud report of Gallaher's clapping Chandler "sonorously" on the back (*D* 79), to the loud laugh of his valedictory (*D* 82), to the echoing roomful of screams and bawls with which the story ends. In any event it reliably produces rain, as a consequence of achieving too high a relative density, of having become saturated with its contents.

"A Little Cloud" ends as follows:

Little Chandler felt his cheeks suffused with shame and he stood back out of the lamplight. He listened while the paroxysm of the child's sobbing grew less and less; and tears of remorse started to his eyes. (*D* 85)

So, finally, the story's gathering storm breaks. Overcharged with the accumulating impulses which in earlier stages of

---

[5]   Thomas A. Blair, *Weather Elements: Texts in Elementary Meteorology* (New York: Prentice Hall, Inc., 1943), p. 130. Blair writes, "If air is perfectly free from dust, it may be cooled far below its dew point without any condensation ... But if smoke or salt spray from the ocean is added, rapid condensation occurs ... Some of the ocean salts and some of the products of combustion have the quality of absorbing moisture from the air and for this reason are said to be hygroscopic. Apparently the presence of hygroscopic, or at least water soluble, particles is essential to the condensation of moisture in the air, and such particles are called nuclei of condensation. Fires, ocean spray, explosive volcanoes, and burning meteors furnish large numbers of dust nuclei."

congestion have suffused and darkened his cheeks, Little
Chandler breaks down and cries. Meanwhile his child is, as they
say, crying himself out, discharging his own load of watery
grief. Chandler's weeping is a culmination, as a cloudburst is the
culmination of accumulated density yielding to gravity. His
story has traced the mounting trajectory of his emotion, from
inception to discharge, employing with remarkably systematic
literalness the conventional comparison of moods to weather, of
rages to storms and of smiles to sunshine, and its governing
conceit has been that emotions like clouds can begin
inconspicuously, can gradually gather mass over the course of
their journeys until they become oppressively heavy, and can
then dissolve in sudden, sometimes violent,
acts of release, thus, as the saying goes, clearing the air. The
title of "A Little Cloud" therefore enjoins attending to a process
rather than to any one point of correspondence — to the
succession of stages by which the fragile and apprehensive
happiness described on the first page drifts, wavers, thickens,
darkens, and breaks down into the tempest of the last page.
Once that is understood, we are I think in a position to
understand as well the relevance of the title's Biblical allusion,
which I would argue should properly be taken as referring not
to one verse alone but to three, I Kings 18:43 through 45:

43 And [Elijah] said to his servant, Go up now, look toward
the sea. And he went up, and looked, and said, There is
nothing. And he said, Go again seven times. 44 And it came
to pass at the seventh time, that he said, Behold, there ariseth
a little cloud out of the sea, like a man's hand. And he said,
Go up, say unto Ahab, Prepare thy chariot, and get thee
down, that the rain stop thee not. 45 And it came to pass in
the mean while, that the heaven was black with clouds and
wind, and there was a great rain.

Seen thus in context, the words "a little cloud ... like a man's hand" pretty obviously have the effect of emphasizing the cloud's contrasting relation to its previous non-existence or invisibility at first and its tumultuous culmination later - what went before it grew to the size of man's hand and what happened afterwards. They function to specify a point in a process, the point just after something has come into noticeable existence and begun its development into something which will eventually prove to be momentous. My primary authority here, by the way, is Stephen Dedalus, who in *Ulysses* uses a version of these words in exactly this sense when he relates how "a matutinal cloud ... at first no bigger than a woman's hand" had by evening swollen into a storm of sufficient magnitude and violence to make him faint with fear (*U* 17:36-41).

Once we recognize that the title "A Little Cloud" directs our attention to questions of developmental process, of growth from near-nullity to dissolving consummation, we may come to notice to what extent the story is concerned with establishing events as stages in a temporal continuum of just that sort. Little Chandler and the narrator are both given to looking before and after. The story begins with the words "Eight years before," by way of relating what Gallaher has made of himself in the intervening time. It ends, by way of relating what Chandler has come to in a comparable period, in a room of furniture bought "on the hire system" (*D* 83), with the wife (in both before and after version — picture and person) of a year-and-a-half-old marriage already beginning to fray badly and a no longer new-born starting to get on the nerves, whose presence is the last straw because it simultaneously embodies to Chandler both what he has done with his life so far and what it will be from now on. The honeymoon is over, the bloom is off the rose, he has made his bed. For Chandler, the meaning of his home is of things ending badly and beginning just as badly, of an ongoing developmental continuum suddenly seen as intolerable rather than as generative, to which the most elemental of responses is the one word he yells at the baby: "Stop!"

In other words, "A Little Cloud" enacts Chandler's growing perception of what he, contrasted with Gallaher, is coming to, over time, and the apparently commonplace but by no means self-evident assumption behind that perception is that life is a testing-ground of coming-to, of inception leading to growth leading or not leading to certain culminative and decisive fulfillments by which all that has gone before may be judged. "His temperament might be said to be just at the point of maturity" (D 73). Behind that statement is a kind of theory of life, among other things.

Among those other things is a poetics. In the course of the story Chandler finds himself wanting to be a poet of a certain type, which can be described with some precision because "A Little Cloud" acts it out. From Chandler's point of view, in fact, the main narrative thread of his story would probably be about the poem not written, the poem which in the course of the evening was conceived, pondered, nurtured, matured, brought to the point of fulfillment, then cruelly aborted in the glare and blare of his home. It is the work of a "sensitive nature" (D 80) whose finely-balanced "equipoise" registers fleeting sensations and transfuses them into an inner repository which then imbues them, over time, with the gentle melancholy of its native spirit. We may possibly glimpse, behind this portrait, the James Joyce of *Dubliners* balefully surveying the James Joyce of *Chamber Music*.[6] Its implicit aesthetic is all Symons and *Silverpoints* and Whistler nocturnes, wispy aperçues swathed in glimmery-shimmery mist, casting — as, incidentally, from a cloud — a "shower" of "kindly golden dust" (D 71) on the locals to transform them, with perhaps a piquant touch of irony,

---

[6] See James Ruoff, "A Little Cloud" in *James Joyce's Dubliners: A Critical Handbook*, ed. James Baker and Thomas Staley (Belmont, California: Wadsworth, 1969), pp. 107-108.

into "cavaliers" and "alarmed Atalantas" (*D* 72).[7]

Implicit to this school of poetics is the principle that such moments must come unbidden. Like the *Symbolistes* and the Romantics before them, Chandler in his poetic role values vagrancy, drift over directedness, neither the cosmopolitan observer holding the mirror up to nature nor the questing spirit seeking out truth in its lair but rather the trembling, sensitively receptive soul waiting to be "touched" by the "poetic moment" (*D* 73) as it comes. That explains, I think, why there should be a suggestion of *sortes Virqiliniae* in the way Chandler allows his left hand to open the volume of Byron which "lay before him on the table" and reads the first poem, a lament for a dead lover which one would think could have little to say to a man one of whose perceived problems at the moment is an all-too-lively wife, but to which he nonetheless, as we would say today, responds as to the call of his lost self, vibrating "to the rhythm of the verse about him in the room" (*D* 84).

Small wonder that someone with a poetic program, however incipient, of this sort, a program of undirected reverberations to "different moods and impressions" (*D* 73), should be "disillusioned" with the Gallaher whose literary code is one of "Always hurry and scurry, looking for copy and sometimes not finding it" (*D* 75-76). Looking and finding is exactly what the Chandlerian poet does not do. "And then, complains Gallaher, always to have something new in your stuff" (*D* 75). The Chandlerian poet by contrast does not "have" the "new," nor think of experience, new or otherwise, as a raw material to be used up. Rather he is a sensitive vessel whose function it is gratefully to receive, nourish, bear and bring to term whatever poetic matter chance may grant it. The metaphor of gestation is in fact quite explicit: "…the thought that a poetic moment had

---

[7]   For the *fin de siècle* and Celtic Twilight origins of Little Chandler's aestheticism, see Torchiana, pp. 131-136.

touched him took life within him like an infant hope." Crystallization, another kind of articulated concretion over time, might also serve as a metaphor for the process, a suggestion perhaps implicit in Thomas B. O'Grady's astute description of Chandler's scene with his child as "the crystallizing point of the story," the baby functioning as a "desperate compression" embodying Chandler's "accumulated frustrations" and in the process displacing and obliterating the story's other baby, "the infant hope" of the earlier "poetic moment."[8]

I would however argue that the most adequate figure for the process is that specialty of clouds, condensation and distillation. Rather than being consumed or enwombed, the moods and impressions which make their way into Chandler's poetic interior are absorbed, randomly, through a permeable surface, to accumulate and combine with other such gatherings until they coalesce into a distilled quintessence which can then be, in Chandler's invariable term for poetic production, "expressed" outward. Like two other resident analogies, the "drum of his ear" "pierced" by the his child's wail or the room in which the story ends, Chandler's poetic vessel has "thin walls," easily perfused, through which impressions pass to be gathered and "echoed" (D 84).

Imagine such a vessel set adrift, like a cloud, and you have, I think, the essential character of Chandler's poetic progress during the story, which can be tracked, meteorologically, as a progressive sequence of points of absorption, condensation, and distillation. The first point would probably be the new feeling of superiority which comes over him as he passes through the "dull inelegance of Capel Street" with his head full of his friend the Great Gallaher (D 73). Still under the influence of that feeling, he then pities, and anthropomorphizes, "the poor

---

[8]   Thomas O'Grady, Little Chandler's Song of Experience," *JJQ*, 28 (1991), 400-1.

stunted houses" which appear to his sight as he crosses Grattan Bridge. Out of this mingling of inner mood and outer impression is engendered his imaginative vision, instantly antiqued with infusions of middle-Yeatsian diction rendering the houses as huddled tramps waiting for night to "bid them arise, shake themselves and begone." It is Chandler's "poetic moment," and its sensed presence yields an "infant hope" taking "life within him," which so suffuses his soul that "a light began to tremble on the horizon of his mind" (*D* 73), and which by the time he reaches Corliss's has by condensing around the conjured image of Gallaher's triumph grown heavy enough — "moods" overbalancing "sensations" to screen out the exterior world.

That world returns in full force when Chandler enters the assaultive "light and noise" of the bar and spends a prolonged period in the presence of what the weather report of *Finnegans Wake*, forecasting "lucal drizzles," calls "A sotten retch of low pleasure" (*FW* 324:32) — a sodden wretch (and wretched sot) given to low pleasures, a sudden reach of low pressure (invariably precipitation-producing), sodden with humidity. Under the influence of Gallaher and his natural environment, through the absorption of water and whiskey, smoke and noise, hot air and low talk (it is here that Chandler concludes he could do "something higher" than Gallaher's work), Chandler's cloud, at the eye of the story's storm, thickens and darkens toward what fancifully inclined weather reporters have long described as the "brooding" or "ponderous" state which will emerge in the concluding section. Large and lowering, "disillusioned" and disengaged from the major mass of nuclei of condensation embodied in Gallaher, its temperature dropping to dew point as it moves from the "warm and excited" (*D* 80) atmosphere of Corliss's to the chilliness of a home in which Chandler "looked coldly into the eyes of the photograph and they answered coldly" (*D* 83), this cloud requires only one last center of condensation around which it can gather in order to erupt. At the end it is as if Chandler, supersaturated with the day's accumulated occasions of grief, were looking, from the volume of Byron to the furniture to the photograph, for such a center of condensation — for, as the saying goes, something to cry about. Wife and child supply it.

In his autobiographical essay "A Portrait of the Artist," the twenty-one year old Joyce envisioned a future fiction in which character would be represented not as set in "an iron memorial aspect" but as exhibiting an "individuating rhythm," "the curve of an emotion."[9] Written two years later, "A Little Cloud" is surely among his earliest experiments in this line. The curve of Little Chandler's emotion is plotted scientifically, meteorologically. It may be that behind what I have called the story's governing conceit is what by Joyce's day was the long-outmoded medical doctrine that an individual's composition of humors is a kind of inner weather, with, for instance, "vapours" rising from liver or blood to cloud the brain; it may even be that Little Chandler's vague antiquarianism can in some way be said to license the application of such theories to his story. It is during a similarly antiquarian period — somewhere between his Byron phase and his Shelley phase, immediately after the "mummery" of his stage performance — that Stephen Dedalus or his narrator similarly takes inventory of Stephen's inner "vapours" in the form of a weather report:

Pride and hope and desire like crushed herbs in his heart sent up vapours of maddening incense before the eyes of his mind. He strode down the hill amid the tumult of suddenrisen vapours of wounded pride and fallen hope and baffled desire. They streamed upwards before his anguished eyes in dense and maddening fumes and passed away above him till at last the air was clear and cold again. (*P* 86)

---

[9]   James Joyce, "A Portrait of the Artist," in *A Portrait of the Artist as a Young Man*, Viking Critical Library, ed. Chester Anderson (New York: Viking Press, 1968), p. 258.

Whatever its local rationale, the interior meteorology of "A Little Cloud" forecasts the work of a writer who will hereafter make it his practice to connect his narratives to the endogenous rhythms and cycles of his human subjects as they absorb or fail to absorb the outer world through membranous surfaces of varying permeability — Gabriel's window, Duffy's wall, Stephen's "prism of language many-colored and richly storied" (*P* 167), Bloom's reflective refraction, the semi-transparent glaucomal "collideorescape" (*FW* 143.28) of *Finnegans Wake*. From now on the stories forged in such convergences will tend to follow an inner-generated dynamic which typically begins with some apparently negligible datum or stimulus and builds by degrees to a dissolving consummation. It may follow the curves of mounting rage and sexual release, as in "Cyclops" or "Nausicaa" respectively, or the larger individuating rhythms involved in gestation, lifetime, day's passage, or any closely related sequence of temporal events, as when Bloom's random "throw it away" comment to Bantam Lyons winds up leading to the Citizen's eruption, or when HCE's answer to a question about the time sets off a chain reaction eventually producing a lynch mob.

Whether determined by the mob psychology at work in these last two examples[10] or the individual psychology, often with a distinctive physiological component, governing a Farrington or a Gerty MacDowell, Joyce's commonest kind of narrative unit will characteristically, in following the course of their interior states, also follow the developmental progress of Elijah's first invisible, then little, then ponderous, then cataclysmic cloud. A self-proclaimed Aristotelian by way of Aquinas, Joyce seems determined almost from the beginning not only to observe the unities within each story or chapter but to extend them, to the

---

[10] According to the OED, the phrase "mob psychology" made its first recorded appearance in 1896, in a letter by William James.

rendering of inner space and its evolving interaction with outer. Indeed one recurring version of this interaction seems to be simply that subjective interior keeps absorbing more and more external influences until it becomes overloaded. Whatever the final outcome, the issue raised by "A Little Cloud," the issue of how optimally to absorb and transmute or distill or alchemize impressions within one's inner self, will be with Joyce until the end, and the meteorological metaphor introduced in that story will frequently recur in other guises. The nebular processes of motion, absorption, collection, contamination, condensation, distillation, reflection, "expression," and discharge, which the title of "A Little Cloud" alerts us to recognize in the consciousness of its subject as he engages his environment, will henceforth return in different combinations as regular features of Joyce's distinctively supple, versatile, mercurial, and collideorescapic brand of *style indirect libre*.

New London

MONEY AND OTHER RATES OF EXCHANGE: COMMERCIAL RELATIONS AND "COUNTERPARTS"

CAROL SCHLOSS

James Joyce was fond of keeping accounts, and many of his fictions are informed by assessments of value and questions of economic management. My concern in this essay is to think about "imaginative economy" — the way in which economic systems are structured by imagination — and, then, "poetic economy" — the way Joyce the artist uses fictive economic discourse as an ordering principle in his work.[1] More directly, I would like to ask how the reader can recognize the assumptions James Joyce makes about the commercial relations between England and Ireland at the turn of the century and how Joyce understood these relationships to affect the conduct of everyday life in Dublin. If money talks, it talked to Joyce in complicated and resonant ways and his sense of what constituted a profitable life emerged out of a series of trade-offs as he sorted out the tensions about money that were created by Ireland's beleaguered place in the British Empire. In this essay, I have selected "Counterparts " — that sometimes contentious story of employer and employee relationships — to illustrate my concerns.

Before turning to Joyce, I would like to present another example of the imaginative use of economic tensions. When E. M. Forster wrote about the English experience of governing in India, he could see quite clearly that conflicts of interest in colonial nations grew out of metaphysical ideas and their structural embodiment. The British and the Indians — Moslems and Hindus — did not simply disagree about material goods, but

---

[1]   Kurt Heinzelman, *The Economics of the Imagination,* (Amherst, University of Massachusetts Press, 1980), p. 11.

about the meaning of the whole system in which they circulated. In *A Passage to India*, Forster dramatized this clash in several conversations between Dr. Aziz, a Moslem and Mr. Fielding, an Englishman teaching school in Chandrapore, who says:

> "Is emotion a sack of potatoes, so much the pound, to be measured out? Am I a machine? I shall be told I can use up my emotions by using them next." eat your cake and have it, even in the world of spirit."
> "If you are right," [Aziz replies] "there is no point in any friendship..., and we had better all leap over this parapet and kill ourselves."[2]

The reader might say that the disagreement expressed by these characters stems from Fielding's failure to make a distinction between a commodity economy and what the noted anthropologist Marcel Mauss has called a gift economy. Fielding assumes that emotion is like money in relation to things: each thing has a fixed and determined price, and one conducts life economically, that is, parsimoniously and without excess. Aziz, on the other hand, understands emotion to be given away without measure, for it is only in this way that it will return and bring benefit to the giver. That is, he knows that the libido is not lost when it is bestowed, but only when it cannot flow.[3] Later in the text, Aziz says, "If money stays, death comes; Did you ever hear that useful Urdu proverb? "To which Fielding replies, My proverbs are" A penny save(d) is a penny earned; A stitch in time saves nine; Look before you

---

[2]   Lewis Hyde, *The Gift: Imagination and the Erotic Life of Property* (New York: Vintage, 1979), p. 21. See also E. M. Forester, *A Passage to India,* (New York: Harcourt, Brace and Jovanovich, 1952), p. 282.

[3]   Hyde, p. 22.

leap; and the British Empire rests on them.[4]

I mention these lines from *A Passage to India* because I think that they can help readers see a similar tension in Joyce's Dublin where differences in economic consciousness are not marked by exotic proverbs but are manifest, instead, by resentments and anxieties whose origin seem to have no clear location for those who experience them. But to Joyce, who shares, I think, Aziz's sense of the erotic life of property, these conflicts can be identified as a result of superimposing British economic ideas onto an Irish culture with very different notions of the value of exchange. That is, Joyce imagined Dubliners to live in a city built from the imposition of one system of economics, or from one discursive superstructure, which has become divorced from the expression of its colony's cultural and spiritual needs. His countrymen struggled within a system of accounting which had ceased by and large to indicate its citizens' inner well-being.

Kurt Heinzelman suggests that, "political economy as a separate discipline, may be seen as [the nineteenth century's] most significant and intricate construct, its greatest and most problematic myth."[5] But as he also points out, such fictions can "have the power of fact"[6] that is, they can work in "prohibitive and prescriptive ways, sanctioning only such arrangements and behavior as are consistent with the ongoing operations of these fictions."[7]

To make these ideas less abstract, I would like to turn to

---

[4] *A Passage to India*, p. 254

[5] Heinzelman, p. 48.

[6] Heinzelman, p. 100.

[7] Heinzelman, p. 100.

"Counterparts." As Joyce's readers know, the story charts one Dublin man's working day and traces its effects into the evening when Farrington appraises his experience and passes on the abuse he has suffered to his young son who cries out in pain and promises to pray for his father. Joyce writes:

> He was full of smouldering anger and revengefulness. He felt humiliated and discontented; he did not even feel drunk; and he had only twopence in his pocket. He cursed everything. He had done for himself in the office, pawned his watch, spent all his money; and he had not even got drunk. He had lost his reputation as a strong man, having been defeated twice by a mere boy. His heart swelled with fury and, when he thought of the woman in the big hat who had brushed against him and said *Pardon!* his fury nearly choked him. (*D* 96-7)

One way to read the sequence of events charted here is to observe that one failure begets another; the man who is brutalized in one situation becomes the brutalizer when the structure of power changes. One cannot strike out at one's north of Ireland employer because such a person has the authority to take away or to limit one's livelihood; but one can hit a child whose livelihood depends on you.[8]

Another way to explain this chain reaction might be to call upon Marx who would tell us that Farrington, as part of a commodity culture, is regarded as nothing more than a commodity himself: he is a "thing" or a machine for producing contracts in a timely manner and on this particular evening he

---

[8] Mr. Alleyne may serve as a manager for the absent Mr. Crosbie, so that Joyce's fictional situation becomes a sort of urban counterpart of the absentee landlord situation that plagued so much of Ireland at the turn of the century. See Cullen.

is bearing the psychological consequences of his failure to perform properly.[9]

But I think both of these ways of reading oversimplify the network of tensions developed within the text, for they do not identify the fictional nature of the economic system that holds sway within the story's frame. I am referring to the power of that fiction to shape lives, not the rudiments of another value system which Farrington inchoately senses but cannot bring himself openly to endorse: although he knows he is violated in some way, he cannot bring himself fully to assert a counter-logic of exchange. Instead, he sneaks around and snipes at Mr. Alleyne while at the same time judging his own life to be a loss. "He felt humiliated and discontented" (*D* 96), the text reads.

Another way to say this is that Farrington's imagination is informed by the contractual economic management that he also spends his time subverting. He subscribes to the very calculus of utility that creates his misery, discrediting himself according to values that are foreign to his nature and to his native culture. For him, the British Empire does provide for the common good.

If we were to name in a very simple way the elements of his employer's political economy, it would probably consist of contracted and institutionalized processes embedded in the commodity market, of all-purpose coinage, of the market mechanism of supply and demand, and of trade markets in foreign and domestic commerce. Since to him, the gaining of wealth pertains to "matters of moral indifference," his principles of economic progress may, in fact, be unprincipled. In saying these things, I am attributing a value system to a fictional character who usually remains silent, but I am inferring this system from the threats that are constantly directed against

---

[9]   In this respect, Farrington reminds us of Herman Melville's copyist, *Bartleby the Scrivener*, whose response to monopoly capitalism, as it is represented by the lawyer whose work he copies is to "prefer not to."

Farrington at the office:

> "Do you hear me now? ... Ay and another little matter! I
> might as well be talking to the wall as talking to you.
> Understand once and for all that you get a half an hour for
> your lunch and not an hour and a half. How many courses do
> you want, I'd like to know ... Do you mind me now?" (*D* 87)

Later Alleyne scolds Farrington in this manner, "You
impertinent ruffian! You impertinent ruffian! I'll make short
work of you! Wait till you see! You'll apologise to me for your
impertinence or you'll quit the office instanter!" (*D* 91-92).
These outbursts and the few remarks Alleyne makes about
Farrington seem to align his attitudes with thinkers like W. S.
Jevons whose book *The Theory of Political Economy,* was
published in 1871 and who was one of the first British
economists to divorce economics from a larger sense of the
well-being of the *polis* and to place it on a purely utilitarian
basis. I would also identify his attitudes with Malthus who had
a "sufficient evil" theory of economic progress. That is, he
assumed all men to be like Farrington: "inert, sluggish and
averse from labor unless compelled by necessity."[10]

The reader should observe that Farrington does not lose a
moment in berating his clerk:

> "Farrington? What is the meaning of this ? Why have I
> always to complain of you ? May I ask you why you haven't
> made a copy of that contract between Bodley and Kirwan ? I
> told you it must be ready by four o'clock."

> "But Mr. Shelley said, sir--"
> "Mr. Shelley said, sir.... Kindly attend to what I say and

---

[10]   Heinzelman, p. 91.

not to what Mr. Shelley says, sir. You have always some excuse or another for shirking work, Let me tell you that if the contract is not copied before this evening I'll lay the matter before Mr. Crosbie.... Do you hear me now?" *(D 87)*.

As a result of these assumptions about labor, price, cost and credit, Mr. Alleyne organizes an office built on privilege for the owner (himself and Mr. Crosbie), strict regulation of work processes, and constant supervision of employees. "Mr. Alleyne has been calling for you," said the chief clerk severely. "Where were you?'" *(D 89)*.

When we look for further circumstances that can account for the dynamics of this Dublin office, we can see the assumptions Joyce made in constituting his story that were not unique to Mr. Alleyne and his business establishment, nor were they simply reflections of economic theories that held sway at the turn of the century, but were buttressed by hundreds of years of commercial relations between England and Ireland. In *A Theory of Literary Production*, Pierre Macherey suggests how we can begin to discern the inscription of such a history, cautioning that "[t]his history is not in a simple external relation to the work: it is present in the work, in so far as the emergence of the work required this history, which is its only principle of reality and also supplies its means of expression."[11]

---

[11] Pierre Macheray, *A Theory of Literary Production* (London: Routledge and Kegan Paul, 1978), pp. 93-94. Macheray continues: "it is not a question of introducing a historical explanation which is stuck on to the work from the outside. On the contrary, we must show a sort of splitting within the work: this division is its unconscious, in so far as it possesses one — the unconscious which is history, the play of history beyond its edges, encroaching on those edges: this is why it is possible to trace the path which leads from the haunted work to that which haunts it. Once again, it is not a question of redoubling the work with an unconscious, but a question of revealing in the very gestures of expression that which it is not. Then the

By 1903, A. E. Murray, one of Joyce's contemporaries and author of *A History of the Commercial Relations between England and Ireland*, could look back and claim that problems in Ireland's current domestic economy had their origins in the terms of the Act of Union in 1800.[12] "The Union" she declared, "has proved but a union of legislatures — not one of hearts, nor even of interests."[13] Looking around her and seeing the financial world with an historical perspective that was denied to Dublin laborers like Farrington, she decided that "[e]conomically speaking, the interests of England and Ireland have never been further apart than at the present time."[14] In her mind, free trade benefited artisans in England while bringing ruin to Irish industries and agriculture;[15] and she considered that the commercial expansion of the British Empire had left Ireland with an increased tax burden without similar benefits. In making

---

reverse of what is written will be history itself.

[12]   Under the Union, each country was to retain and service a separate national debt and Ireland was to contribute 2/17th of the common expenditure of the United Kingdom. When the respective national debts of the two kingdoms reached a proportion of 2/17ths, the two exchequers were to be amalgamated. In 1800 a future of peace had been envisaged, and the British national debt, it was expected would fall from its abnormally high level. In fact, however, the fifteen years after the Union were years of almost uninterrupted war. The Irish contribution to the expenditure of the United Kingdom rose sharply. Revenue, despite tax increases, rose less sharply, and by the end of the war, the Irish exchequer was covering the deficiency in its 2/17th share of the common expenditure of the United Kingdom by borrowings amounting to roughly half the size of its contribution" (Cullen, *Economic History,* p. 104).

[13]   A. E. Murray, *Commercial Relations between England and Ireland,* (London: P.S. King and Son, 1903), p. 2.

[14]   A. E. Murray, p.3.

[15]   A. E. Murray, p. 3.

her own assessment of Ireland's commercial status at the turn of the century, she took into account social practices and political economies as well as import/export statistics, pointing out that the British viewed Ireland as they did other possessions; assuming the subservience of the colony to the Mother Country.[16] Given the unstated values that supported such an assumption — those of hierarchy, control, and materialism — it was little wonder, she argued, that England feared Roman Catholicism, for it threatened the very pillars of the Empire. "When Catholic Emancipation at last came," she concluded, it was too late; *the gift* had lost its grace and was powerless to remove the terrible bitterness that religious persecution had caused"[17] (my italics).

Departing, once again from the standards of strict utilitarian economics, she also claimed that one could not fully understand the commercial relations between England and Ireland without taking the penal code into account.[18] "For over a century," she reminded her audience,

the Irish people were ground down by laws which Edmund Burke described as "a machine of wise and elaborate contrivance, and as well-fitted for the oppression, impoverishment and degradation of a people and the debasement of human nature itself, as ever proceeded from the perverted 'ingenuity of man.'"[19]

---

[16] A. E. Murray, p. 9.

[17] A. E. Murray, p. 2.

[18] A. E. Murray, p. 14.

[19] A. E. Murray, p. 13. Quote from "Letter to Sir Hercules Langrishe." See Matthew Arnold's edition of Burke's *Letters on Irish Affairs* (London, 1881).

Our contemporary, the economist L. M. Cullen disagrees vehemently with Murray's views and argues that commercial ideas during the time of Union could not be trusted because they tended to become mixed with the various ideological positions of the Irish before their independence.[20] Murray would not have disagreed with him, for her claims were unabashedly founded on political premises. Like Marcel Mauss, she believed in a gift economy and on an expanded understanding of community well-being: one could not claim to have described a culture unless all of its transactions had been identified. To look only at fiscal exchange, was, from her perspective, to see money as the only unit of value and consequently to mute the complications of all other human interactions. For her, all community transactions, including those that involved religious values, the management of the body, and the creation of self-esteem (the very things that are sacrificed in Farrington's life), had to be accounted for in making generalizations about national well-being. "When Catholic emancipation came," she had reckoned, "it came too late. *The gift* had lost its grace"[21](my italics).

Even in matters of fact, in cases that involved statistical science, she pointed out that "there is only a small gulf between fact and fiction; and between the figures that are facts and the figures that are fiction, there are numerous figures that are partly fact and partly fiction, and that can only be accepted with supplying us with more or less trustworthy indications of tendencies not as giving us sufficient material for arriving at any

[20] L. M. Cullen, "Irish Economic History: Fact and Myth" in *The Formation of the Irish Economy*, L. M. Cullen, ed. (Cork: Mercier Press, 1969).

[21] A. E. Murray, *Commercial Relations between England and Ireland* (London: P.S. King and Son, 1903), p. 2.

practical conclusions."[22] When she wrote this, she was referring to the conclusions of the Financial Relations Commission of 1894-96, known as the Childers Report which had tried to address the widespread belief that Ireland suffered under a heavier burden of taxation than did Great Britain. While she considered the report to be favorable to Ireland, she also harbored reservations about the trustworthiness of its evidence. Countering the Commission's methodology with private knowledge of the practices of the laborers, renters, and land owners in Ireland, she concluded that "to get at the true figures of the revenue derived from imperial taxation, so many allowances and conjectures have to be made that the statistical basis of the whole inquiry is much weakened."[23]

Murray's goal was to show the imaginative substructure of statistical science when it was applied to problems of parity between Ireland and England; and we might say that Joyce's goal, insofar as he "read" economics in a similar historical light, was to reveal the power of such fictions to structure imaginative life. Whatever the actual status of Mr. Alleyne's wealth in "Counterparts," he relies on it to establish and to enforce his superiority in the eyes of his employees.

While it is not surprising to find these ideas in the owner of a business or in his representative, I do find it interesting that Joyce creates a Dublin workman who subscribes to the same code. Farrington assumes the naturalness of wage labor and the necessity of usury: the need to pawn his watch for lack of adequate pay. He accepts economies of size, efficiency, and the use of time, the need for hierarchy, the naturalness of property rights and the ubiquity of cash purchase. As a consequence, he assumes there to be something radically wrong with his own desire to be with friends in a pub and he also assumes he is a

[22]   A. E. Murray, p. 401.

[23]   A. E. Murray, p. 402.

worthless person. "Mr. Alleyne would never give him an hour's rest; his life would be a hell to him. He had made a proper fool of himself this time" (*D* 92). Never does Farrington see himself as someone with a different but equally appropriate value system, nor does he come to understand that utility economists like Jevons and Malthus offered only one way of imagining the proper conduct of economic life. That is, Joyce shows us the nature of imperialist economics as an imaginative or poetic activity and then demonstrates to us that poetic constructs can have the force of fact: they can compel behavior and ideals about self-worth. "Farrington felt humiliated and discontented" (*D* 96).

Given Joyce's exposure of this fiction in "Counterparts" it is interesting to tease out the suppressed and only partially acknowledged value system behind Farrington's dissatisfactions and to assert that his desire to be in the pub is based on the felt experience of what is sacrificed in Mr. Alleyne's economic world view and on an alternative sense of the proper nature of exchange.

Here I would like to return to a more deliberate study of the work of the anthropologist Marcel Mauss whose influential book, *The Gift*, was like an injunction to record the entire credit structure of a community. "He offered the theory of the gift as a theory of human solidarity and considered that field work would be below standard unless a complete account could be given of all transfers, that is, of all gifts, inheritances and successions, tributes, fees, and payments. He was looking at every transaction that affected human well-being; he was not just looking at cash transfers. Although Mauss was observing primitive cultures, he was convinced that this morality and organization still functioned in surreptitious ways in modern society.[24]

It is this sense of the gift exchange that motivates Farrington in "Counterparts:" where Mr. Alleyne robs him of feelings of self-worth, honor and even *eros* itself:

> The moist pungent perfumes lay all the way up to Mr. Alleyne's room. Miss Delacour was a middle-aged woman of Jewish appearance, Mr. Alleyne was said to be sweet on her or on her money. She came to the office often and stayed a long time when she came. She was sitting beside his desk now in an aroma of perfumes, smoothing the handle of her umbrella and nodding the great black feather in her hat. Mr. Alleyne had swivelled his chair round to face her and thrown his right foot jauntily upon his left knee. The man put the correspondence on the desk and bowed respectfully but neither Mr. Alleyne nor Miss Delacour took any notice of his bow (*D* 89-90).

The pub works toward restoring values (for Farrington) and with these values a voluntary cycle of exchange and the benefits of a culture based on reciprocity can be seen. In some inarticulate way, Farrington gropes to understand that gifts allow one to feel part of a larger, self-regulating system and that each donation is an act of social faith. That the gift exchange falters in this case — Farrington does not recoup his self-esteem or a sense of abundant friendship — need not impair the applicability of this construct, for Farrington's frustrations allow us to see the power of a predominant economy to mute dissident thoughts and practices.

Another way to say this is to observe that Joyce's *Dubliners* shows us an historical world in which the business of Empire

---

[24]   Marcel Mauss, *The Gift,* trans. W. D. Halls (New York: Norton, 1990).

has interrupted the cycle of gift exchange so that what is passed on is neither reciprocal nor beneficent.[25] At the end of the workday in Dublin Farrington finds his abused and terrified child. 'O pa!' he cried. 'Don't beat me, pa! And I'll say a *Hail Mary* for you, pa, if you don't beat me ... I'll say a *Hail Mary*" (*D* 98). But beyond this dark image of violation, Joyce manifests a second knowledge: that scarcity and abundance have as much to do with the form of exchange as with how much material wealth is at hand (see Hyde).[26] In this regard, his scrupulously mean picture of Dublin working life was itself added to the wealth of nations.

If we extend Ireland's economic system to include Joyce's contribution to it, and think of the social function of art, we might consider his work to be offered in the spirit of the gift — as a return to Ireland, an exchange which pits one artist's imaginative economy against the British commodity culture which had so disrupted the lives of his characters. Imagination can have the force of fact. In writing, Joyce raised a challenge in two directions, daring both England and Ireland to face their relations in new ways and to acknowledge the values inherent in the commerce of the spirit.

Philadelphia

[25] As the Drummond Commission of 1838 admitted, "these signs of growing prosperity are, unhappily, not so discernable in the condition of the labouring people as in the amount of produce of their labour. The proportion of the latter reserved for their use is too small to be consistent with a healthy state of society. The pressure of a superaboundant and excessive population ... is perpetually and powerfully acting to depress them" (Cullen, pp. 109-110).

[26] See Lewis Hyde, *The Gift: Imagination and the Erotic Life of Property* (New York: Vintage, 1979).

THE CRAFT OF "A PAINFUL CASE": A STUDY OF REVISIONS

JANA GILES

As a writer, I am fascinated by the way in which James Joyce composed his work. The conceptualizing of crucial encounters, the development of character, setting and tone, the organization of symbol and meaning — all are part of the creative process of writing fiction, and Joyce not only chose a fascinating subject in "A Painful Case" — the death of love and its ramifications — but he also left his stamp on the story by his quest for perfection and skill in editing. The purpose of this paper is to compare the revisions in the Yale manuscripts and the story published in *Dubliners*.

I. A Fine-Tuned Character

Joyce seems to have known from the beginning how he wished to present Duffy's home and surroundings. On the first page of the draft copy, only two words differ from the later version: the draft copy reads, "he lived in an old gawky house" (*JJA* 4, 95) while the *Dubliners* story replaces "gawky" with "sombre"(*D* 107), and further Joyce emended "two or three cane chairs" to read first "three cane chairs " and finally "four cane chairs (*D* 107). While "gawky" gives the impression that Duffy's taste is awkward, or out of step, it does not suggest that he is deliberately misanthropic. "Sombre," on the other hand, reinforces Duffy's character as Joyce has described it. But why did Joyce increase the number of chairs in Mr. Duffy's room? The gesture at first seems to contradict Mr. Duffy's anti-social habits — two chairs imply intimacy, three suggest the proverbial crowd, but four are a complete and ordered set — one for each side of the table — and suggest a sense of material symmetry and completion rather than a habit of entertaining. His life with neither "companions nor friends" (*JJA* 4, 99; *D* 101) tells the reader that Duffy never entertains guests: one chair would have served just as well as four.

Joyce fine-tunes Duffy's character on the third page of the draft copy. Joyce writes, "His cheek-bones gave his face a harsh ~~expression~~[1] character" (*JJA* 4, 99; *D* 108), insisting that Duffy's facial expression is not transitory but reflects his inner nature. The description originally reads as follows —

Joyce's Notes in Revision	*Joyce's Original Text*

He lived at a little distance
from his body and regarded his
own acts with doubtful
He had an odd
sideglances. Every
autobiographical habit
two or three days
he added a short
composed
sentence ~~to an~~
~~He never gave to beggars~~
~~alms on principle;~~
unwritten story containing a
subject in the third person
and a predicate in the past
tense.
~~This odd habit grew on him~~
~~unawares.~~ He never gave alms
to beggars, on
principle. He walked firmly,
carrying a thick
hazel stick. (*JJA* 4, 99; *D* 108)

black hair and a tawny
moustache did not quite
cover an unamiable
mouth. His cheek-bones
also gave his face a harsh
~~expression~~ character but
there was no harshness in
the eyes which, looking at
the world from under
their tawny eyebrows,
gave the impression of a
man ever alert to greet a
redeeming instant in the
lives his soul spurned^:
He walked firmly,
carrying a thick hazel
stick.

---

[1] Words crossed out with a line through them indicate Joyce's revisions in the draft. Words underlined in the quotations indicated Joyce's insertions between the lines of his own text of the draft.

In rewriting this passage, Joyce added vital information about Duffy: he excised the harsh "lives his soul spurned," which too obviously makes Duffy a detestable snob, and the substitute, "but often disappointed" is more likely to garner the reader's sympathy for Duffy's idealism. Having solicited our compassion, Joyce pulls us away from too much empathy by emphasizing Duffy's abstraction from the sensual world of bodies and beggars, the world of physical need. And while the change in the draft copy suggests that Duffy's story is in the third person and past tense, Joyce makes Duffy's distancing from himself more immediate in the *Dubliners* story: "He had an odd autobiographical habit which led him to compose in his mind from time to time a short sentence about himself containing a subject in the third person and a predicate in the past tense" (*D* 108).

Furthermore by removing "this odd habit grew on him unawares" (*JJA* 4, 99), Joyce took away the possibility that Duffy is victim rather than master of his own emptiness. And Joyce juxtaposed Duffy's behavior towards beggars with the now "stout hazel" (*D* 108), reiterating Duffy's firmness of purpose and suggesting that if a beggar were to be over eager, Duffy might not hesitate to use his stout hazel on the beggar's back.

Three more alterations establish music as Duffy's sole "dissipation." The draft states:

His evenings <u>were</u> spent either roaming about the outskirts of Dublin, or before his landlady's piano. His liking for Mozart brought him sometimes to a concert or to an opera (*JJA* 4, 99).

The story in *Dubliners*, however, reads:

His evenings were spent either before his landlady's piano or roaming about the outskirts of the city. His liking for Mozart's music brought him sometimes to an opera or concert (*D* 109).

Contrary to Duffy's solitary habits, his landlady's piano takes precedence over lonely wanderings; it is not Mozart the man, but his music Duffy likes; Duffy seems to prefer the very human theatrics of opera to the more exact quietude of chamber music, for instance; and in both versions Dublin becomes just another abstract "city."

In the early draft Duffy has "neither friends nor companions" (*JJA* 4, 101), but he comes to be lacking in church and creed as well: this is solitude extraordinaire. "[He] ... conceded nothing further to the conventions which regulate one's civic and personal life" (*JJA* 4, 101) becomes "conventions which regulate the civic life" (*D* 109). The effect of this is clearly to distance Duffy and the reader from any emotional implications whatsoever and keep all interactions on a strictly formal basis. The revision reads,"He even allowed himself to think that, in certain circumstances, he would rob his bank: but such circumstances never arose. His life rolled out evenly, an adventureless tale"(*JJA* 4, 101). In the final version Joyce smooths over the full stops in the original version so that the sentence rolls out as evenly as Duffy's life, coming to the first full stop at the ironic wall of Duffy's futility.

II. The Temptress and the (At)Tempted

Duffy first meets Mr. Sinico at a poorly attended concert. She is introduced to Duffy and the reader through her empathic action: "The lady who sat next to him surveyed the empty benches once or twice... (*JJA* 4, 101). Joyce rewrites this passage less clinically: "The lady looked round at the deserted house..." (*D* 109). The substitution of "deserted" for "empty" augments the atmosphere of desolation which pervades the finished story. Joyce tightens "He was surprised that she seemed so free from awkwardness" (*JJA* 4, 101) to read "so little awkward" (*D* 109), removing any possible suggestion of slatternly behavior on the part of the lady. Joyce began to describe Emily Sinico with a rather odd focus,

> Her eyes were very dark blue and steady. Their gaze began with a note of defiance but was confused by what seemed a deliberate swoon of the pupil into the iris, revealing for a moment a temperament of extreme sensibility. In a moment the pupil reasserted itself, this half-disclosed temperament fell again under the control of prudence, and the astrakhan jacket.... (*JJA* 4, 103)

In *Dubliners*, Joyce gives Mrs. Sinico's eyes a life of their own, and they seem to acquire a character all the more compelling because of their defiance. To gain speed, he changes "In a moment" to "for an instant" and adds "quickly." Joyce foregrounds the notion of defiance. While "extreme" seems to promote a subtle hysteria about Mrs. Sinico, "great" seems noble, and a similar dignity governs the substitution of "reign" for "control." And the substitution of "her astrakhan jacket" for "the astrakhan jacket" brings the reader's attention away from her eyes and back to the person of Mrs. Sinico and her coming defiance of socio-sexual norms hiding even then in her bosom. The finished description of Emily Sinico reads:

> The eyes were very dark blue and steady. Their gaze began with a defiant note but was confused by what seemed a deliberate swoon of the pupil into the iris, revealing for an instant a temperament of great sensibility. The pupil reasserted itself quickly, this half-disclosed nature fell again under the reign of prudence, and her astrakhan jacket.... (*D* 109)

In the ensuing paragraphs, Joyce's growing subtlety in handling the developing relationship between Emily Sinico and James Duffy becomes apparent. The first draft contains the obvious explanatory sentence, "Such was the beginning of their acquaintance"(*JJA* 4, 103), and this is omitted from the story in *Dubliners*. Another example of Joyce's growing sense of nuance can be seen by comparing the two versions of their first date. Duffy makes an appointment with Emily Sinico, and in the draft version this reads, "She came — without her daughter (*JJA* 4, 103) to simply "She came" (*D* 110) in the *Dubliners* text, entirely eliminating the coy tone of insinuation.

I would now like to discuss the third person in the triangle — Captain Sinico. Joyce sets out to describe his ingenuousness in the original draft in the following manner:

> Captain Sinico encouraged his [Duffy's] visits as he imagined that his daughter's hand was in question and, as he had in his own mind, dismissed his wife so thoroughly from the gallery of pleasure that it did not occur to him for a moment that anyone else would take an interest in her. As the captain was often away and the daughter often out giving music lessons Mr. Duffy had opportunities to enjoy the lady's society. (*JJA* 4, 105)

Joyce alters "as he imagined," which implies the captain could have had his suspicions, had he bothered to think about them, for the decisive "thinking," and underscores the captain's true ignorance and obtuseness by ending the sentence at "question." The complexity of the situation is not sacrificed in Joyce's revision, "Captain Sinico encouraged his visits, thinking that his daughter's hand was in question. He had dismissed his wife so thoroughly from his gallery of pleasures that he did not suspect that anyone else would take an interest in her" (*D* 110).

The lack of clauses set off by commas in this sentence adds to its irony and sureness. Deleting "in his own mind" removes the possibility of the captain's heart knowing what his mind forgets. "Sincerely" is less abrupt than "thoroughly" and also serves to exonerate Mrs. Sinico from a crime of passion. This is reinforced by the substitution of *his* gallery of pleasures for "the gallery of pleasures": now the reader wonders if the captain has sexual interests elsewhere. Regardless of Sinico's rank, he is a seafaring man, and echoes of Eveline's father's statement — "I know those sailor chaps" — still ring in the reader's ear. In the last sentence Joyce substitutes" As the captain," with "As the husband." This change distances the reader from the captain's frame of reference, and returns the focus to Duffy and Mrs. Sinico. The reader is forcibly reminded of the irony of the Sinicos' marriage, because the use of "husband" in the *Dubliners* story is coupled with "He had dismissed his wife...." These two are nominally and legally, but not actively, husband and wife.

The next sentence begins the account of the blossoming of the relationship between James Duffy and Emily Sinico. In the draft, Duffy lent her books, provided her with new ideas, but in the final version 'new" is deleted, and it appears that he is now Mrs. Sinico's sole source of food for thought. Joyce also altered "she became his confessional" to the more personal "his confessor" *(D* 110).

When Joyce has Duffy speak of his involvement with the Socialist Party, he emends the passive "the interest taken in the question of wages was excessive" *(JJA* 4, 107) to the more active and less arrogant "the interest they took in the question of wages was inordinate" *(D* 111), and puns on the workers' unrest when he substitutes, "No social revolution ... would be likely to affect Dublin..." *(JJA* 4, 107) for "strike Dublin" *(D* 111). Joyce resists the temptation to portray Mr. Duffy as an entirely unsympathetic stuffed shirt, so he inserts the phrase "with careful scorn" when Duffy responds to Mrs. Sinico's inquiry about his failure to write down his thoughts. Here Duffy is disingenuous since we already know he is an autobiographer who keeps writing materials available on his desk, and translates

Hauptmann. Duffy's curmudgeonly criticism of phrasemongers and policemen is that of a failed artist (like Little Chandler) as well as a romantic afraid to test his ideals. Moreover, the irony of Mrs Sinico's death will resound again when the evening paper delivers that news realistically and unsparingly. Joyce excises in the draft itself what would have been the last sentence of the paragraph which reads, "I, he said, will receive with disdain every advance on the part of this civilisation which is unworthy of me but which seeks to entrap me" (*JJA* 4, 107). It is a good thing that Joyce removed it, for one glance at this comic vainglorious statement, and the sensitive reader would cease to respect Mr. Duffy's moral predicament.

Joyce deletes "fertile" from the phrase which originally said "her companionship was like a warm fertile soil" (*JJA* 4, 107), since the union of the lovers comes to nothing.

> [A]s he attached the fervent nature beside him more and more closely to him, he heard his strange unimpassioned voice say that in man's soul loneliness ~~has never yielded to any love~~ outlives all its longings, ~~He held on to his~~ We cannot give ourselves: we are our own (*JJA* 4, 109).

In the *Dubliners* story, the passage reads:

> [A]s he attached the fervent nature of his companion more and more closely to him, he heard the strange impersonal voice which he recognized as his own, insisting on the soul's incurable loneliness. We cannot give ourselves, it said, we are our own (*D* 111).

Clearly the substitution of "his companion" for "beside him" personalizes Mrs. Sinico, while the other changes are meant to further separate Duffy from himself. At last arriving at the moment of passion, Joyce rewrites, "...Mrs. Sinico threw her arms around forward into his lap and seemed to faint" to read

"...Mrs. Sinico caught up his hand passionately and pressed it to her cheek" (*D* 111). The last version is less melodramatic, less sexual, and more poignant. Chances are Mr. Duffy would be more repelled by a fainting woman in his lap than by an impulsive yet restrained tenderness.

III. The Force of Habit

The reader is returned to life as James Duffy knew it, and Joyce takes pains to sustain the sense of his protagonist's tense calmness. The draft of Duffy's return to habit betrays traces of Mrs. Sinico's emotionalizing:

Four years passed. Mr. Duffy lived four more years of his even adventureless life. His father died; the junior partner of his bank retired. ~~During these years Mr. Duffy retreated more into himself as the accentuated lines on his face testified.~~ He kept away from concerts and theatres lest he should meet her ~~and consoled himself with his piano and books.~~ (*JJA* 4, 111; see *D* 112)

Any sign of grieving is removed in the revision.

IV. Phrasemongers and Paramours

The bulk of the revisions to "A Painful Case" occur in the newspaper account of Mrs. Sinico's death. It does not seem necessary or desirable to analyze every sentence of the intertext. Joyce, as is evident from his letter of c. 24 September 1905 (*L* II 109) to his brother Stanislaus, was mainly concerned with checking the details of the fictional accident, and with producing an utterly objective reporting tone which would show Mr. Duffy his own failings.

The minor alterations which do seem noteworthy concern proper names. The names of the railway and city officials are no more arbitrary than those of James Duffy and Emily Sinico. Duffy is from the Gaelic *dhu*, and Irish *dubh* meaning "swarthy; dour; one who scowls, looks black,"[2] — a suitable choice for one of saturnine humor. Many have speculated on the meaning of "Sinico." Some have suggested that it puns on "sin," *"sine coitone*," or "sinecure" or that the name was borrowed from a composer Joyce knew in Trieste.[3] Sinico could also imply "sinister" from the Italian *sinistra*, meaning the left hand or side, often associated with maligned or ill-omened forces. Further, "Emily" may be the feminine form of *Aemilius*, meaning "rival." If Emily Sinico is Mr. Duffy's rival at all, it is in rivalry over his soul.

I found the alterations of names within the newspaper article noteworthy. The Deputy Coroner who holds the inquest is Leveret in both the draft and the later version of the story. "Levret" is derived from the Old and Middle English and means "dear or beloved counsel."[4] It seems appropriate that he should bear the official message of death. Lennon, the name of the driver of the engine which strikes Mrs. Sinico is similarly unaltered. This surname means 'lover,' 'paramour' or 'concubine.'[5] Perhaps we can see him as a stand-in for Duffy.

---

[2]   See Patrick Hanks and Flavia Hodges, *A Dictionary of Surnames* (Oxford: Oxford University Press, 1988), p. 156 and Henry Alfred Long, *Personal and Family Names* (London: Hamilton Adams and Co., 1883) rpt. (Detroit: Gale Research Co., 1968), p. 33.

[3]   Bruce Bidwell and Linda Heffer, *The Joycean Way* (Dublin: Wolfhound, 1981) p. 126 and 128. See also Epifanio San Juan, Jr., *James Joyce and the Craft of Fiction* (Rutherford New Jersey: Fairleigh Dickinson University Press, 1972) p. 160.

[4]   Hanks, p. 324.

[5]   Hanks, p. 322.

Kilbride was the original name of the railway porter, but Joyce may have seen this as too blatant a choice[6] because Joyce changes his name to Dunne. Higgins, the railway official becomes Patterson Finlay. "Finlay" from the Gaelic means "fair warrior" and "Patterson," "of Patrick."[7] On a more superficial level the double patronymic seems to show the authoritativeness or substantiality of the railway company official. It seems to correspond to "magniloquent" name of the journalist — "O'Madden Burke — in "A Mother." Then, there are the substitutions of Dr Halpin for Dr. Cosgrave and Dublin City Hospital for St. Vincent's Hospital. Vincent Cosgrave, was of course, a friend of Joyce's, who tried to betray him with Nora (*JJII*, 160 and 279). Joyce found out from Stanislaus that St. Vincent's Hospital would not serve accident victims at Sydney Parade, and the etymology of "Halpin" is obscure.

No one seems to have considered Mrs. Sinico's death a suicide, but the name itself as the characters involved seem to implicate both Duffy and Dublin.

V. Decline and Autumn

It seems to the reader that a century has passed, that time has telescoped and Duffy is suddenly aged when he raises his head from the page after his final reading of the evening paper, and it is not until the article has been "digested" that Joyce slows time down by examining Duffy's reaction.

---

[6] See Patrick Hanks and Flavia Hodges, *A Dictionary of Surnames* (Oxford: Oxford University Press, 1988) and Henry Alfred Long, *Personal and Family Names* (London: Hamilton, Adams and Co.); rpt. (Detroit: Gale Research Co., 1968). The Kilbride of this early draft appears, I think, as the engine-driver in "Circe" (*U* 15:96).

[7] See Long, p. 271 and Hanks, p. 183.

Disgust and disbelief characterize the first period of Duffy's decline, and Joyce's alterations to the text seem to be made with this in mind:

> The whole narrative of her death revolted him and it revolted him to think that he had ever spoken to her of what was sacred to him. The threadbare phrases, the inane expressions of sympathy, the mild commonplaces covering such a commonplace vulgar collapse attacked his stomach. He felt that in her nightly excursions to buy spirits she had degraded him ~~and~~ or she had degraded herself. He had been foolish enough to imagine that he had found in her his soul's companion. And now her image was superseded by the recollection of the babbling wenches he had seen carrying cans and bottles to be filled by the barman. Just God, what an end !------ Evidentally, she had been unfit to live, lacking in strength of purpose, an easy prey to habits. Civilisation has been reared upon such wrecks. And yet he was astonished and almost incredulous. How could she have sunk so low ! He could not have deceived himself utterly about her. (*JJA* 4, 123 and 125)

"[W]hat was sacred to him" is, changed to "what he held sacred" (*D* 115), but what that is we are never told; we must assume it is the same "principle" which required him to withhold arms from mendicants. "[T]he mild commonplaces covering such a commonplace vulgar collapse" becomes "the cautious words of a reporter won over to conceal the details of a commonplace vulgar death," which is more explicit and brings to mind Duffy's own sin of excessive caution. The rest of the passage in the final copy reads:

> Not merely had she degraded herself; she had degraded him. He saw the squalid tract of her vice, miserable and malodorous. His soul's companion! He thought of the

hobbling wretches whom he had seen carrying cans and bottles to be filled by the barman. Just God ! what an end! Evidentally she had been unfit to live, without any strength of purpose, an easy prey to habits, one of the wrecks civilization had reared. But that she could have sunk so low! Was it possible that he could have deceived himself so utterly about her? (*D* 115)

Duffy is sure she has degraded him — the vision of her vice confirms it; "His soul's companion!" may imply a mocking, ironic stance, and, of course, he does not see the irony of accusing her of being a prey to habit. Though the paragraph ends with Duffy thinking, "He had no difficulty now in approving of the course he had taken"(*D* 115-6), the first sign of doubt has already crept in: Duffy's bewilderment over his possible self-deception is the first sentence he phrases as a question in the entire story.

As Duffy's disgust gives way to memory, doubt, and then remorse, Mrs. Sinico returns to haunt him with ghostly touches. "The cold air struck him on the threshhold: he felt it in the sleeves of his coat" (*JJA* 4, 125) is altered to read, "The cold air met him on the threshold: it crept into the sleeves of his coat" (*D* 116). In the *Dubliners* story the air has its own power, and "met" is substituted for the melodramatic "struck" of the draft, yet in Mr. Duffy's memory, the working men in the pub at Chapelizod seem more threatening in the published story than in the first draft. Rather than drinking from "big pint glasses" and "pulling the sawdust over their spits with their heavy boots" (*JJA* 4, 127), the published story reads they drink from "huge pint tumblers," "dragging the sawdust" (*D* 116). If these revisions seem to suggest that James Duffy is overpowered by the elements, and either dwarfed or threatened by the workers in the pub, it is interesting to note that in the *Dubliners* story Duffy is referred to from this point forward as simply 'he.' The use of the pronoun shows his submergence as well and is consistent with the other changes.

Joyce works on the progress of Duffy's self-doubt and remorse as Mrs. Sinico's death makes a growing impression on him. The draft copy (*JJA* 4, 129) shows that Joyce felt Duffy's explanations were too lengthy to be in character:

> The ~~thought~~ fact discomposed him because his own statement of it to himself seemed something of an accusation. He asked himself what else could he have done — carried ~~on~~ a ~~comedy of~~ furtive comedy which must have ended in mutual disgust or gone away with her out of Ireland. Either course would have been ~~ridiculous He thought of the pain~~ impossible the one of an undignified intrigue the other a ridiculous elopement. He had acted for the best: ~~and yet her death had revealed to him her loneliness. He too would be lonely now.~~

No other course had been possible. And yet he understood now how lonely her life must have been and how lonely he would be until he, too, died, ceased to exist, became a memory. But who would remember him?

Joyce gets away from Duffy's self-accusation in the later version and substitutes for the first sentence the simpler, "He began to feel ill at ease" (*D* 116). Similarly, Joyce removes the question of an elopement entirely; perhaps he felt this was too close to his own experience, and too uncharacteristic of Duffy[8] who scarcely ever varies his routine. Joyce rephrases the last sentence to form a statement that is more fatalistic than the original — "if anyone remembered him" (*D* 116) — than the original question. Duffy may already know the answer. In the final draft most of the sentences begin with "he," and the

[8]   John William Corrington, "Isolation as Motif in "A Painful Case," *JJQ* 3 (1966), 182.

repetition of the pronoun suggests his stultification or diminishment.

In the last two paragraphs of the story, Joyce reduces the number of sentences, and sharpens the imagery. Hence, "deserted alleys" (*JJA* 4, 131) becomes "bleak alleys" (*D* 117). For "her voice seem [sic] touched his ear so and he stood still to listen" (*JJA* 4, 131) Joyce writes "he seemed to feel her voice touch his ear, her hand touch his" (*D* 117) which emphasizes the tactile. "He felt his morality falling to pieces" (*JJA* 4, 131) becomes "his moral nature" (*D* 117), which reminds the reader that the story's fatalism may lie in Mr. Duffy's unfortunate temperament. In the original draft the light of Dublin seem "human and hospitable" (*JJA* 4, 131), but Joyce rewrites this as "burned redly and hospitably in the cold night" (*D* 117) perhaps to avoid the implication that Duffy is not human. He alters the description of the goods train so that the word "winding" occurs three times, and retains the double occurrence of "laborious" (*JJA* 4, 133; *D* 117). The train that some commentators have designated "the worm of conscience"[9] also recalls the actual rupture of the relationship between Mr. Duffy and Mrs. Sinico, as well as the metaphorical interruption of the train incident. Joyce seems to take pains to assure readers the train was moving slowly, and had in fact stopped before moving on again to strike Mrs. Sinico in what the doctor said was not a fatal blow. It seems to have be the lack of direct contact, the absence of the sexual *petit mort*, which killed her. Finally Joyce removes the literal repetition of "Emily Sinico" and simply states that the train moved on — reiterating the syllables of her name. (See *JJA* 4, 133 and *D* 117.)

Joyce's rewriting of "A Painful Case" takes two directions. One is to refine the character of Mr. Duffy, emphasizing his taciturn and repressed nature while refraining from making him

[9]   Corrington, p. 190.

a caricature in the eyes of the reader. Joyce wants us to both sympathize with and judge James Duffy. Second, Joyce seems to exonerate Mrs. Sinico for attempted adultery through his portrayal of her husband and by pointing to the responsibility of both Duffy and Dublin society in her spiritual and literal death.

In October, 1905, Stanislaus Joyce wrote to his brother in the same letter which contained research for "A Painful Case," "Do you write out of rough copy these stories? Like a Shakespeare manuscript there is scarcely ever a correction in them and yet I can hardly imagine that astonishing unravelling of the sodomite's mind [in "An Encounter"] was written offhand." On the other hand, in August, October and November, 1906, James Joyce grumbled to Stanislaus in his letters of his own adjustments to "A Painful Case" and of his dissatisfaction with it: "I wish someone was here to talk to me about Dublin. I forget half the things I wanted to do. The two worst stories are "After the Race" and "A Painful Case" (*SL* 127).

I think that readers can look on "A Painful Case" — draft and finished versions — and appreciate Joyce's growing control of his characters and fiction. This exercise has taught me a great deal about the need for simplicity and of the appropriateness of thought to character, and that Joyce succeeds — even when he is least pleased — because he is an outstanding editor of his own work.

Albuquerque

THE STORIES OF PUBLIC LIFE

MARY POWER

Joyce's original plan for *Dubliners* involved four distinct groupings of stories within the collection. In a letter to his brother Stanislaus, Joyce explained:

> The order of the stories is as follows. *The Sisters, An Encounter* and another story which are stories of my childhood: *The Boarding-House, After the Race* and *Eveline*, which are stories of adolescence: *The Clay, Counterparts*, and *A Painful Case* which are stories of mature life: *Ivy Day in the Committee Room, A Mother* and the last story of the book which are stories of public life in Dublin. (*L* II 109-112)

Except for the stories of childhood, brought together by a common narrative voice, discussion of Joyce's internal groupings of the stories has been neglected. The last set, the stories of public life, is the only division which is not chronological. What did Joyce mean by the phrase "public life"? The easy answer is that he showed Dubliners participating in political, theatrical and religious spheres rather than caught up in the tangle of their personal and domestic fortunes. Though the term "public life" is now diluted because it is applied to anyone of celebrity status, historically, the notion of a public life has momentous connotations. It suggests the time at which young noblemen in ancient Rome began political apprenticeships at the forum or even more commonly, Christ's three-year ministry of preaching and working miracles from the time he was thirty until he died on the cross three years later. Any Dublin reader contemporary with Joyce would have immediately

made the connection to Christ.[1] I read the phrase "public life,"
then, to mean that Dublin offered little opportunity for the
interplay of heroes, lofty ideals and grand action and that the
motley players in that urban arena were a lot older than their
early thirties.

The three stories that concern public life are reserved until the
end of the collection to stress that groups, even if they convene
for significant purposes, are no better than the individuals that
comprise them. If the first eleven stories of the volume portray
individual Dubliners who are self-conscious, ineffective, and
fragmented, these three stories show that collective endeavor
undertaken by such people is almost doomed. Indeed, the
Dubliners seem to know less about being public than about
being private. Trevor Williams suggests, "all three stories, in
turn, reduce Irish politics, culture and religion to a shambles
and a farce, suggesting in their composite picture, that this is the
Ireland that would emerge if the Irish were left to organize their
own lives."[2]

I do not go as far as Trevor politically, but I think these last
three stories close the door on any elegant platitude about Irish
patriotism, culture or religious faith. "Ivy Day" shows that the
Dubliners are graceless and clumsy in mourning their heroes,
and inept about proposing a slate of candidates for civic offices.

---

[1]   See Joyce's letter to his brother Stanislaus, dated 11 Feb. 1907 (*SL*
147-148). See also Florence L. Walzl, "Dubliners" in *A Companion to Joyce
Studies,* ed. Zack Bowen and James F. Carens (Westport Connecticut:
Greenwood Press, 1984) p. 180. James Joyce wrote his brother Stanislaus
that in the construction of "Ivy Day" he was influenced by Anatole France's
story "The Procurator of Judea" in which "Pontius Pilate relates memories
of his years of administrative service in Judea but never once mentions
Christ. When asked about Jesus of Nazareth, he cannot recall him. Yet Jesus
dominates the story."

[2]   Trevor Williams, "Resistance to Paralysis in *Dubliners*" MFS, 35
(1989), 444.

"A Mother" demonstrates that musical presentations are uneven and raggle-taggle, and that the financial backing for such enterprises is worse than shaky. The message of "Grace" is even more discomfiting. Religious observance has become casual and prosaic. Retreat priests are nothing but conciliatory crowd-pleasers, and they depict a Christ who is as laconic, worldly and impervious as the Dubliners themselves.

The stories resemble each other thematically in showing that group endeavor is doomed. All three feature expanded casts, and show that money is *a* basic, if not *the* basic, motivation for action. Furthermore, the stories have similar plots and epiphanies. The technical repetition forcibly emphasizes the encroachment of collective paralysis. The three stories go a long way to providing closure to the volume; in fact, they were Joyce's original ending to the collection before the composition of "The Dead." By showing the inadequacy of groups and institutions in Dublin, Joyce indicts the Dubliners for failing to provide their city with excellence in politics, the performing arts, and religion.

The stories of public life contain more characters than their predecessors. Though not quite amounting to the casts of thousands of the old Hollywood boast, the number of participants in each story has risen dramatically. While there are only four characters in "A Painful Case" (ten, if those named in the report of the inquest are included), "Ivy Day," the next story, the first of public life, has twenty participants; "A Mother," eighteen, and "Grace," a high of twenty two.[3] But these stories are not set apart by expanded casts alone; the characters have complex allegiances. For example, in "Ivy Day" the reader has to sort out a whole range of political affiliations — Labour, Conservative and Nationalist — and match them with the canvassers; then gauge the length of time each man has

---

[3]   See the table at the end of this essay.

supported the Nationalist candidate, Tierney. It is no mean feat to identify each stripe of wavering political identity. After all, for a few of the canvassers party affiliation has little to do with deeply-held convictions; rather, it seems to hinge on nothing more than the hope, if not the expectation, of a few quid.

In "A Mother" a similar task of sorting characters is needed. The reader would do well to separate the amateur performers who, like Kathleen, have stepped out of the drawing rooms of upper middle class Dublin, from the rather scruffy assortment of professional *artistes*, all the while keeping their respective talents in mind. Though the *artistes* stand about in small groups waiting to go on stage, it should be noted that anything resembling that prized theatrical virtue — *esprit de corps* — is sadly lacking.

In "Grace," the characters have few of the affiliations of the characters in the preceding pair of stories; however, the outward form of groups is carefully, even artfully, staged. For example, bystanders arrange themselves around Tom Kernan's unconscious body in a circle; later Martin Cunningham urges Tom Kernan to join him, Jack Power and M'Coy at the retreat under the guise that they'd be "a four-hand reel" (*D* 163). Later that same group of retreatants appear in church as a quincunx, (*D* 172), and certainly this is the fanciest geometrical figure since the gnomon of "The Sisters." These carefully arranged groupings may be Joyce's way of showing that the characters are little more than bodies or masses whose only function is decorative, taking up physical space at the right place and the right time.

If groups are artfully arranged in "Grace," it is significant that in all three stories of public life, characters cheerfully and complacently lose their individualities and blend into larger social units. Mrs. Kearney is an exception. In the earlier stories in the collection, the characters who serve as central consciousnesses define their reality against the crowd. Individual awareness sets each apart from the throng. On the other hand, in the last story of public life, "Grace," the main character Tom Kernan has passed out cold. That a person of such fictional importance would succumb is surprising and it also serves a contrastive function in the collection.

It is instructive to trace the play of the individual consciousness and the crowd throughout the collection. In the stories preceding the group on public life, crowds have the allure of the romantic unknown, whether the narrator identifies with them or not. For example, the young narrator of "Araby" takes pleasure in defining himself against all the other Dubliners. While out shopping with his aunt, he basks in his heightened sensitivity, thinks of Mangan's sister, and recalls:

We walked through the flaring streets, jostled by drunken men and bargaining women, amid the curses of labourers, the shrill litanies of shop-boys who stood on guard by barrels of pigs' cheeks, the nasal chanting of street singers, who sang *come-all-you* about O'Donovan Rossa, or a ballad about the troubles in our native land. These noises converged in a single sensation of life for me: I imagined that I bore my chalice safely through a throng of foes (*D* 31).

The narrator feels that his rich interior life sets him apart from all the others who are, as he sees them, engaged in the base activities of buying and selling.

Frank finds Eveline in the crush at the North Wall, even though she will not hear him. In "Two Gallants," the word "crowd" occurs five times. The Sunday promenaders in central Dublin are an ever-present backdrop for the main action. They serve as a reminder that Corley has no resources, and provide the setting for his cheap date. They may also increase Corley's bravado with the girl. He may have felt he could try practically anything — even ask for money — because he knew that if the girl rebuffed him, he could be off in a flash, anonymous to her as she is to him and to the reader. The crowd also gives the voyeuristic Lenehan cover and allows him to keep track of the pair. The story ends in a cinematic tableau, as the people thin out to focus on the three main characters.

Even Farrington in "Counterparts" incongruously and unexpectedly savors liberation from his job and a transitory reprieve from his financial woes as he joins the anonymous urban throng. Unlike the boy in "Araby," Farrington enjoys the crowd, and is relieved to join with it in spirit:

In Westmoreland Street the footpaths were crowded with young men and women returning from business and ragged urchins ran here and there yelling out the names of the evening editions. The man [Farrington] passed through the crowd, looking on the spectacle generally with proud satisfaction and staring masterfully at the office-girls. (*D* 93)

Farrington is freed from the shackles of his petty servitude in Mr. Alleyne's office as he becomes part of the street scene. He can think of himself as a Dubliner, out on the town, not as an oppressed clerk. This brief glimpse of Farrington in the work-day crowd anticipates the magnificent renderings of all the Dubliners on-the-town in "Wandering Rocks" in *Ulysses* or even the concept of HCE — Here Comes Everybody — in *Finnegans Wake*.

Farrington, the urban man, sounds momentarily like the observer in Baudelaire's essay, "Les Foules":

Le promeneur solitaire et pensif tire une singulière ivresse de cette universelle communion. Celui-là qui épouse facilement la foule connait des jouissances fièvreuses, dont seront éternellement privés l'égoiste, ferme comme un coffre et le paresseux, interne comme un mollusque. Il adopte comme siennes toutes les professions, toutes les joies et toutes les misères que la circonstance lui presente.[4]

[The solitary and thoughtful walker derives a special excitement from this general mingling. The person who easily joins the crowd in spirit knows the heady joys which are forever lost on the egoist locked up like a chest, or the lazy man confined within himself like a clam. The walker claims as his own all the declarations, joys and miseries that circumstance presents (Translation mine).]

My point is that the characters in earlier parts of the collection place a high value on their personal views of reality or they at least have a perspective. Each stands apart from the crowd, the masses, all those other Dubliners. In contrast, the characters in the stories of public life generally make no special claim to uniqueness or individual consciousness. They are all parts of groups; they blend in. For the most part, the characters in these stories merge into committees, casts, or the churchgoing public. Beyond even the most extreme case of individual surrender to the group is poor Tom Kernan, out cold. Instead of having a sense of his individual consciousness, even a Sisyphean one, he has become an object, a cynosure, a spectacle for a crowd to observe.

The flatness of group membership gives the reader practically no opportunity to identify with a particular character. Cues on how to read the story come from careful attention to manners, names and affiliations. Joyce creates tension by balancing formality against casualness in the use of proper names. In "Ivy Day," for example, everyone calls the old caretaker Jack, while he refers to them by surname — apparently because of a difference in their status. Mat O'Connor and Joe Hynes are on

[4]   Charles Baudelaire, "Le Spleen de Paris," *Oeuvres Completes* ed. Claude Pichois (Paris: Gallimard, 1961) pp. 243-4.

a first-name basis, though they distance Crofton and Lyons in greeting them by surnames, thereby showing their distrust of the latecomers. Each of the stories contains a name of resounding caricature. "Ivy Day" has Tricky Dicky Tierney; "A Mother," Hoppy Holohan; and "Grace," more artily, allusively and meanly, Father Purdon. With each of these characters, naming is used to suggest rather than denote. The names raise doubts about the possessor's character, and the reader is alternately amused and suspicious, as in the spirit of Jonsonian comedy. Within the stories, however, Joyce never gives the reader enough information to condemn; he works instead by innuendo. The very nicknames Hoppy and Tricky Dicky suggest the impossibility of getting a grip on the character. Father Purdon is, of course, named for a street in Dublin's Nighttown; but what he says from the pulpit has nothing to do with sex, and the reader knows nothing about his private life. The reader infers that this priest's treatment of Scripture is so debased that it amounts to a kind of prostitution — but the reader must make the link.

Joyce emphasizes the importance of naming in "A Mother." In fact, there seems to be an almost hypostatic connection between proper names and their bearers' essences. Mrs. Kearney, with her gilded manners and prepossessing stance, seems to be more comfortable in thinking of herself and everyone but her elder daughter by surname. Joyce undercuts her formidable demeanor by supplying Hoppy Holohan by way of contrast. His nickname seems so apt — morally, physically and stylistically — that his Christian name, like Mrs. Kearney's is lost to the reader.

Mention of the name Kathleen Kearney conjures up the heroine of an old Irish song — " O, did you not hear of Kate Kearney?/ She lives on the banks of Killarney," — and inadvertently perhaps, a popular Cockney music hall *artiste* of the day, Kate Carney. While many starlets invent stage names to suit their theatrical aspirations or metaphysical ideas of self, here the appropriate name may precede both mother's and daughter's ambitions. Kathleen Kearney is a name which predestines its bearer for a musical career, though the Kathleen of Joyce's story is never referred to casually as Kate.[5] Similarly, the substitute journalist O'Madden Burke seems to have a reputation around the city not because of the stories he has written, but because he is distinguished-looking, and his west of Ireland name sounds substantial. The text calls attention to this point: "His magniloquent western name was the moral umbrella upon which he balanced the fine problem of his finances" (*D* 145). It is impossible to know exactly what attracted Joyce to this name. It might have been because it was strongly accented metrically, or because a surname as a first name sounded gentrified, or because it followed the same pattern as O'Donovan Rossa. In any case, Joyce makes it appear that few writers are as fortunate in their pseudonyms as this character is with his given name. The surface qualities of name and demeanor were all this man needed to appear to be the final voice of authority in the Antient Concert Rooms the night of the last concert. Unquestionably, Joyce took extraordinary care with naming in "A Mother." A list of the performers would have provided a marvelous fictive playbill had Joyce gone no further. Even the lesser *artistes* have names worthy of a nudge or, at least, a wink. Mr. Bell, the tenor, probably had a voice as clear as one. Madame Glynn of London shared her name with a popular melodramatic novelist of the day, Elinor Glyn, and Mr. Meade, the comic turn, quaintly conjures up thoughts of the ancient brew.

With the exception of Father Purdon, naming in "Grace" lacks the suggestiveness and colorfulness of "A Mother." Joyce may be trying to show that Kernan, Cunningham, and M'Coy

---

[5]   See my note, "The Naming of Kathleen Kearney," *Journal of Modern Literature,* 5 (1976) 532-4.

are ordinary Dublin surnames of only a shade more distinction than the Paddy Stink and Mickey Mud scorned so bitterly by Simon Dedalus in *A Portrait*. However, since such flimsy items as Tom Kernan's silk hat and suspenders are signs of respectability in this story, it is not surprising that characters are touchy about the way in which they are addressed. Mr. M'Coy, who has a reputation for being an opportunist, offends Mr. Power by calling him Jack. When the fabric of life is as thin as it is here, details of naming, clothing and manners assume an exaggerated importance.

These Dubliners, out in public, are very guarded and stiff. It almost seems as if Joyce has them respond to each other Eliza Doolittle-style from some contemporary manual of polite conversation. The characters engage in conventional chitchat only; they are ill-at-ease, uninformed and risk very little of themselves. They are perfectly, almost comically, superficial. Given such a banal state of affairs, the reader has to pay attention to details apart from dialogue to see what is going on and how the action of the story is furthered or obstructed.

I would like to turn now from questions of character to questions of theme. The stories preceding these three show that lack of money can lead to embarrassment, mean-spiritedness, resentment and bad judgement, while having money can serve as a source of petty power or control. In the stories of public life, money assumes even greater importance. In "Ivy Day," Joyce shows that politics is more about money than ideals. The canvassers have no particular faith in Tricky Dicky; most of them have taken on the job for the money. Yet skepticism about the political process is so thorough-going and pervasive, that twice Mr. O'Connor wonders aloud if Tierney will pay him. This anxiety betrays a lack of trust in the candidate and by extension in the Nationalist party. The problem of money and the public trust deepens in "A Mother. " Mrs. Kearney demands immediate payment for her daughter under the terms of a contract. Hoppy and Fitzpatrick bluster, prevaricate and feign anger because they feel she has done the unthinkable; she has upset the *status quo*. In fact, she has realistically dared to question the honor and financial solidity of the Eire Abu Society while they think such an institution still provides complete safety as a hiding place or an excuse. At the outset, membership in this group seems to make otherwise questionable dealings legitimate, but as with political life in "Ivy Day," the moral character of the members of an organization puts the organization itself in question. The cameo appearance of Father Keon casts aspersions on the ministers of the Church as well as the representatives of the city.[6] The fiction of the autonomy of the "cometty" in "A Mother" seems to prefigure the role of clumsy, faceless, obstructive bureaucracies that thwart nearly every aspect of twentieth century public life, not only in Dublin but in every other city.

In "Grace," money also plays an important role. The story shows paradoxically how financial problems can be transformed into spiritual ones. As the story begins, Tom Kernan has been conferring with Harford and another man, both known to be money lenders. The deliberation is apparently so stressful that Tom gets very drunk. Mrs. Kernan's actions upon his return show how dire the family financial situation must have been. The kitchen cupboards are bare, and she has nothing to offer Jack Power in the name of hospitality after he has so kindly helped her husband home. Later, she is reduced to going through her husband's pockets in search of petty cash. When Tom's friends come to call several nights later, they discuss his accident and determine he was associating with Harford. This piece of information is significant, but Tom's cronies are too embarrassed or too stingy to pursue the subject. Instead, they

---

[6] Cheryl Herr, *Joyce's Anatomy of Culture* (Urbana: University of Illinois, 1986). This study offers a valuable discussion of the interchangeability of the theatrical, religious and political spheres in *Dubliners*.

change the conversation to something harmless — small talk about the Church and its dignitaries. In order to "help" Tom they try to persuade him to join them in a businessman's retreat. They become excited about the idea, and claim it will make Tom a new man. But in the course of the narration, Joyce has managed to characterize Tom Kernan's four friends in terms of their respective financial problems. Jack Power has "inexplicable debts "(*D* 154) and besides, he has bailed Tom out on previous occasions. Martin Cunningham's problems with a wildly alcoholic wife are common knowledge. Mr. M'Coy is a real chancer, as they say in Dublin, and Mr. Fogarty is standing on shaky financial ground: he has recently set up a small grocery store, and is recovering from a previous business failure. Given their financial profiles, it is easy to see why these men would just as soon avoid Tom's immediate problem of insolvency.

It must have been cold comfort for Tom Kernan to hear Father Purdon say that Christ was a businessman like themselves. If one of the worries in "The Sisters" concerns simony, the buying and selling of religious things, "Grace" brings a reversal of the theme which is equally insidious — the replacement of the material by the spiritual. There are times when material demands come before spiritual ones. Starving people want a meal before a prayer. Tom Kernan has pressing financial problems which need to be relieved. His friends ignore his immediate predicament because it would cost them, and they are all strapped for cash themselves. They substitute the spiritual help of institutional religion in the form of a retreat because it is easy, inexpensive, and *looks* like the right thing to do. Mrs. Kernan, a devout Catholic herself, tells the well-wishers skeptically that the retreat can "do no harm" (*D* 158). She probably would have considered a cash contribution the answer to her prayers or manna from heaven.

If Joyce had uncharacteristically shown an urchin begging and passers-by who urged the child to pray rather than offering him a coin or a crust of bread, the moral would have been cruel and obvious. In "Grace" Joyce shows another kind of callousness. He points out that middle-class dignity is precious, and saving face is so important that it obscures real need. Tom Kernan is financially embarrassed to the point of silence, perhaps deliberately. His credit with his friends is exhausted — he simply can't ask for help directly any more than he can appear in public without his silk hat.

Money plays a broader and more disturbing role in the stories of public life than in earlier stories. It is disillusioning that the canvassers in "Ivy Day" are more concerned with finances than politics, and do a lot less to earn their money than committed followers would gladly do for their ideals alone. It is disgraceful that Mrs. Kearney and the Eire Abu Society cannot stop bickering about a small amount of money, for a higher purpose — the success of the benefit concerts. Finally, in a reversal of emphasis, it is both clever and mean-minded of Tom's cronies to ignore his immediate financial need and substitute religious observance.

The stories of public life present a united front technically as well as thematically. The plots of the stories of public life are similar in that they all revolve around absent, ineffectual or diminished centers.[7] In "Ivy Day," Joyce works around a center that is doubly absent. Parnell is ill-remembered and clumsily eulogized on the anniversary of his death, and the present candidate, Tierney, is missing from the Committee Room as well. Tierney's workers have no campaign spirit or rallying cries. They worry about being paid for their paltry services, and anticipate the delivery of the bottled stout from the Black Eagle with more enthusiasm than Tierney's projected victory. Thus, Joyce makes a point about the vacuousness of political institutions and their ability to endure in spite of themselves. He

[7]   See Walzl, "Dubliners," pp. 180-181.

further trivializes the situation by presenting an election for a minor city official rather than a contest for a successor to Parnell at Westminster.

In "A Mother," the reader would gather from the narration rather than the title, that the story is about the series of events leading up to a recital in the Antient Concert Rooms. There must be something terribly the matter if the entertainment was overshadowed by the behind-the-scenes haggling of Mrs. Kearney and Hoppy Holohan. Mrs. Kearney, whose consciousness dictates the narration, considers Kathleen the center of events. However, she is misguided, because accompanists never have top billing. When one of the *artistes* mentions that Mrs. Pat Campbell, a real star of the London stage is in town, a further distraction is introduced. Shouldn't she be center stage? The competing varieties of displacement challenge the reader's expectations about the narrative. By showing that the clamor and acrimony of business arrangements overshadow the actual recital, the status of the performing arts in Dublin is brought into question.

In "Grace," the plotting is more complicated. Literature usually chronicles characters who develop; occasionally a point is made about those who resist change. Tom Kernan flies in the face of narrative tradition — and Catholic theology — by telling his friends he will have nothing to do "with the magic candle business." He stubbornly refuses to do the expected as a literary character — and a good Catholic — he balks at the very idea of change by declaring he will not renew his baptismal vows, which is the first and least troublesome step in regenerating a spiritual life. A reluctant penitent is exposed to a popular and reputedly dynamic retreat master, yet every detail suggests that nothing is going to happen to Tom Kernan's heart and soul: he wills that it will not. Given his interior disposition, the retreat is almost guaranteed to have no effect on him . Unlike the retreat sermons in *A Portrait,* through which Stephen is moved to repentance, the sermon in "Grace" seems to be lost on Tom

Kernan. He is bodily present; he is just a member of a group in the Jesuit Church on Gardiner Street; he cannot even properly be called a worshipper.

The plot of "Grace" is a variation on that of "The Sisters." Father Flynn serves as the absent center of the first story and Joyce must have played off that design for the sake of symmetry in what was to be, at least for a time, the final story in the collection. The description of Tom Kernan's unconscious body reminds the reader of Father Flynn's corpse, and if the focal point of Tom's body is a bloody tongue rather than furry nostrils, the effect is equally bizarre. Both stories trace how other characters minister to injured or dead bodies, but here the comparison ends. While Father Flynn exerted great but undetermined influence on the young narrator, Tom Kernan has influenced no one. Others try to persuade him to seek spiritual help — to *be* influenced — but this half-hearted collective gesture has no effect. Father Flynn's crisis came from being too scrupulous, while superficially, Tom Kernan appears too complacent. Actually, he is preoccupied with his financial woes and has reason to be so. He has gone on the retreat at the urging of his friends, but his material circumstances are so grim, he would be better off attending to them first. As Father Flynn's ghostly face haunts readers of "The Sisters," so Father Purdon emerges as the final horrifying specter in "Grace." He has won celebrity as a pulpit orator and is known as a man of the world in contrast to humble Father Flynn, who has told the boy with biblical solemnity that he was not long for this world. At worst, Father Purdon seems the embodiment of the fears of simony present in "The Sisters." It might be more accurate to say that, for all he is a fine figure of a man up in the pulpit, his message is anti-climactic and he scarcely lives up to his reputation.

A final unifying technical characteristic of the stories of public life is the similarity of their epiphanies. In each, a text or performance is interpreted by a character who is totally unqualified to make a judgment. In "Ivy Day" Crofton declares that Joe Hynes's poem is "a very fine piece of writing" (*D* 135). Crofton has become a canvasser for Tierney only after the Conservative candidate has withdrawn, and the inference is that he has taken the job with Tricky Dicky and the Nationalists solely for the money. His reception in the Committee Room is cool. When Mat O'Connor prompts him to say something complimentary about Parnell, he makes the bland comment that Parnell was a gentleman. He ignores Parnell's enormous contribution to Irish history, but his thoughtless statement shows that no one in the room is paying too much attention, because whether or not Parnell was a gentleman was the cause of his political downfall. Parnell's involvement with Mrs. O'Shea had, of course, been the ruin of his career. In other words, Crofton had picked exactly the wrong pleasantry for the occasion. The mere fact that Crofton was a Conservative -- a party Parnell was always at odds with--should have disqualified him from having the last word at a ceremony in Parnell's honor.

In "A Mother" O'Madden Burke is pressed into service because the regular *Freeman* journalist had a more important story to cover. Burke has gotten far on his good looks and substantial name. He offers the judgment that the fracas over the concert will mean the end of Kathleen Kearney's musical career. As the Kearneys make their dramatic exit, O'Madden Burke is supportive of Hoppy Holohan and tells him he has done the right thing. No one bothers to ask O'Madden Burke for his credentials; he is accepted as an insider, even as a spokesman for the Eire Abu Society. The reader should realize he is telling the group what they want to hear, and that the real epiphany is the silent conspiracy of the remaining *artistes* and the Eire Abu Society . Another important realization is the simple but painful truth that incompetent, bungling groups have enormous power over individuals.

Father Purdon has the last word in "Grace." The subject of his sermon is the parable of the unjust steward. It is a puzzling text in which the reader has to decide in what context the master praises the steward. An orthodox view is that the master applauded the steward, meaning that his actions would stand him in good stead in this world, not in heaven or God's eyes. Father Purdon misinterprets the text by making the master's commendation seem altogether favorable, both on earth and in heaven. In this way, he has sought to appeal to his businessmen-retreatants. Joyce's irony perfectly captures the length to which such a preacher would go to win a wide following. This misinterpretation — which is also the epiphany of the story — perfectly captures the behavior of Tom Kernan's friends. They, men of the world as they are, have wisely avoided lending Tom money and have, instead, brought him on the retreat. They will only win approval in a world in which real charity has been deposed and appearances reign.

In conclusion, I would like to offer an observation on collective behavior. In the stories of public life there is no such thing as group dynamics — group lethargics seems to prevail instead. If it has often been said that the narrator of the first three stories is more or less the same young boy, so here in the last three stories both the groups and the individuals who comprise them seem interchangeable. They are all what pass in Dublin for ordinary, decent, well-educated businessmen. In the earlier stories in the collection, age seems to be the main principle of organization, but in the stories of public life this distinction seems to have been erased. The characters are of indeterminate age. In "Ivy Day," Joyce introduces a gray-haired young man, as if deliberately to set the precedent for the blurring of characters' ages as well as their personalities. Intellectually, the men all seem to seek the lowest common denominator as they reduce ideas to truisms. They avoid complexity or qualifications. All these men come from much the same mold — and it is a curious literary challenge for Joyce or any creative writer to set out to create a whole brigade of mediocre men with an emotional and intellectual range from A to B.

Joyce took no lessons from George Eliot's *Felix Holt* or Zola's *Germinal* on the depiction of group action. Joyce shows no group or crowd contagiously excited about matters of social injustice. Individuals, living and dead, however famous, do not spur the Dubliners to meaningful action — or if they do, it translates awkwardly. Parnell becomes the subject of bad poetry, and Father Purdon is not in top form as a pulpit orator. In "A Mother" no one backstage pays much attention to the audience's response to the *artistes*. Even if an act or two did bring down the house, the sponsors are oblivious. Groups never inspire or reach any sort of an emotional pitch in these stories. Rather the clusters of men in the committee room, the green room and Tom Kernan's bedroom — seem affable, clumsy and platitudinous. They are polite and distant and out to offend no one — with the exception of the "commetty's" attitude toward Mrs. Kearney. These groups are almost exclusively male, but unaccountably, the individuals do not seem to bond, or have very much fun together. The laundresses in "Clay" are Joyce's only sizeable group of women in *Dubliners* and they are atypical of his characterization of individual women. Nevertheless, these workers enjoy teatime and show a real spirit of camaraderie. Then again, they are outcasts of society, and do not have to keep up appearances as the men in the public life stories do. Put another way, the groups of men seem to be trying to achieve some mutual kind of anonymity in getting together. Perhaps they simply find safety in numbers out on the town removed from domesticity. In all three stories, characters quote public opinion or the newspaper, and never volunteer a private notion; the conversations are riddled with misinformation and are painfully close to parody and caricature. The only time a group is ready to mobilize is in "A Mother" where they band together against the threat of a formidable woman — Mrs. Kearney. The reader is hard pressed to find a leader in any of these groups; they defer to each other in bumbling ways as the blind lead the lame. An odd brand of democratization prevails, if it can pass for anything that positive.

Perhaps an outside perspective would help to illuminate the diffident behavior of Joyce's men in groups. In 1895, Gustave Le Bon's classic work of sociology, *The Crowd*, appeared. One of Le Bon's observations seems to be especially relevant to Joyce's characters. It reads "in the collective mind, the intellectual aptitudes of the individuals, and in consequence, their individuality are weakened."[8] This statement can be applied to *Dubliners* to mean that if individuals suffer from paralysis of the will, groups are positively stultified and directionless. In "Ivy Day," the group meeting retards the work of campaigning; in "A Mother" the group prevents Mrs. Kearney from going further; and in "Grace," the group takes Tom Kernan on a pointless excursion to church.

In the first eleven stories of *Dubliners*, Joyce exposed the thwarted sensitivities of individuals, and perhaps inadvertently aroused readers' sympathy. I have tried to show the thematic and structural similarity of the public life stories is very important for the design of the collection as a whole. By featuring expanded casts and turning to the political, theatrical, and religious institutions of Dublin, Joyce indicts the city as a whole. He shows that money is the basic motivation of the characters in these stories, a factor more disturbing than human incompetence or reticence. There is little if any room for emotional involvement on the part of the reader. The three stories show convincingly that private frustration and inhibition lead to devastating public incompetence and consequently, Dublin as a metropolis is diminished inadvertently by its own citizens. Aesthetically, the three stories provide a logical and appropriate ending to the collection but such closure would have been unrelievedly grim and perhaps unduly emphatic. In adding "The Dead" as a coda to *Dubliners* Joyce offered new

---

[8]   Gustave Le Bon *The Crowd* (New York: Viking, 1960), p. 129.

possibilities, vitality and surprise.

Albuquerque

Table

	Participants	Others Mentioned	Total
"The Sisters"	6	2	8
"An Encounter"	3	4	7
"Araby"	9	1	10
"Eveline"	3	2	5
"After the Race"	7	-	7
"Two Gallants"	3	1	4
"The Boarding House"	4	5	9
"A Little Cloud"	4	1	5
"Counterparts"	11	4	15
"Clay"	5	1	6
"A Painful Case"	4	6	10
"Ivy Day"	18	2	20
"A Mother"	18	0	18
"Grace"	22	0	22
"The Dead"	19	15	34

FROM PARALYSIS TO PARA-LIRE: ANOTHER READING OF "A MOTHER"

MARIE-DOMINIQUE GARNIER

"A Mother" like most stories in *Dubliners*, is read in connection with three interpretive signposts that overshadow the beginning of "The Sisters" — paralysis, simony and a gnomonic lack. It is tempting to read the story within the conceptual frame delineated by the three terms, as yet another tale of "scrupulous meanness." The Joycean phrase, however, deserves more than a cursory, straightforward reading. Meanness obliquely relates to mean-ing — like "owing" is at the heart of knowing.

My essay uses the concepts of *differance/difference* developed by Jacques Derrida — particularly in *The Postcard* — and in rather dissonant terms by Gilles Deleuze in *Repetition and Difference*. "A Mother" — but the same might apply to other stories — resists frontal, plain approaches; it refuses to be contained within the prophylactic framework posted at the beginning of "The Sisters," or simply reformulated as the tale of a mother who paralyzes her daughter's musical career after trying to sell her talents under cover of an Irish patriotic cause — namely, the language movement.

Though the most common meaning of "scruples" is "thought(s) or circumstance(s) that trouble the mind" or "causes(s) of uneasiness," it may also mean, according to *The Oxford English Dictionary,* small weights, small details, or small pebbles. A number of scruples in both senses, haunt the story, return with a vengeance to titilate meanness into meaning, in an ongoing process of textual harassment. "A Mother" functions, like all of Joyce's deceptively plain stories, as a pre-Wakean exercise, as an end-negating drill — an exercise in repetition, with a difference, or a differential. Jacques Derrida devotes an entire section of *The Postcard* to the concept of paralysis where the term becomes a synonym for differance, for endless deferrals of movement and mean-ing. Postcards abound in "A Mother" as elsewhere in Joyce: "Kathleen and her sister sent Irish picture postcards to their friends and these friends sent back other picture postcards"(*D* 137). In the same vein, the character of Mr. Kearney shifts from obvious meanness to rampant meaning: "She respected her husband in the same way as she respected the General Post Office, as something large, secure and fixed; and though she knew the small number of his talents she appreciated his abstract value as a male" (*D* 141).

GPO and "abstract value" point to "other" alternative readings of "A Mother" just as the words of the title gesture towards a possible "am other." The sentence, if read "scrupulously," offers two arresting details which open up different, or deferring interpretive vistas, whether Derridean — the GPO — or Deleuzian — "abstract value" — where abstraction calls forth Deleuze's reflections on differential mathematical avenues.

Although paralysis-oriented readings of the text appear to be fully supported by the Joycean letter, much is left aside — details, minute notations, which are literally "scruples," or possibly "litter." Alternative readings such as the one promoted by Jean-Michel Rabaté,[1] (who most convincingly compares the mother to a Medusa, mère medusée et medusante") or by Jane F. Miller[2] and Sherril E. Grace,[3] hardly avoid the interpretive lures of the first page of *Dubliners*. Miller writes, " 'A Mother'

---

[1]   "Joyce, Portrait de l'Auteur en autre lecteur," *Citre-essais*, 1984, p. 40.

[2]   Jane F. Miller, "'O, she's a nice lady!': A Rereading of 'A Mother'," *JJQ* 28 (1991) 407-426.

[3]   Sherril E. Grace, "Rediscovering Mrs.Kearney: An Other reading of 'A Mother'" in *James Joyce: The Augmented Ninth,* ed. Bernard Benstock, (Syracuse: Syracuse University Press, 1988), pp. 273-281.

deals with the major themes present in the other *Dubliners* stories, but as they specifically relate to a woman: it is a tale of paralysis — of the trap not only of Dublin, but of gender; it is a tale of simony — of the influence money exerts over art and relationships between men and women; it is a tale of a gnomon — of romantic disillusionment and unfulfilled incomplete lives."[4]

All three interpretive signposts can indeed be read into the story — perhaps too easily. Simony stares at the reader from the start; Kathleen Kearney is being sold as a second best clone to Cathleen ni Houlihan, the epitome of Irishness. Kathleen is a mere understudy, an uncopyrighted version, a fraud in "blush-pink charmeuse" (*D* 138). Her concert is interrupted. Money is paid back before the completion of the musical intercourse. Musical notes are displaced by bank notes. The story is, one should conclude, written under the sign of the gnomon, the figure of lack inscribed as a frontispiece to the work. Half of the concert is missing; only about half the money is paid and only half of the story is told. Like the incomplete parallelogram at the beginning of "The Sisters," "A Mother" exhibits its lack. However probable and plausible the standard approach, it ignores a number of pregnant details, and makes use of three terms which Joyce's text in "The Sisters" deconceptualizes and renders unstable. Joyce's gnomon provides notoriously unsteady interpretive ground, vacillating as it does between several semantic poles as well as between several paranomastic readings — from *no-man* to *know-man*. Simony is also rendered unstable through the return of its less substantial body double, the more uncanny, soluble, or chemical form "simoniac" found in "The Sisters."

Paralysis is the least conceptual of the three signposts. *The Oxford English Dictionary's* etymological analysis provides the

---

[4]   Miller, p. 410.

following paraphrase: "to loose from beside, to enfeeble."
Webster's offers, "to loosen (i.e. disable) on one side." Father
James Flynn's disease in "The Sisters" seems to be a case of
paralysis agitans, akin to (James) Parkinson's disease[5] — an
instance of rhythmic, repetitive gesturing, which may not only
be "a symptom of the pathology of Dublin, but also, possibly,
an instance of what Derrida calls in the wake of Nietzsche,
"serial differance and rhythm. Here is Derrida's reading of
Nietzsche: "We are henceforth in a logic of difference — which
can be radical alterity — and no longer in a logic of opposition
or contradiction: "Pain is something other than pleasure, I mean
it is not the opposite of pleasure."[6]

Paralysis re-emerges in Derrida's analyses as yet another
word for deconstruction. His reading of Freud's *Beyond the
Pleasure Principle* in two chapters of *The Postcard*, namely
"Freud's Legacy" and "Paralysis," echoes, paraphrases,
paralytically repeats or parareads[7] Joyce's own texts. Both
Joyce's stories and Derrida's rereading of Freud seem to stress
"all these steps which do not advance " (my italics). Each step
lets itself be registered, as a step for nothing in the athesis of
this scene of writing. I recognize in this an exemplary
movement of what was elsewhere named paralysis."[8]

Derrida relates this forbidden step or de-marche to Freud's
analysis of the *fort-da,* or repetition-compulsion. Joyce's text in
"A Mother" begins where Freud left off in *Beyond the Pleasure
Principle,* with an appendix, a supplement, a poetic reference to

---

[5] The priest's hands "trembled too much..." (*D* 12).

[6] Jacques Derrida, *The Postcard,* trans. by Alan Bass, (Chicago:
University of Chicago Press, 1987), p.408.

[7] "Parareads" translates my French induced notion of para-lire.

[8] Derrida, p. 336. Derrida's "elsewhere" can be found as the footnote
makes clear, in *Parages* (Paris: Galilee, 1986).

limping. Derrida writes, "The allusion to limping, on the last line of the book (*Beyond the Pleasure Principle*) has an oblique, lateral, winking relation to Freud's very procedure ... It is suddenly immobilized over limping at the moment of stepping across the last line of the text."[9]

Holohan's "game leg" and useless legwork, like Freud's legacy, call for a differa/ent reading, which will emphasize this oblique *lateral* rather than *literal*, winking approach — a para-*lire*, as it were, a reading of the loose ends, or para-literal details of the text, where some dubbing or dub-lining effect is at work.

"A Mother" presents a number of uncouth details or scruples that add to the mean-ness of the whole. The first lines are strewn with pebble-sized "scruples": Mr. Holohan ... had been walking up and down Dublin ... with his hands and pockets full of **dirty pieces of paper**.... He had **a game leg**." (*D* 136 — Boldfacing is mine). Derrida's leg/legacy coupling casts a new light on these lines, as does the following commentary on a sentence by Freud: "Let us make a bold attempt at another step forward" einen Schritt weiter zu gehen) which he paraphrases as "un pas d'écriture," either a "step in writing" or a no-writing, an unwriting, in other words, either construction or deconstruction. The steps of Holohan, if scrupulously followed, lead the reader on similar tracks — tracks which will read either as a step in writing or as unwriting, or no writing. The last words uttered by Holohan are an instance of repetitiveness, of dub-ling — or of what Heidegger terms "dublette."[10] Beyond the paralysis and staleness of neurotic repetition, looms a differential repetition.

The following quotation provides an almost tailor-made close

---

[9]   Derrida, p. 406.

[10]   *Being and Time,* trans. John Macquarrie and Edward Robinson (New York: Harper and Row, 1962).

commentary on "A Mother." Though Derrida analyzes Freud's *Beyond the Pleasure Principle*, the Joycean story reacts as does the Freudian script because both somehow share the same theme. Both treat paralysis in terms of a de-marche, an un-walking, repetitive, stalling, deconstructive process.

In the fate neurosis the repetition has the characteristics of the demonic. The phantom of the demonic, and even of the diabolical, reappears measuredly in *Beyond the Pleasure Principle*. Coming back — subject to a rhythm — this phantom deserves an analysis of the passages and procedure, of everything that both makes him come back and conjures him up cadentially. This very procedure of the text is diabolical. It mimes walking but does not cease walking without advancing, regularly sketching out one step more without gaining an inch of ground. A limping devil, like everything that transgresses the pleasure principle without even permitting the conclusion of a last step. Limping is the devil, but also absolved of who knows what debt by the one who at a given moment calls himself the "advocatus diaboli" of the death drive, and concludes with a citation in which each word can be remarked with Scripture and with literature. Scripture says that it is no sin to limp — in 'the words of the poet.'

The figure of the diabolical simultaneously looks in the direction of *Beyond* and in the direction of *das Unheimliche*. Elsewhere I have described the systematic and kinship ties between these two essays.[11] In them the devil limps, comes back in a mode which is neither that of an imaginary representation (of an imaginary double) nor that of an apparition in person. His way of coming back, *revenance,* defies such a distinction or opposition. Everything occurs and proceeds as if the devil "in person" came back in order to double his double. So as a

---

[11]   Limping should here be connected with Rabaté's deciphering of the imp of the perverse, in the vicinity of text-geared implications... imprimatur, impresson, writing (in *Portrait de l'auteur en autre lecteur).*

doubling doubling his double, the double of this double, the devil overflows his double at the moment when he is nothing but his double, the double of this double that produces the unheimlich effect."[12]

A process of de-lire, parallel or oblique reading — from swerve of shore to bend of bay — seems to be called for — an ill-mapped navigation around elements of textual flotsam and jetsam. The GPO and the game leg in "A Mother" beckon toward the Derridean corpus (or textual corpse); Holohan's dirty pieces of paper point towards litter/rature, and the house, later, will be filled with paper"(*D* 140). The text is punctuated or punctured by a number of stray, recurring terms such as "point" and "interval."[13] The title "A Mother" also lends itself to a scrupulous kind of surgery or to the pointed steel of interval reading: it becomes AM/OTHER, am/author that is, in the limited space of overlapping sound and sense effects, a differance as well as a restance — a case of *paralysis agitans* as redefined through Derrida's cogitations. Mrs. Kearney's "I am not finished with you" signals Joyce's own compulsion to author other Fin-negans, end-negating texts. The word "end" is here perceived as meaning "telos" as well as end. Derrida rephrases this in pristine words: "Tele — without telos. Finality without end, the beauty of the devil."[14]

---

[12]   Rabaté, pp. 269-70.

[13]   His conversation ... took place at *intervals* (*D* 137); Mrs Kearney said curly at intervals (*D* 146); the men went out for the *interval* (*D* 147); Holohan "stood ... arguing the point" (*D* 136); Mr. Fitzpatrick, who did not catch the *point* (*D* 141); Mr. Holohan *pointed* ... towards the hall... and Kathleen looked down, moving the *point* of her new shoe (*D* 146).

[14]   Derrida, p. 341.

The/A

An ontological drop or loss seems to be at stake in Joyce's choice of the indefinite article in the title of the story. It appears to be suitably mean and scrupulous. "A" reacts against a substantification (/) and determination, while providing oblique inroads into motherhood as a form of otherness, or other/authorship, once a pre-Wakean exercise in verbal cut-up has been carried out on the title. In the last segment of *Finnegans Wake* — "A way a lone a last a loved a long the" (628 15-16) — linguistic molecules and particles resist the return of the substantive, the law of "the," the deixis of fatherhood — which might be called THE-ology. Conversely, (m)other/ness implies an absence of determination, or more exactly a status of A-hood — not exactly a lack. An excess, rather than a lack informs the story, in which Joyce, as in his later works, operates as a clever cleaver, a butcher's daughter of sorts, by doing many "an improper thing" and providing the reader with an *opus interruptum*. One of the most thought-provoking critical statements about this short story was made by William York Tindall, who quite inconclusively concludes: "Mrs. Kearney is an unassigned symbol — that is ... a meaningful thing of uncertain meaning."[15]

The body of the text, the character as type, "character'd in the (type) face," provides a fairly reliable corpus for interpretation and deciphering. "A Mother" is not only concerned with gender issues, but also with "the language movement," or more precisely with Mrs. Kearney as a variation on the old Cotter theme. Mrs. Kearney is the female cutter, the (m)other or (m)author. The story's rather uncouth insistence on the paradigm of the umbrella (a well recognized and exploited Joycean

---

[15] William York Tindall, *A Reader's Guide to James Joyce* (New York, Farrar, 1959), p. 37.

obsession) is neither peripheral nor decorative. The "A" of the title can be seen to reverse, upend itself, and subvert (or as at the beginning of "The Dead" phrases it, literally 'run [it] off its feet') the phallic umbrella of male/linguistic balance. In other words, "A Mother" does something to language which is close to what Alice Jardine has named "gynesis" — or putting into the discourse of woman — which she defines as " a reading effect, a woman-in-effect that is never stable and has no identity."[16]

Instability is a feature of "A Mother"; the Kearney façade rests on the Devlin disestablishment. Devlin is not only a pregnant name, but also a pregnant body or at least a corpus. Mrs. Kearney's maiden name, Devlin, connects her with recurring concepts or patterns in the Joycean matrix: Eve, the line, the borderline, boarding, verging on, becoming,[17] as well as with Dublin to which Devlin is etymologically linked. Beneath the Kearney cognomen, a "Devlin" identity, the name of no-woman, an early Ulyssean female type. The Devlin/Dublin stubbornly surfaces and later "dyoublong "series opens up alternative avenues — or blind alleys perhaps — though the name Devlin reappears on the very first page of *Finnegans Wake*, and seems to have been there all along "since devlins first loved livvy"(*FW* 3.24).

The Devlin-based approach rests in yet another theoretical ground than the Derridean — which somehow remains fascinatingly glued to romantic polarities such as lack, negation, or the concept of origin. Another logic, not so much that of differance as that of difference and repetition (rather than paralysis) is at stake. Effects of difference and repetition —

---

[16]   Alice A. Jardine, *Gynesis: Configurations of Woman and Modernity* (Ithaca: Cornell University Press, 1985), p. 25.

[17]   I am thinking here of possible philosophical links with concept of "devenir" as developed by Gilles Deleuze and Felix Guattari, in *A Thousand Plateaus,* (Minneapolis: University of Minnesota Press, 1987).

Deleuzian concepts[18] — are generated in the last, repetitive words of the story. "—That's a nice lady! he said O, she's a nice lady!"(*D* 149). Holohan's redundancies are framed in between other rhythmical, iterative patterns such as Holohan's pacing up and down, or the swift tit-for-tat exchange of words between himself and Mrs. Kearney. Such effects are poised between actual paralysis and the Derridean version of paralysis, between "A Mother" and "Am/Other." Derrida defines limping "as the very rhythm of the march," in which he reads the return of Nietzsche: "pleasure is a kind of rhythm, says a fragment from 1884."[19]

Drawing near the Limit

In "A Mother" the title character functions as a body double for the m/author, one who has a contract honored and broken at the same time, one who subverts the law of the fathers. A number of misleading points or minor disturbances in the story contribute to prevent straightforward readings of the unscrupulous kind. In the "swift struggle of tongues" many things which would have seemed to go without saying, are left unsaid. Unwanted questions arise such as, "Who is Kathleen's father? Why does Kathleen have a sister? Why does Holohan hop first in and last out of the story? What has Turkish Delight got to do with motherhood? Why does the number eight recur here and elsewhere?"

One of the most puzzlingly "mean" sentences in *Dubliners* is the following: "However, when she [Miss Devlin] drew near the limit and her friends began to loosen their tongues about her she silenced them by marrying Mr. Kearney, who was a bootmaker on Ormond Quay" (*D* 137). "[D]rawing near the limit" implies

---

[18]   Gilles Deleuze, *Difference et Repetition* (Paris: PUF, 1968).

[19]   Derrida, *The Postcard,* pp. 405-6.

a variety of limits, from the age limit to actual spatial boundaries such as those imposed by extra-large hips. But in both cases, why should friends "loosen their tongues"? The sentence calls forth some unmentionable sin, implying a distant suspicion of "greatness." One remembers similar effects in "The Dead," in which Gretta was "great with" Michael Furey. This could suggest she is a really good friend of his, yet also, possibly, that she is great with child. Turkish Delight might very well function as a screen for Devlin's blooming or booming maternity — the candy subtly glazing over the "topping" by screening it off as mere icing. Devlin's pregnancy would then parody Mary's.

The mention of Turkish Delight, a prefiguration of Molly Bloom's *sweets of sin,* connects Miss Devlin with the rest of Joyce's para-lyzing, fort-da creatures — forever on the borderline between *differance* and *restance*, *tele* and *telos*, forever embodiments of undecidability or rhythm. Turkish Delight has made Miss Devlin — a name which etymologically duplicates Dublin yet echoes Eve and Eveline — "draw near the limit." The phrase itself is pregnant with logical, philosophical and mathematical implications.

The text offers a possible key to Miss Devlin's maternity by having Holohan hop first into the story. He is an unlikely candidate for fatherhood since the reader, quite inescapably cliché-contolled, will think of Cathleen ni Houlihan, the traditional personification of Ireland, at once a poor woman and a queen, here turned into a "quean" in the older sense of a prostitute. Houlihan is worded or voided differently, hollowed out into hollow/han. Hoppy Holohan, however hollow, singles himself out as possessing a lot of Joyce's own mania: he is a street-walker who makes notes, a singer and a writer, one who walks about with his pockets full of dirty pieces of paper (lit[t]erature). Mrs. Kearney draws near the limit much in the way Joyce's sentences do, by rewriting the law of the father (of the Committee) in different/deferring terms, by unsettling the relationship between sentences and sentencing. The phrase appears in a pregnant context — linked to the birth of language, and the "loosening of tongues." The loosening of tongues stands in close, though oblique relationship with the "language movement." Joyce evidently caricatures the *Eire Abu* society as the purveyor of mere gossip. Yet beneath this surface reading, another lateral meaning emerges. Joyce's own tongue loosens the traditional frames of storytelling, here turned into "a swift struggle of tongues." The text hardly manages to silence its own "distant music." The sound reduction effect ("she silenced them") is challenged by the next boisterous phrase referring to, of all professions, a bootmaker — yet another Joycean, fetishistic, perverse pleasure and a paralysis-ridden ploy. The author haunts the m/author.

"A Mother" which is opposed to "a nice lady," comes close to functioning in the way that Deleuze calls a plateau, a threshold, a space of microfissures, of multiplicities connected to other multiplicities by superficial underground stems in such a way as to form a rhizome. Here is a portable definition of the term: "A plateau is always in the middle, not at the beginning or the end. A rhizome is made of plateaux. Gregory Bateson uses the word "plateau" to designate something very special: a continuous, self-vibrating region of intensities whose development avoids any orientation towards a culmination point or external end."[20]

More micro-fissures or disconcerting echoes can be heard in the apparently ludicrous portrait of the husband, Mr. Kearney, whose "conversation, which was serious, took place at intervals in his great brown beard"(*D* 137). "Interval," like "drawing near the limit," adds one more element to a series of related, musical or mathematical terms. Much hair-splitting or cleaving goes on in Joyce's text; "A Mother" is a study in intervals,

[20]   *A Thousand Plateaus*, p. 22.

interval-playing, and limits. It is an early exercise in serial organization, where excess, rather than lack, rules.

Mrs. Kearney draws near the limit in a mathematical sense, by her careful keeping accounts: the sum she asks for is eight guineas; the one she receives is four, minus four shillings. An equivalence is established between telling and telling, i.e. between, keeping accounts and making accounts, story-telling and book-keeping. "A Mother" prefigures "Penelope" and its many references to number eight, the figure of the Virgin Mary disestablished into a horizontal pair of breasts. Devlin/Kearney cleaves, disrupts, creates "intervals" for conversation — in more than one sense. Kathleen Kearney's singing career strangely resembles Joyce's own, as Miller points out.[21] It is yet another interval for yet another *struggle of tongues*.

The Matter Before the Committee

"A Mother" subverts committees into *cometties*. The word occurs and recurs here and there in the story. Joyce subtly brings the matter/mother before the Committee, giving it (her) precedence over the self-appointed, male powers. Such a precedence reformulates in Deleuzian terms, what he calls the becoming-woman, or the molecular woman, or "the girl": "She is an abstract line, or a line of flight. Thus, girls do not belong to an age group, sex, order, or kingdom: they slip in everywhere, between orders, acts, ages, sexes; they produce molecular sexes on the line of flight in relation to the dualism machines they cross right through. The only way to get outside the dualisms is to be-between, to pass between the

---

[21]   Miller, p.423. Bell, the second tenor, is compared with Joyce who also sang second tenor, and "like Bell, was awarded a bronze medal at the Feis Ceoil." The actual concert took place on August 27th, 1904. Bell is the only character who speaks up for Mrs. Kearney.

intermezzo...."[22]

Dev-lin — the name — can be read as a line of flight, a becoming (devenir)-line. Devlin functions like a plurilingual pun on the fringe between French and English — *devenir*, to become, a line. It rewrites Eveline — the maternal version of the spinster.

Transformation takes place in the story, between gender barriers. Womanhood or maternity or ladyhood is revised into this curious word-formation by which Mrs. Kearney gives an unwitting definition of herself/ the other or the (m)other. Like Joyce's "a great fellow fol-the-diddle-I-do" this is a linguistic exercise in the gynesis of a feminine language, made up of intervals. To diddle means several things in English: to waste time (time and money are wasted in the story) but also to jerk up and down or back and forth, to jiggle, hence to coit a woman or to masturbate. Richard Spears's dictionary of slang[23] notes that the noun also designates the penis, and the female genitals — a linguistic plateau of sorts. In "fol" another subterranean meaning emerges. It could possibly be to write and draw near the limit of madness. Mrs. Kearney stands all the closer to the figure of the (m)author since she has married the GPO and a bootmaker to boot. As a body without organs — yet another Deleuzian line — she connects the organs of literary creation — hand and foot, pen and phallus, in an open-ended structure. The conjunction is made syntactically in the following sentence: "She will get four pounds eight into her hand or a foot she won't put on that platform" (*D* 148).

The sentence may refer to the mother's cliché-ridden language. In this case, it shows an instance of good saleswomanship, which points to the mother-as-pimp

---

[22] *A Thousand Plateaus*, p. 276.

[23] Richard Spears, *Slang and Euphemism* (New York: Signet Books, 1981), p. 108.

interpretation. Conversely, one might muse on the proximity of hand and foot, or promiscuity rather, where Kearney displaces an interval, and creates the impish body of the creator — *her hand or a foot.* The sentence verges for an instant on the undecidable; a *differance* sets in, a space between occurs, a middle voice between passive and active, is heard. This logic of in-betweenness connects with Kristeva's definition of maternality as *"the ambivalent principle that is bound to the species on the one hand, and on the other stems from an identity catastrophe that causes the Name to topple over into the unnameable that one imagines as femininity, non-language or body."*[24]

Kristeva adds that "it is ironic that the orthodox constituent of Christianity, through John of Chrysostom's golden mouth, among others, sanctioned the transitional function of the maternal by calling the Virgin a 'bond', a 'middle' or an 'interval.'" Kearney actually loses her proper name to wear the improper name of "A Mother." She provides intervals, breaks, difference and undecidability as in the paragraph: "He went out at once. Mrs. Kearney wrapped the cloak around her daughter and followed him. As she passed through the doorway she stopped and glared into Mr. Holohan's face (*D* 149).

"Him" is in a state of syntactical suspension between two possible fathers, a postman and a penman, a shem and a shaun — unless the pronoun is uncannily tied to the daughter; Joyce's insistence on the cloaking and wrapping process might abortively suggest some undecidable moment of in-betweenness — the daughter being at the same time sped off into the world in a (French) letter and yet covered and cloaked in a virginal veil, given and taken back, woven and unwoven in the same process of a pen-eloping.

In *Giacomo Joyce,* the following fragment floats into the reader's line of vision: *My words in her mind: cold polished*

---

[24]   "Stabat Mater," in *A Kristeva Reader*, ed. Toril Moi, pp. 161-162.

stones sinking through a quagmire' (*GJ* xiii). According to the *Oxford English Dictionary*'s second mother entry, mother precisely means quagmire, mud, matter: Mud, mire, scum, dregs — alchemical sense. The original crude substance which remains after a substance is refined. (The OED also quotes an entry from Killian's Dutch or Flemish dictionary of 1598 where mother is spelt modder and defined as limus, faeces, mollius and crassamen.)

Mollius provides an interesting sidelight on possible connections between Joycean versions of the maternal, Kearney and Bloom. At the end of "A Mother," Kearney turns to stone, though not necessarily to a figure of Medusa. She merely draws very near the limit — verges on the status of a writer, the figure of the other/author. The "cold, polished stones" sinking into the quagmire, emblematize "the scrupulous meanness" advertised as constituting *Dubliners:* they are, literally, small pebbles, scruples, scruples that will haunt the text and fissure mean-ness into mean-ing — as well as pure "tele without telos."

Paris

"GRACE" AFTER *PIERS PLOWMAN*
A COMPARISON OF "GRACE" AND THE MEDIEVAL
ALLEGORY
OF GLOTOUN IN WILLIAM LANGLAND'S
PIERS PLOWMAN

YVONNE STUDER

In *My Brother's Keeper*, Stanislaus Joyce explains that in "Grace,"" the fall, repentance, and rehabilitation of Thomas Kernan follow the progress of Dante through Hell, Purgatory, and Heaven."[1] However, there is more to "Grace" than Dante's tripartite structure. Apart from the obvious references to the New Testament and to Chaucer's "Pardoner's Tale," Tom Kernan's fall and pseudo-conversion might also be based on William Langland's *Piers Plowman*, especially on the allegory of Glotoun, one of the deadly sins Langland parades in Passus VI of the C-text, which dates from c. 1387.[2] To corroborate this view, I shall be looking at similarities in the two narratives: the plots and use of language, the characters' names and functions, especially at the protagonists and their wives. There is also a fair amount of external evidence from *Ulysses* and *Finnegans Wake* which points to the connection between the two stories. Nevertheless, I do not mean to imply that "Grace" is exclusively about gluttony but agree with Brewster Ghiselin, who writes: "In the twelfth through the fourteenth stories, the subversion of the cardinal virtues of justice, temperance, and prudence, and

---

[1]   Stanislaus Joyce, *My Brother's Keeper*, ed. Richard Ellmann (New York: Viking, 1959), p. 228.

[2]   Subsequent quotations are from William Langland, *Piers Plowman. An Edition of the C-text*, edited by Derek Pearsall (London: Edward Arnold, 1978). The date of the C-text is discussed on p. 9. All quotations from the allegory are documented within parentheses in the text; translations are mine.

the contradiction of reason, upon which they are based, is displayed in those narratives that Joyce intended to represent 'public life' in Ireland. ... Certainly the culminating subversion of the three virtues is represented in the third story of this group, 'Grace,' in the sermon of 'a man of the world' recommending worldly wisdom for the guidance of 'his fellowmen'."[3]

It is helpful to read "Grace" in the wider perspective of *Ulysses*. In "Lotus Eaters," Joyce presents an outsider's view of conversion and gluttony by making Bloom consider these themes. Intemperance, the Irish version of gluttony, is neither excused nor condemned. But its extent and usefulness for certain people are exposed when Bloom calculates the amount of porter consumed to make Lord Iveagh's fortune. The link with the earlier short story is established as soon as M'Coy, one of the characters from "Grace," comes to Bloom's mind while he is entering All Hallows Church. A notice on the door announcing Father Conmee's sermon on Saint Peter Claver and the African mission triggers off thoughts both about conversion and Martin Cunningham. It is hardly surprising that Cunningham, the chief missionary from "Grace," happens to know Conmee. Whether or not the priests' drinking wine and the old popes' hedonism are associated with gluttony is hard to say. But the eunuchs Bloom eventually recalls are "Gluttons..." (*U* 5: 411).

The word "grace" or elements from "Grace" are combined with the word or the fact of gluttony in some other places in *Ulysses*. In "Lestrygonians," Bloom considers the prayers said before and after meals. However, the ambiguity of the word "grace" favors a smooth transition of his thoughts from prayers to the looks of the greedy eaters he is watching. He ironically

[3]   "The Unity of Joyce's *Dubliners*" in *"Dubliners": Text, Criticism, and Notes*, ed. Robert Scholes and A. Walton Litz (New York: Viking, 1969), p. 324.

comments: "Grace after meals" (*U* 8:674). The description of Tom Kernan in "Wandering Rocks" shows that he is still as much of a glutton in *Ulysses* as he was in *Dubliners* : his body is "stumpy," his strut "fat," and his face of "High color, of course" (*U* 10:755-7). Later, in "Cyclops," the narrator turns out to be another glutton for, as he reckons in the backyard, he has drunk "about a gallon." No sooner has he relieved himself than Cunningham and Power turn up in the pub. Finally, with a mind bent on gluttony, one might even discover a cannibalistic message in "Eumaeus." The cryptic line of "bitched type" in the pink edition of the *Telegraph*, .")eatondph 1/8 ador dorador douradora...," is inserted exactly between the names of Cunningham, Power and Kernan (*U* 16:1258-9). Meaningless though the line seems to be, the word "eat" stands at its beginning; so the passage may suggest subliminally that Cunningham and Power eat Kernan.

The two antithetical terms can be found together in *Finnegans Wake* as well, e.g. in the elliptical "Grace before Glutton" (*FW* 7). Among many other things, this might be a comment on the reading history of the two stories about Tom Kernan and Glotoun: it is "Grace" *before* Glutton since most readers will come across Joyce's story before reading the medieval allegory. This sentence is placed two lines after the word "patterjackmartins," by which the patron saint of Ireland, Patrick, as well as the leaders of the Protestant Reformation, Jean Calvin and Martin Luther are brought to mind. In addition, the word might allude to St. Patrick's contemporary "Catholic" successors Jack Power and Martin Cunningham, who are trying to undo Calvin's and Luther's work in Dublin.

The search for sources of "Grace" need not lead straightaway to Langland's dream vision. Chaucer's Pardoner, whose tale is told in the *Canterbury Tales*, might more readily be remembered. At least as corrupt as Father Purdon, the Pardoner hypocritically preaches against gluttony, wrath, and lechery, but especially against covetousness, on which he prides himself in his Prologue. Nevertheless, *Piers Plowman* accounts for more elements in "Grace" than "The Pardoner's Tale" does, from Tom Kernan's fall to the character of Father Purdon.

Langland's dreamer-narrator starts by condemning the corruption of a number of spiritual leaders in his Prologue:

> Ac sith charite hath be chapman and chief to shryue lordes
> Mony ferlyes han falle in a fewe Zeres,
> And but holi chirche and charite choppe adoun suche shryuars
> The moste meschief on molde mounteth vp faste. (Prologue, ll. 62-5)

> But since Charity has become a tradesman and mainly hears the confession of lords,
> Many strange things have happened in recent years,
> And unless the holy Church and Charity reject such confessors,
> The greatest mischief in the world will soon be heaped up.

He then mentions a pardoner who sells cheap forgiveness to the "Lewed," that is, to ignorant men who believe him well enough and "lykede his wordes" (Prologue, l. 70), as Father Purdon's congregation of businessmen like his. The narrator goes on to warn his readers: "Thus Ze gyue Zoure gold glotons to helpe" (Prologue, l. 74) — such fellows are gluttons who do not care about the spiritual welfare of those they rob of their money. If Purdon is first identified by Tom Kernan's cronies in the sick room as a "fine, jolly fellow ... Rather red face, tall" (*D* 164), there can be little doubt later of his corpulence and probable gluttony. His "bulk" all but prevents him from beginning mass in a dignified way, for everyone can see him "struggling up into the pulpit" (*D* 173).

After his initial strictures, the narrator in *Piers Plowman* continues to relate, in the text following the Prologue, how forgiveness must be earned by means of a long and tiresome quest for virtue. In "Grace," on the other hand, the Purdon episode is placed at the end of the story, to provide an anti-climax to the bungling attempt at making Tom Kernan a "good holy pious and God-fearing Roman Catholic" (*D* 170) after his graceless fall in the pub. The quest for virtue, if ever there was one, ends here. Forgiveness is thrown to the congregation and need not be earned at all unless to "set right [one's] accounts" (*D* 174) means to earn it. The name Purdon was anything but an accidental choice, as a note in Richard Ellmann's biography shows: "...as Stanislaus Joyce notes, the name was given him sarcastically because Purdon Street was in the brothel area."[4] Fritz Senn has complemented this interpretation: "Once ... you start to look into the priest's name, you may realize that if it were French it would mean 'pure gift', and that grace is a divine gift, so that Joyce's choice might somehow span a Dublin hell and a French heaven."[5]

Both Glotoun's and Tom Kernan's drinking tours start on Friday. Glotoun is actually on the way to confession, but Betty, the breweress, tempts him to taste her ale. The two protagonists get so drunk that they have accidents in their respective drinking establishments. While Tom Kernan falls down the stairs to the lavatory, a detail that emphasizes the disgrace of the accident, Glotoun stumbles over a threshold. Since neither of them is in a position to get up on his own, they have to accept the help of bystanders. Glotoun genuinely regrets his sins on the sickbed[6]

---

[4]   Stanislaus Joyce, pp. 227-8. See also *JJ II* 133n.

[5]   Fritz Senn, "A Rhetorical Account of James Joyce's 'Grace,'" *Moderna Språk,* 54 (1980), 123-4.

[6]   Derek Pearsall, the editor, is more skeptical about Glotoun's intentions, as his footnote to 1. 441 shows: "Gluttony's last words are a backward look at his old life. His penitence seems peremptory and mechanical, and the allegorical suggestion is that formal confession will not

and swears an oath that he will be abstinent henceforth, however painful this may be for him:

> For y vowe to verray god, for eny hungur or furste,
> Shal neuere fysch in пe Fryday defyen in my wombe
> Til Abstinence myn aunte haue Zeue me leue -
> And Zut haue y hated here al my lyf-tyme. (Passus VI, ll.438-41)

> For I swear to God, in spite of hunger or thirst,
> Never shall fish be digested in my womb again on a Friday,
> Until Abstinence, my aunt, has given my leave -
> And yet I have hated her all my life long.

Kernan, on the other hand, becomes the "victim" (*D* 157) of a plot of his visitors, who have conspired to lead him back to the fold of the Catholic Church, or rather, to tie him more firmly to their network of obligations. He joins their retreat because he can only win by doing so; there will be no reproachful sermon but merely a "friendly talk ... in a common-sense way" (*D* 165). Moreover, the admirer of eloquence thinks he may be rewarded by a piece of perfect rhetoric, for Father Purdon is of the "educated order" (*D* 163) of the Jesuits.

Language plays an important role in both stories. Langland, who is obliged to "Treuthe," calls a spade a spade even if the facts he reports are disgusting. Before Glotoun stumbles, "His gottes gan to gothly as two grydy sowes" (Passus VI, l. 398), his guts began to grunt like two greedy sows. "A pissede a potel in a *pater-noster* whyle" (Passus VI, l. 399), he pissed a pot full in the time it takes for praying the Lord's Prayer. After his breakdown, he "cowed vp a caudel in Clementis lappe" (Passus

---

prove adequate to cleanse society as a basis for reform" (p. 128).

VI, l. 412), he was sick over Clement's lap (Clement is a cobbler who comes to his aid after his fall). These descriptions sound ribald even today, yet nobody appears to have felt a need to censor *Piers Plowman* because of them.

At the time Joyce wrote *Dubliners*, however, such frankness was considered offensive. The publication history of the collection illustrates to what extent the use of language is subject to social and political conditions. Although vulgarity, false swearing and cursing were no doubt as common at the beginning of this century as they are today or were in Langland's days, publishers and printers would not have them printed; they were "subject to criminal prosecution" for the publication of "objectionable material."[7] Joyce had to fight for every swearword that he insisted on retaining in a book concerned with moral corruption. Especially in "Grace," they are indispensable since gluttony is traditionally linked with cursing and idle swearing.[8] When Glotoun acknowledges his sins, he admits to swearing as well as to eating and drinking to excess, for he is guilty of having "trespased with tonge" (Passus VI, l. 426) in general and "Sworn 'Godes soule and his sides!' and 'So helpe me, god almyhty!'" (Passus VI, l. 427) when there was no need to swear. Neither Kernan nor Cunningham, however, seem to be aware of committing a sin when they season their stories with such expressions as "bloody" (*D* 161), "damned ... faith ... tell you God's truth" (*D* 165), and similar intensifiers.

Idle swearing and cursing might be called irresponsible uses of language. In "Grace," Joyce shows that language is being

[7]   Ellmann, p. 220.

[8]   See Pearsall's note to ll. 361: "Swearing is one of the 'sins of the tavern'traditionally associated with gluttony (II 97n), along with drunkenness and gambling (see 376-93 below), in homiletic literature (Owst, 1933, 427-41), as in the sermon of Chaucer's Pardoner (CT VI. 463-660)" (p. 125).

used irresponsibly and inaccurately most of the time, not only in cases condemned by the Church. In the narrative passages, he mocks the pomposity and linguistic hypocrisy of those characters who imitate the language of "educated" people without altogether mastering it and who tend to dress crude realities they are unwilling to acknowledge in euphemisms. At the beginning of the story, Kernan is not found in the vulgar "jakes" but in the "lavatory," and its floor is all the same covered with "filth and ooze" (*D* 150). Later on, a veritable effusion of words disguises Kernan's financial misfortunes: "Modern business methods had spared him only so far as to allow him a little office in Crowe Street..." (*D* 154). Archaic and precious words land "Grace" an ostentatiously stilted tone, especially when the text reads: "The manager at once began to *narrate* what he knew" or the constable "made ready to *indite*" (*D* 151, emphasis added). Such a style cannot fail to alert readers to the fact that language is a social tool and makes them pay more attention to the way it is used in the dialogues and the sermon at the end.[9] Only occasionally did Joyce "upgrade" factual details borrowed from the medieval allegory: though Kernan, like Glotoun, makes a "grunting noise" (*D* 150) while lying on the floor, though the sound comes from his nose, not from his guts. Usually, however, details that are more infamous than in the original story are told in a style less obligated to truth than to euphemism and snobbery. I suspect that "narrate" and "indite" would have been the verbs used by Kernan had he written down his story. For he is the character most conscious of language and its effects on an audience (*D* 171). Even with his tongue bleeding, he thanks the young man most elaborately: "- I' 'ery 'uch o'liged to you, sir. I hope we'll 'eet again. 'y na'e is Kernan" (*D* 153). Language to him is a means of aggrandizing

---

[9]   For a thorough analysis of the language of "Grace" see Fritz Senn's "A Rhetorical Account of James Joyce's 'Grace,'" 121-128.

himself — he does not realize how ridiculous he often is. But in the "Hades" chapter of *Ulysses*, Kernan's style will be mocked, by Cunningham and Power of all people, who poke fun at his use of the word "trenchant" (*U* 6:145-150). Mrs Kernan's view that there is a "curious appropriateness" (*D* 157) in her husband's biting off a piece of his tongue is right: it is a crucial part of his body that has been punished since he depends on it both professionally, when tasting the teas he sells, and socially, as his tongue enables him to drink and play the character everyone expects him to be.

The secularization of religious terms (besides those used as oaths and swearwords) is another issue of "Grace." Joyce has interspersed the story with a large number of words that might have both a secular and a religious meanings, starting, of course, with the programmatic title "Grace" and its derivations in the text. Other examples are "fallen" and "curate" (*D* 150), "*bona-fide*" (*D* 159), "Christian name" and "crusade" (*D* 160), or "officiate" (*D* 161; 167). Except in the sermon, the meanings of such words are exclusively secular. How could it be otherwise in a story in which a plot of conversion turns out to be no more than a "conversation" (*D* 161), or a sermon, "a friendly talk ... in a common-sense way" (*D* 167)? Purdon is by no means the man to stop such a development; he even appears to promote it actively by "translating" the text he has chosen into the language of businessmen and thus trivializing the message — and what is worse, by first falsifying the passage, as Fritz Senn has found out: "Father Purdon, we know, is better at eloquent poise than close to the spirit of the Gospel as he 'develops the text.' The text itself, taken from Luke 16: 8-9, has one strange feature: '...*so that when you die...*' (*D* 173). This you won't find in the Douay Version of the Bible, which reads: '...when you shall fail...', nor in the Authorized Version, which has '...when ye fail...', nor in the Vulgate, '...*cum defeceritis...*', or else the Greek New Testament, '...*hotan eklipé...*' — a difficult text indeed. An authorized translation which actually says 'died' may still come to light, but until then we are left to wonder why a professional expounder of Scriptures, preaching to men of the world, should substitute something else for a word that has reverberations in the territory ruled by Mammon, as in 'He had failed in business...' (*D* 166)."[10] Some of the less conspicuous words would no doubt be fraught with religious overtones, too, if they did not appear in "Grace," the point of which is that its characters, all but one, are incapable of re-en-act-ing crucial moments of the Gospels or the Mass: "lift ... up" (*D* 150) might refer to the Ascension, or to the elevation of the Host at Mass for adoration; "turning ... over" (*D* 150) to the conversion of a heathen or a sinner; "air" (*D* 156) and "wind" (*D* 153) besides various alcoholic beverages mentioned in the story to the friendly or evil spirits which assist or attack humankind. When Langland's dreamer-narrator describes the Tree of True Love, the latter image is still valid: the tree, whose blossoms symbolize "Benigne-speche" (Passus XVIII, l. 11) and whose fruit is charity, may be attacked by three "wikkede wyndes" (Passus XVIII, l. 29), that is covetousness, lechery, and slander (Passus XVIII, ll. 32-47).

The reader faces a real problem with the dialogue of "Grace." In conversation, language is bandied about: words are used and abused for all kinds of purposes, and they are fairly unreliable indices by which to judge characters.[11] I do not think that reading faces is any more reliable, although Kernan admires Martin Cunningham for his skill in that art (*D* 164). Except in fiction, the thoughts of other people are beyond the observation of others so we are left with their actions alone. In Passus XVI of *Piers Plowman*, the need to act according to, rather than talk

---

[10]   Senn, p. 126.

[11]   Only Christ is capable of doing this, as Ulrich Schneider points out quoting Matthew 12: 36-7 in *James Joyce: Dubliners* (Munich: Wilhelm Fink, 1982), p. 55.

about, God's will is pointed out to the dreamer, too. Hence, a special light is thrown on the character in "Grace" who is known by his actions alone: the laconic young man in the cycling suit who administers first aid to Kernan. The cyclist is a stranger without the slightest intention of getting recognized or recompensed for his services — he does not even introduce himself (*D* 153) — he resembles the good Samaritan, another outsider, whose story is told by Christ to illustrate what it means to love one's neighbor.[12] Clearly, the reticent young man is the antithesis of the imposing figure of Father Purdon, who speaks at length in an inflated style. The Samaritan is a figure of importance in *Piers Plowman* as well. In Passus XIX, the narrator meets him on his way to Christ. But already earlier on, in the allegory of Glotoun, Clement the cobbler acts as a Samaritan assisting the drunken protagonist. His name is significant: Clement is a merciful and lenient man, but he is also gullible and partly to blame for Glotoun's condition. Having proposed and "won" the first of a series of games of exchanges, Clement had to pay for a round of drinks to appease the loser and please the audience in the tavern. An umpire also set up the rule that whoever regretted an exchange later on would have to "grete syre Glotoun with a galon of ale" (Passus VI, ll. 376-93).[13]

---

[12]   See Luke 10:25-37. Biblical quotations are from the King James Bible.

[13]   Pearsall's note to l. 377 provides further information on this game: " *Þe newe fayre* seems to have been a game of exchanges. The two 'players' offer objects for exchange, which are appraised by selected *chapmen*, and the winner of what they deem the more valuable object offers compensation to the other player (382). If there is further argument, an umpire is appointed (388). Here the argument is settled, to everyone's satisfaction, by having Clement, who seems to have gained by winning Hick's hood, pay for a round of drinks. Anyone who wants his property back has to pay for a gallon of ale for the privilege (392-3). The point of the game is to 'beat one's neighbor',

If the nameless stranger were the only helper in "Grace" corresponding to the biblical Samaritan or the medieval Clement, Dublin would not be an altogether hopeless case incapable of salvation. But early in the story the young man is ousted abruptly by Jack Power, who begrudges him the slightest token of gratitude from Kernan. When Kernan starts to praise the young man, Power interferes: "- O, only for him, said Mr Power, it might have been a case of seven days without the option of a fine" (*D* 160). An allegorical reading of this change of helpers might lead to this interpretation: ineffectual legal Power (the constable who keeps repeating questions nobody is willing to answer) and selfless Charity (the young man) cannot possibly sustain their influence on a sinner so as to make him change his ways; for there are other Powers (e.g. Jack) who need sinners as puppets they can manipulate as they please after ingratiating themselves. Power's nickname is Jack and it is common knowledge that a jack is a face card of considerable value, and also a knave, "an unprincipled crafty man" — according to *The American Heritage Dictionary*. The full name, then, is an allusion to male power games. It also suggests the British "Union Jack,"and may indicate that the character's political loyalties are certainly not the author's.

Power is "outgeneralled" (*D* 171) when Cunningham, his elder colleague, takes the lead in the conversion of Tom Kernan. If we put aside Martin Luther and St. Martin of Tours, we might speculate that his "Christian" name, Martin, is derived from the Roman god of war, Mars. It relates him as much to Power as his employment in the Royal Irish Constabulary Office in Dublin Castle. Yet, Cunningham's part corresponds to

---

presumably by getting one's friends to acts [sic] as appraisers (379). The game had a bad name, and was probably used as a form of confidence trick. It was perhaps named after 'The Neue Feyre', the nickname of a disreputable street-market in Soper Lane, put down in 1297 because it was infested with thieves and beggars (Riley's *Memorials* 33)" (p. 126).

another element in Langland's allegory, that is to "inwit" (Passus VI, 1. 421), or conscience. Unlike the reproaches of "inwit," Cunningham's reproaches do not crush the sinner. Instead of arguments, he offers "monosyllables [with] a moral intention" (*D* 159), or euphemistic hints: "- It happened that you were peloothered, Tom, said Mr Cunningham gravely" (*D* 160). The response to such a surplus of lenience resembles the humble admission of a businessman who has just been found guilty of overcharging one of his customers: "- True bill, said Mr Kernan, equally gravely" (*D* 160). "Cunning"-ham is described as a "...thoroughly sensible man, influential and intelligent. His blade of human knowledge, natural astuteness ... had been tempered by brief immersions in the waters of general philosophy. He was well informed" (*D* 160). He evidently embodies worldly wisdom, as does the unreliable steward in the parable from Luke 16, from which Purdon has borrowed the two sentences on which his pseudo-sermon is based. The steward, who has lost his master's trust, arbitrarily diminishes the sums that debtors owe his master so as to remain popular with them after his dismissal. Quoted out of context, the two sentences seem to praise the behavior of the steward who squanders his master's property for his own sake. But if the master is God, the property he squanders is nothing less than the souls of those he ought to remind of their debts. Had Purdon quoted one more sentence, the seeming praise would have been unmasked: "He that is faithful in that which is least is faithful also in much: and he that is unjust in the least is unjust also in much."[14] As unreliable as the steward and Father Purdon, Cunningham squanders Kernan's soul for his own sake. For if cunning, or worldly wisdom, replaces conscience, true insight into faults is impossible; self-delusion[15] and the promise of new

---

[14]   Luke 16:10.

[15]   See Kernan's "...I'm not such a bad fellow..." (*D* 170).

profit - a "friendly talk" instead of a sermon - may temporarily alleviate the state of disgrace but they do not remove it. Cunningham's motive for "helping" Kernan is less one of augmenting his personal power than one of assuring himself of his friends' respect and pity. Even Bloom likes him: "Sympathetic human man he is" (*U* 6:344-5). Nevertheless, Cunningham does not really help his friend or do his job properly. Instead of reminding Kernan of his personal responsibility for his actions, he twice conjures up the spirit of collective guilt:

> - Yes, that's it, said Mr Cunningham, Jack and I and M'Coy here - we're all going to wash the pot.
> He uttered the metaphor with a certain homely energy and, encouraged by his own voice, proceeded:
> - You see, we may as well all admit we're a nice collection of scoundrels, one and all. I say, one and all, he added with gruff charity.... (*D* 163)

> - We'll all renounce the devil, he said, together, not forgetting his works and pomps. (*D* 171)

Whatever his motives, the fruits of his activities bear testimony against him: his own wife is an "incurable drunkard" (*D* 157), and as Kernan's reappearances in *Ulysses* illustrate, the confession of his "little tale of woe" (*D* 171) did not cure his gluttony either.

The names of Cunningham's assistants are no less telling than his own. Apart from Power, there is M'Coy, whose name gives rise to associations such as "affectedly shy, evasive" or "modest," and indeed, so are his contributions to the conversion. M'Coy has held many posts throughout his life (*D* 158) but is incapable of doing anything well but withdrawing. Thus, the only time a contribution of his is sincerely appreciated by the others is when he humbly abstains from having a second measure of whisky because there is not enough to go round (*D* 169). He generally fails to "enter the conversation" (*D* 161), however hard he tries. When he succeeds in taking part, his role is restricted to dealing keywords to the others, or to assenting to what they have said. But even these entries lack perfection; in the example below, he foolishly breaks the rule of coherence in conversational turn-taking:

- It's like everything else in this world, he [Cunningham] said. You get some bad ones and you get some good ones.
- O yes, you get some good ones, I admit, said Mr Kernan, satisfied.
- It's better to have nothing to say to them, said Mr M'Coy. That's my opinion. (*D* 161)

Unconsciously, however, he tells the truth about the behavior of corrupt Dubliners towards outsiders more perfect than themselves.

Another unexpected helper is Fogarty, whose presence and gift of whisky — derived from Irish Gaelic "uisce beathadh," i.e. "water of life" — gives new spirit to the party. He is "announced" by Mrs Kernan and, with his "neat enunciation" and "grace," resembles an angel "stepping forward into the light" (*D* 166) — but it is not clear whether his appearance is supposed to parody the Annunciation, as the vocabulary strongly suggests, or if Fogarty — with his gift — is the fourth Wise Man at a sham Epiphany. He might as well represent a debased Dublin type of Holy Ghost, Fog, who is invoked by regular consumption of alcohol and now appears to crown by his presence Kernan's initiation into the community of Dublin businessmen. It is certainly no accident that Cunningham's words about renouncing the devil (*D* 171) echo those of a Catholic baptism. Foggy though his role may be, he is welcome to skeptical Thomas Kernan: "- I wouldn't doubt you, old man..." (*D* 166). Fogarty's spirit restores Kernan's male dignity after his wife's refusal to serve him porter has reduced him to the helplessness of a baby, maybe a small-time copy of Christ in the manger: "- Nothing for poor little hubby!" (*D* 162).

In Langland's allegory, it is the wife who plays the most important part in the conversion of Glotoun.: "His wif and his inwit edwitede him of his synne" (Passus VI, l. 421) - she and conscience reproached him for his sin until he "wax ashamed" (Passus VI, l. 422). Her motives are not mentioned, of course, since the text is too early to display a psychological interest in the characters. She stands for all the wives who do their Christian duty by their husbands. We know, however, that she and the maid carry him to his bed "With alle πe wo of this world" (Passus VI, l. 415), which points to a genuine concern for his welfare.

Mrs Kernan's motives are open to the readers' scrutiny since her thoughts are represented in the text. Although she is not the worst of wives (cf. Mrs Cunningham), she is as superficial and materialistic as her husband. As long as the salary is secured, she does not object to "his frequent intemperance" (*D* 156). "Such a sight!" (*D* 154), she comments on her husband's state when Power brings him home; his looks apparently worry her most. It is also his looks she remembers when thinking of their wedding, which to her never meant a sacrament, i.e. a ceremony conferring religious grace. "Religion for her was a habit" (*D* 157), an established custom, or a costume. Yet, Mrs Kernan is less exposed to laughter than the would-be missionaries at her husband's sickbed because she is free from their pretensions. Uneducated as she appears to be, she cannot be blamed for the lack of sophistication in her religious beliefs or her language, and in spite of all difficulties, she has always been a practical housewife and mother: "The part of mother presented to her no insuperable difficulties and for twenty-five years she had kept house shrewdly for her husband. Her two eldest sons were launched. One was in a draper's shop in Glasgow and the other was clerk to a tea-merchant in Belfast"

(*D* 156). Mrs Kernan has to suffer most when her husband squanders his money on drinks and clothing. But what is absent from Joyce's description of her is love for, or at least tokens of a friendly attachment to, her husband. Renewing her "intimacy with her husband" means no more than "waltzing with him to Mr Power's accompaniment" (*D* 156). Power's "good offices" are also necessary "during domestic quarrels, as well as many small, but opportune loans" (*D* 155). Real intimacy, however, in the sense of a close, harmonious relationship has never been built up between husband and wife: "After three weeks she had found a wife's life irksome..." (*D* 156). Joyce criticizes her for her lack of sympathy and the malicious joy she barely succeeds in concealing. He does so by granting us insight into the thoughts which incriminate her: "She was tempted to see a curious appropriateness in his accident and, but that she did not wish to seem bloody-minded, she would have told the gentlemen that Mr Kernan's tongue would not suffer by being shortened" (*D* 157-8). Such a wife is as incapable of curing her husband's gluttony as are the Church or his "friends."

I have already tried to establish that Glotoun and Tom Kernan are gluttons who can easily be diverted from their purposes by drink. Now I would like to look at them as literary types. Since an allegorical character is by definition subservient to an idea, psychological depth and detailed information on appearances are not to be expected. The description of Glotoun offers no surprises: he is a "greet cherl" (Passus VI, l. 441), a big fellow. Another detail about the drunken protagonist is slightly more original: without a staff, he "myhte noпer steppe ne stande" (Passus VI, l. 403), he is unable to walk or stand. Expectations are higher when "realistic" characters are examined. In "Grace," there is no shortage of information on Kernan's looks. Not only do we learn (from Mrs Kernan's memories) that she got married to a "jovial well-fed man, who was dressed smartly in a frock-coat and lavender trousers and carried a silk hat gracefully balanced upon his ... arm" (*D* 156), but we get to know excerpts from his philosophy of dressing: "He had never been seen in the city without a silk hat of some decency and a pair of gaiters. By grace of these two articles of clothing, he said, a man could always pass muster" (*D* 154). If we look for depth of thought, however, Kernan does not pass muster at all. Significantly, his friends do not esteem his character but "him as a character" (*D* 154), that is, they appreciate the role he plays in their circle. The principles he deems worth defending are all designed to protect either his looks or his reputation, not his religious or other beliefs. Thus, when protesting against the candles at the end of the second part of "Grace," he is skeptical about the least disputable part of the retreat as far as theology is concerned; he swallows "the retreat business and confession" (*D* 171) but won't have that "magic-lantern business" (*D* 171), presumably because he would look ridiculous with a candle in his hand. His rejection of a source of light is a symbolic act, though: he stubbornly opposes anything that might "illuminate" him; he is perfectly impervious to spirituality.[16] Because of his concern for outward grace it seems that he has never been able to experience, or merely estimate moments of internal grace when epiphanies, religious revelations manifest themselves to a sensitive mind.

The associations evoked by Kernan's family name support this view of the protagonist. A "kernel" is the seed of a fruit, or the grain of a cereal, in short, the essential part of anything that grows. Hence, Kernan might be seen as the essential Dubliner growing on the "untilled field" of Ireland, as Joyce once called his home country alluding to the title of a book of Irish short stories by George Moore.[17] This kernel or center of the story is quite hollow inside if his lack of character, his inability to be

[16] Incidentally, "Illumination" was the term for baptism with the early Christians. See Ghiselin, p. 321.

[17] See Ellmann, p. 217.

filled with anything but alcoholic spirits, and his concern for appearances are considered.[18] On the Day of Judgment, the lightness of his soul may prove disastrous, for Christ is a harder taskmaster than Father Purdon wants him to be, at least this is what John the Baptist's metaphor suggests: "...he shall baptize you with the Holy Ghost and with fire: whose fan is in his hand, and he will throughly purge his floor, and will gather the wheat into his garner; but the chaff he will burn with fire unquenchable."[19] Joyce's instrument for defining and evaluating characters is not the fan; he passes judgment by the degree to which he exposes them to his irony. With regard to Kernan, his sense of irony could be no more in evidence than in equipping this spiritual lightweight of a protagonist with the heavy body of a glutton.

Both Langland and Joyce are dissatisfied with the state of spirituality in their own countries, yet Langland nevertheless displays an unshakeable belief in conservative Christianity and the theological authority of the Church.[20] In his dream vision at least, though his choice of that genre might indicate that reality was quite different, it is possible to convert a sinner. In order to impress his readers with the power of Christian belief, Langland starts by describing Glotoun in the worst possible terms. After this, it is a real achievement when his wife and his conscience succeed in persuading him to give up his former life. "Grace," on the other hand, leaves no doubt about Joyce's disillusion with his former compatriots and with the Church in particular: in Dublin, under the conditions exposed, conversion and spiritual

[18] Perhaps it is useful to remember that *Dubliners* was written in pre-Lacanian times when the self had not yet been replaced by the split subject forever barred from wholeness.

[19] Luke 3:16-7.

[20] See Prologue, ll. 59, 64, and 76-80.

rebirth are impossible. The businessmen of Dublin — who pass for solid citizens — are unable even to acknowledge their depravity. And if a look into the distorting mirror held up to them by Joyce were able to open their eyes, there wouldn't be a Church of sufficient integrity to lead them to salvation. Their souls are condemned to die. The position of "Grace" as the second-to-last story in the collection underlines this verdict, for, as Ghiselin points out: "...the entire sequence represents the whole course of moral deterioration ending in the death of the soul."[21]

Joyce must have been winking when he called *Dubliners* "a chapter of the 'moral history' of his country and a first step toward its 'spiritual liberation.'"[22] Obviously, he preferred the hazards of exile to waiting for the spiritual liberation of Ireland, or to submitting to the false security Tom Kernan starts enjoying in church when all the "familiar faces" eventually make him feel "more at home" there (*D* 173).

Zurich

---

[21]   Ghiselin, p. 322.

[22]   Letter to Grant Richards, 20 May 1906, (*LI* 62-63).

CRUXES AND GRACE NOTES:
A HERMENEUTIC APPROACH TO "GRACE"

ULRICH SCHNEIDER

> For the artist the rhythms of phrase
> and period, the symbols of word
> and allusion were paramount things
> (*Ur-Portrait*)

If the course of getting *Dubliners* published had run more smoothly, "Grace" would have been the final story and a priest would have had the very last word, and this would have been appropriate in Joyce's Dublin. In his sermon to a congregation, the Jesuit Father Purdon, ready to "wash the pot" (*D* 163), starts *in medias res* with a passage from Luke:

> For the children of this world are wiser in their generation than the children of light. Wherefore make unto yourselves friends out of the mammon of iniquity so that when you die they may receive you into everlasting dwellings (*D* 173).

Father Purdon is aware that he is dealing with "one of the most difficult texts in all the Scriptures ... to interpret properly" (*D*173). Nevertheless, as a professional biblical exegete he does not seem to have the slightest difficulty in understanding the passage. In fact, he makes short work of it and presents it to his congregation as a "text for business men and professional men" (*D* 174). In a trice he manages to present the "very worshippers of money" (*D* 174) as models of behavior to his congregation. Father Purdon seems to be a particularly fine specimen in the "distinguished and world-honoured company of Christian Mammonists" which appeared to Coleridge "as a drove of camels heavily laden, yet all at full speed and each in the confident expectation of passing through the *eye of the needle*, without stop or halt, both beast and baggage."[1] Listening to Father Purdon's sermon and its bravado we can still feel some of Joyce's annoyance after hearing a sermon on grace in which "the preacher had not even tried to know what he was talking about, but assumed that anything was good enough for his listeners."[2]

The narration follows Father Purdon's exegetic legerdemain without any authorial comment and renders the sermon in indirect speech, culminating in a passage of direct quotation. The narration tells us nothing about the congregation's reaction to the sermon, so that, as readers, we are left alone with Father Purdon's words. As in his other stories, Joyce uses the satirical strategy of letting the characters expose themselves, and challenges the reader to form his or her own judgment.

1 "To interpret properly"

By including a difficult biblical passage at the very end of his cycle of short stories, Joyce highlights the hermeneutic question of "[how] to interpret properly" (*D* 173), a question which has often enough been answered by his own critics "with resonant assurance" (*D* 173). In the history of interpretation there has been disagreement about whether we should read *Dubliners* as a series of realistic stories or as allegories, possibly with a Dantean fourfold meaning, whether we should read them in the light of Joyce's later works, and, last but not least, about how much importance we should attach to his allusions. The tide of

---

[1]   Quoted in *Religious Controversies of the Nineteenth Century*, ed. A. O. J. Cockshut (London: Methuen, 1966), p. 43.

[2]   Stanislaus Joyce, *My Brother's Keeper*, ed. Richard Ellmann (London: Faber, 1958), p. 225.

symbolical and allegorical interpretations in the 1960's, which swept up every allusion or quotation, provoked some vehement reactions. Thomas E. Connolly invoked the principle of Occam's razor in his plea for a "straightforward reading" of "The Sisters,"[3] and in similar terms Robert P. Roberts attacked Harry Stone's interpretation of "Araby," in particular the basic assumption that in *Dubliners* Joyce already employed the allusive method of his later works.[4] But what looks extravagant to one critic seems plain to another and the plea for straightforwardness has often led to belaboring the obvious and tedious paraphrasing.

The question of allusion remains crucial. Bernard Benstock complained that "...Joyce's allusive method, however, has often eluded the allusionists"[5] and, in a similar vein, Fritz Senn warned us that whenever we say "this is an allusion, a reference to..." we are transforming a dynamic process into some reified meaning.[6] The same caution is even more appropriate when we try to turn allusions spread out over a text, which absorb different meanings in their different contexts, into a straightforward "parallel." (Lenehan's pun about transforming something as dainty and fragrant as a rose of Castile into solid rows of cast steel comes to mind.)

Most interpretations of "Grace" take their cue from Stanislaus's comment that the story was "so far as I am aware,

[3]   Thomas E. Connolly, "Joyce's 'The Sisters': A Pennyworth of Snuff," *College English*, 27 (1965), 189-90.

[4]   Robert P. Roberts, "'Araby' and the Palimpsest of Criticism," *Antioch Review*, 26 (1966/67), 469-89.

[5]   Bernard Benstock, "Text, Sub-Text, Non-Text: Literary and Narrational In/Validities," *JJQ*, 22 (1985), 355.

[6]   "Protean Inglossabilities," p. 3. I want to thank Fritz Senn for letting me read the typescript of his essay.

the first instance of the use of a pattern in my brother's work. It is a simple pattern not new and not requiring any great hermeneutical acumen to discover — Inferno, Purgatorio, Paradiso."[7] According to Marvin Magalaner "Grace" is Joyce's first experiment "with gentle juxtaposition of a public and universal mythical structure, on the one hand, and, on the other, a sordid contemporary narrative." The moral intention behind this juxtaposition is to expose "the deterioration in the quality of response to religion."[8] Carl Niemeyer carries this approach a step further when he finds Joyce's characters guilty of the sins of fraudulence and flattery and when he takes Joyce's parody for a method to show that "the world is deteriorating from the greatness of its past."[9] Stanislaus's comment seems to have led critics to see Joyce in the role of a stern Dante who indicts modern life in strong moralistic terms.[10] This is a far cry from Joyce's attitude in his early essay on "Drama and Life":

> Even the most commonplace, the deadest among the living, may play a part in a great drama. It is a sinful foolishness to sigh back for the good old times, to feed the hunger of us with the cold stones they afford. Life we must accept as we see it before our eyes, men and women as we meet them in the real world, not as we apprehend them in the world of fairy. The great human comedy in which each has share, gives limitless scope to the true artist, today as

[7]   Stanislaus Joyce, *My Brother's Keeper*, p. 225.

[8]   Marvin Magalaner, *Time of Apprenticeship: The Fiction of Young James Joyce* (London: Abelard-Schumann, 1959), pp. 129 and 138.

[9]   Carl Niemeyer "'Grace' and Joyce's Method of Parody," *College English*, 27 (1965), 196.

[10]   For the relation of Joyce's story to medieval allegory see Yvonne Studer's' essay in this collection.

yesterday and as in years gone. (*CW* 45)

2 The parable of the unjust steward

The pursuit of the Dante connection might well be the reason why critics have tended to neglect the basis of Father Purdon's sermon, the parable of the unjust steward. Magalaner associates the young man in the cycling suit who comes to Kernan's rescue with the Good Samaritan and finds the first part of "Grace" "almost a parable."[11] Strangely enough he makes no mention of the parable actually quoted in the text. Robert S. Jackson's "parabolic reading" connects the biblical parable with Paul's doctrine of grace and identifies Tom Kernan with the unjust steward: "Kernan appears of course as the unjust steward, who has wasted the worldly substances he has been attempting to manager [sic]. He is simply a bad business man. Furthermore he drinks too much."[12] Neither the parable nor Joyce's story lend themselves to such a narrow moralistic judgement, however. We do not know how much worldly substance there was to be wasted in the first place, and in spite of Tom Kernan's drinking bouts, his wife has to admit "that he would walk to the end of Thomas Street and back again to book even a small order" (*D* 156). Joyce does not overlook the possibility that sharp "modern business methods" (*D* 154) might be just as responsible for Kernan's social decline as his moral shortcomings. Donald T. Torchiana finds Jackson's identification of Tom Kernan with the unjust steward unconvincing, but agrees that Father Purdon distorts the parable completely by "making out of it the point exactly the reverse of

[11]   Magalaner, *Time of Apprenticeship*, p. 132.

[12]   Robert S. Jackson, "A Parabolic Reading or James Joyce's 'Grace,'" *Modern Language Notes*, 76 (1961), 722.

its plain literal sense."[13] If only we knew what "the plain literal sense" of the biblical parable was! It is no accident that the parable Joyce chose has long had the notorious reputation of a *crux*. In his epoch-making study of the parables in the New Testament, Adolf Jülicher declared the "bankruptcy" of traditional interpretation when faced with this parable and, without having heard of a Father Purdon, spoke of the "acrobatics of a god-forsaken exegesis."[14] A recent monograph on the parable of the unjust steward finds it impossible even to systematize the hundreds of different and contradictory interpretations.[15]

One of the difficulties is that the parable has always given moral offense and has indeed been thought to be "at variance with the lofty morality elsewhere preached by Jesus Christ" (*D* 173). Jülicher quotes Renan's caustic comment, "dans ce royaume nouveau il vaudra mieux s'être fait des amis parmi les pauvres même par l'injustice que d'avoir été un économe correct."[16] It is not without irony, that in 1900 a Westphalian merchant was so incensed by the new exegetical attempt of a theologian from Strasbourg that he wrote the following letter to the editor of a Protestant Sunday paper:

> Although a merchant I occupy myself very seriously and frequently with the Bible. I am familiar with the various attempts to make Luke 16:1-8 palatable and cannot see how

---

[13]   Donald T. Torchiana, *Backgrounds for Joyce's "Dubliners"* (Boston: Allen and Unwin, 1986), p. 219.

[14]   Adolf Jülicher, *Die Gleichnisreden Jesu*, I/II (Darmstadt: Wissenschaftliche Buchgesellschaft, 1963), pp. 495 and 502.

[15]   Michael Krämer, *Das Rätsel der Parabel vom ungerechten Verwalter* (Zürich: Pas, 1972), p. 237.

[16]   Jülicher, *Die Gleichnisreden*, p. 495.

Herr Smend's explanations should improve the matter. I am firmly convinced that Jesus should never have spoken as in the parable handed down to us. Its moral keynote is and remains highly dubious."[17]

That the unjust steward should be praised for his behavior was clearly incompatible with the code of honor of the Protestant merchant. There are other questions. If there is a "mammon of unrighteousness," as the Greek "mamonas tes adikias" is translated in the Authorized Version, is there a "mammon of righteousness"? And if one sees the parable as an exhortation to be charitable, the question remains, as John D. Crossan put it: "If it is the master's money, should one give alms from another's property? And if it is not the master's money but the steward's exorbitant profits which are being reduced, is it alms to reduce large amounts of usury to smaller ones?"[18]

Exegetical difficulties arise, in particular, at the end of the parable. The verses 8b-13 seem so contradictory in themselves that C. H. Dodd could remark with the approval of most modern interpreters: "We can almost see here notes for three separate sermons on the parable as text."[19] We know from Mark about the difficulties which Jesus's first listeners had with his parables, and we can assume that by the time the parables were written down various sayings had already been added. Most probably Luke also had his difficulties with the parable and, looking for a strong unambiguous ending, added the saying he

[17]   See Krämer, p. 33; my translation.

[18]   John D. Crossan, *The Parables. The Challenge of the Historical Jesus*, repr. (San Francisco: Harper and Row, 1985), p. 109.

[19]   C. H. Dodd, *The Parables of the Kingdom*, (London: Nisbet, 1953), p. 30.

found in Matthew about the impossibility of serving two masters. However that may be, Joyce found these words convenient for criticizing the "church diplomatic" and its disastrous influence on Irish history. He writes in "Ireland, Island of Saints and Sages" (1907): "Ireland ... has fulfilled what has hitherto been considered an impossible task — serving both God and Mammon, letting herself be milked by England and yet increasing Peter's Pence" (*CW* 190). He certainly expected the reader to recognize the incompatibility of this statement with the passage quoted by Father Purdon.

The priest's neglect of Luke's concluding comment upon the parable appears less objectionable, however, if we assume that he did not take his text from the Bible, but from the Missal, where only Luke 16: 1-9 is given as the gospel for the Eighth Sunday after Pentecost.[20] If we accept this assumption it is less astonishing that he ignores Luke's conclusion than that he ignores the actual parable. The quoted passage from which he sets out is already an interpretation of the parable; his final comments are thus an interpretation of an interpretation to which Joyce critics add still more interpretations. It begins to look like an infinite regression, in which the original meaning of the parable can never be grasped. Instead of giving us a key for the "correct" interpretation of Joyce's story, the biblical parable presents more riddles, and multiplies the hermeneutical difficulties and the challenge to the interpreter. Perhaps its point lies not in any "plain literary sense" after all, but in its function to tell us something about the enigmatic qualities of a story which looks simple enough at first sight.

One way to deal with such difficulties has been allegorical interpretation. While such interpretation of Joyce had its heyday in the sixties, in biblical hermeneutics it went out of fashion a

---

[20]   *The Missal in Latin and English* (London: Burns and Oates, 1949), pp. 571-72.

century ago. In the first volume of *Die Gleichnisreden Jesu* (1888), A. Jülicher made a clean sweep of the prevailing allegorical interpretations of parables. He emphasized that each parable had a single point to make and had no use for obscurity. Later on, in search of the ur-parables, Joachim Jeremias formulated ten "laws of transformation" which, he thought, explained the shift from the original eschatological meaning of Jesus' parables to the hortatory interpretation which suited the changing conditions in the early Church. Originally, the parable of the unjust steward was addressed to the hesitant, unconverted crowd as "a summons to resolute action in a crisis," whereas the primitive Church applied it "to the Christian community ... and drew from it a direction for the right use of wealth, and a warning against unfaithfulness." In order to bridge the gap between the original and the newly acquired meaning of the parables, allegorical interpretation had been employed to an increasing degree. If we want to find out what Jesus actually meant, Jeremias argues, we first have to clear away the allegorical additions of a later period. The reaction against allegorical interpretation in parable research has been so strong that in 1979 it was still provocative to write that "the time to recall allegory from the exile imposed upon it by such scholars as Jülicher, Jeremias, and Crossan has come."[21]

In recent times the founding fathers of modern biblical parable research have, in their turn, come in for criticism. Contemporary scholars would dispute the view, for instance, that the one and only function of a parable is to drive home a certain point. Such a view lends itself too easily to a didactic streamlining and a disregard of the poetic qualities of the parables. Instead, these scholars emphasize the narrative complexity and sophistication of the parables and give more

---

[21]   Mary Ann Tolbert, *Perspectives on the Parables: An Approach to Multiple Inter-pretation* (Philadelphia: Fortress, 1979), p. 28.

attention to their stylistic and dramaturgic qualities, their rhetoric of exaggeration and irony, their skill in creating suspense and disappointing expectations, and their configurations of characters. Thus, in the parable of the unjust steward we have a typical triangular constellation of rich man, steward, and debtors which gathers dramatic momentum because the main character plays the double role of creditor and debtor.[22]

John D. Crossan rightly calls our parable "a carefully formed mini-drama ... constructed in three scenes each of which is an internal diptych."[23] Dan O. Via reads it as the story of a successful rogue who dupes conventional society without having any positive moral principles to offer; the steward's conduct is part of an aesthetic constellation which is a miniature in the picaresque mode.[24] Seen in this way, the parable offers an example of how to survive in an amoral world: a kind of negative morality, rather than a moral dogma. It may, in fact, betray a highly developed sense of irony, a quality Jackson wanted to rule out in his consideration of the parable.[25]

In *The Genesis of Secrecy: On the Interpretation of Narrative*, Frank Kermode points out that in the Greek of the Bible the word "parable" has the meaning of "dark speech" or "riddle,"[26] and surely the parable of the unjust steward offers sufficient

---

[22]   See Wolfgang Harnisch, *Die Gleichniserzählungen Jesu,* (Göttingen: Vandenhoeck, 1985), pp. 15-41.

[23]   Crossan, *The Parables*, p. 109.

[24]   Dan Otto Via, *The Parables* (Philadelphia: Fortress Press, 1967), pp. 159-62.

[25]   Robert S. Jackson, "A Parabolic Reading," p. 721.

[26]   Frank Kermode, *The Genesis of Secrecy: On the Interpretation of Narrative,* (Cambridge, Mass.: Harvard University Press, 1979), p. 23.

evidence that biblical parables can be as enigmatic as any of Kafka's. Like Kafka, Joyce must have been much aware of the affinities between parables and enigmas. In *Ulysses*, Joyce has Stephen pondering another dark Biblical saying: "To Caesar what is Caesar's, to God what is God's. A long look from dark eyes, a riddling sentence to be woven and woven on the church's looms" (*U* 2:86-87). Jesus's evasive answer is given when the Pharisees seek to "entangle him in his talk" (Matthew 22:15-21). It is obviously related to Jesus's saying about God and mammon, but instead of an "either/or" it offers an "as well as." Not surprisingly, it has taken a considerable amount of hermeneutic weaving on the Church's looms to reconcile such incongruent statements. Jesus's enigmatic saying leads Stephen on to an Irish riddle, which remains insoluble for his students and has been "solved" by Joyce scholars only with considerable effort. Later in the morning, Stephen bewilders his listeners with a story which he calls "A Pisgah Sight of Palestine or the Parable of the Plums" — which continues to tease Joyce's readers up to the present day. A new dimension of obscurity is reached when we come to the parables of "The Mookse and the Gripes" and "The Oondt and the Gracehoper" in *Finnegans Wake*. The latter brings us by a commodius vicus of recirculation back to "Grace."

If the parable of the unjust steward does not offer a pat solution to the difficulties in Joyce's story, it can nevertheless, like an Elizabethan play within the play, elucidate the text in which it is embedded, and vice versa. Reconsidering the story in the light of the parable, it strikes us that not only Tom Kernan, but most, if not all, of the other characters can be seen as embodiments of the same type. Tom Kernan spends money on drink which should support his family, and he and his wife neglect the education of their children. Mrs Cunningham has pawned the furniture on her husband six times, but if her alcoholism drives him out of the house, it might well be the consequence of his neglect of her. Mr Power is cast in the double role of creditor and debtor which is typical of the biblical steward. He has "inexplicable debts" (*D* 154) and "giv[es] many small, but opportune loans" (*D* 155) to the Kernans. M'Coy has been "driven to live by his wits" (*D* 158) and has fallen into disgrace among his friends because of his shabby trick of borrowing valises and portmanteaus and taking them, as we may assume, to the pawnshop. There is Mr Harford, Tom Kernan's drinking companion, who has made his money by "lending small sums of money to workmen at usurious interest" (*D* 159); there is Mr Fogarty who has "failed in business in a licensed house" (*D* 166) and now, as a small shopkeeper, "flatter[s] himself, his manners would ingratiate him with the housewives of the district" (*D* 166). Undoubtedly, with the same purpose he brings the Kernans a gift of "a half-pint of special whisky," although "there was a small account for groceries unsettled" (*D* 166). Among the "gentlemen" gathered in the church are "old Michael Grimes, the owner of three pawnbroker's shops" (*D* 172) and "poor O'Carroll ... at one time a considerable commercial figure" (*D* 172-173). Mr Hendrick is present as well. He is the chief reporter from *The Freeman's Journal,* who, as we found out in "A Mother," decided to report on the speech of an American priest rather than on the Irish concert. His choice seems to uphold the unholy alliance of the press and the Church at the same time it belies the emancipatory promise of the newspaper's title. And last but not least in this series, comes Father Purdon, who wants to ingratiate himself among his congregation, by meeting their expectations of "just a kind of friendly talk" (*D* 165) more than half-way.

The parable might also tell us something about Joyce's attitude towards his characters. Often enough critics have seen it as "ruthless irony ... that diminishes and ridicules its object."[27] But, in fact, Joyce was much concerned whether he was perhaps "plainly mischievous" or "unnecessarily harsh" (*L II,* 99, 166), and these self-doubts certainly contributed to his wariness in condemning his characters in moral terms. The parable can be read as an illustration of Jesus' saying: "Judge not that ye be not judged" (Matt. 7:1), and if the unjust steward found grace in spite of his misdeeds, it would have been rather pharisaical of Joyce to judge his characters too harshly. If Joyce finally decided to end his short story cycle with the image of snow falling "upon the living and the dead," he does not only point towards the "interrelationship of dead and living," (*JJ II* 252), but he also suggests adjourning a final moral judgement until Doomsday.

3 The Semantics of "Grace"

Although Jesus does not use the word, the idea of grace is very central to his parables, in which, as Thomas F. Torrance puts it, "both debit and credit accounts with God are quite ruled out, for grace means the complete under-cutting of the human status based on ordinary ethical rights."[28] The idea is contrary to the religious practice in which Stephen temporarily seeks refuge in *A Portrait*: "...he seemed to feel his soul in devotion pressing like fingers the keyboard of a great cash register and to see the amount of his purchase start forth immediately in heaven" (*D* 148). In spite of his devotional zeal, he cannot help beginning to wonder whether the grace which he had refused to lose was not being filched from him little by little. The clear certitude of his own immunity grew dim and to it succeeded a

---

[27]   See Homer O. Brown in his otherwise excellent *James Joyce's Early Fiction* (Hamden, Conn.: Archon, 1975), p. 32.

[28]   Thomas F. Torrance, *The Doctrine of Grace in the Apostolic Fathers* (Edinburgh: Oliver and Boyd, 1948), p. 24.

vague fear that his soul had really fallen unawares. It was with difficulty that he won back his old consciousness of his state of grace by telling himself that he had prayed to God at every temptation and that the grace which he had prayed for must have been given to him in as much as God was obliged to give it (*D* 153).

If the notion of a free, undeserved gift is essential to the idea of grace, it is highly ironical, as Fritz Senn points out, that the priest's name is Purdon, which, read in French, has exactly this meaning.[29] No doubt, like the unjust steward, the priest expects to get something back by remitting the spiritual debts of his congregation.

In the *Dubliners* story the word "grace" is given a religious meaning only in the final scene in the church. Before that, it is associated with external things such as manners and clothes. In English, the word "grace" has accumulated so many different meanings that it would have certainly deserved to be included among William Empson's "complex words."[30] It is "a name [which] is comprehended in a Monosyllable, but in its nature not circumscribed with a world," as Sir Thomas Browne says of "pride."[31] In Christianity alone, it has become a cipher for such an intricate complex of ideas, that it would be possible to unravel the great theological controversies from the Church Fathers to the Reformation just by pursuing its history. But the word existed before it entered the New Testament, and was in Greek originally applied to whatever awakens pleasure and joy.

[29]   Fritz Senn, "A Rhetorical Account of James Joyce's 'Grace'," *Moderna Sprak*, 74 (1980), 123-24.

[30]   Wolfgang Wicht, "'Grace': Purdon and Vaughan," *Anglistentag 1993 Eichstätt*, Vol XV,(Tübingen: 1994), 402-414, deals thoroughly with the intricacies of "grace."

[31]   Sir Thomas Browne *Religio Medici*, in *The Major Works*, ed. C.A. Patrides (Harmondsworth: Penguin, 1977), p. 146.

It was regarded as a life-enkindling pneumatic potency, a notion that points to the connection between *charis* and *charisma* or the gifts of the Holy Spirit in the New Testament.[32] From antiquity to Neo-Classicism it was also used in relation to artistic inspiration, connoting, in M. H. Abrams's words, "a quality, difficult to describe, which is a free gift of nature or heaven, hence to be achieved negligently, if at all, and never by effort or rule."[33] Mr Fogarty's sententious "*Great minds are very near to madness*" (*D* 168) is trivial enough in itself, but could, without too much effort, be traced back to Dryden's famous dictum, "Great wits are sure to madness near allied" and even further to the passage on inspiration in Aristotle's *Poetics*: "Poetry demands a man with a special gift for it, or else one with a touch of madness in him."[34]

4 "Seeing quincunxially"

The peculiar seating arrangement of Tom Kernan and his friends — "in the form of a quincunx" (*D* 172) — is plausibly explained on the narrative level; since the scene takes place in a church, however, we might associate this chiastic formation with the initials of Christ and his crucifixion. And since the Greek word for grace, *charis*, also begins with a *chi* it may also remind us that, according to the New Testament, God's grace manifested itself through the crucifixion (See for instance Hebrews 2:9: "...that he by the grace of God should taste death for every man.")

If we want to find out more about quincunxes, the first author

---

[32] See Torrance, pp. 1-6.

[33] M. H. Abrams, *The Mirror and the Lamp* (New York: Norton, 1958), p. 193.

[34] *Poetics* 17, 1455; quoted in Abrams, p. 188.

we will probably consult is Sir Thomas Browne, who, according
to Coleridge, saw "Quincunxes in Heaven above, Quincunxes
in Earth below, & Quincunxes in the water beneath the Earth;
Quincunxes in Deity, Quincunxes in the mind of man;
Quincunxes in bones, in optic nerves, in Roots of Trees, in
leaves, in petals, in everything."[35] Like Stephen (and Jakob
Boehme) in "Proteus," Sir Thomas was an eager reader of the
"signatures of all things" (*U* 3:2) and he found Christ's initials
written all over the "orderly book of nature" (Browne 360). For
him gospel truth was never plain and the Bible, just as the
creation, "full of Meanders and Labyrinths" (Browne 81).[36] He
acknowledges that "though many ordinary Heads run smoothly
over the Scripture, yet I must acknowledge, it is one of the
hardest Books I have met with."[37] He must have been familiar
with the Father Purdon type of biblical interpreter since he
complains that the "unspeakable mysteries in the Scriptures are
often delivered in the vulgar and illustrative way"
(Browne 117).

If the "greatest mystery of Religion is expressed by
adumbration" (Browne 376), it cannot be the task of biblical
exegesis to explain that mystery out of existence. Sir Thomas's
animadversion against "all deductions from Metaphors,

[35] *Coleridge on the Seventeenth Century,* ed. Roberta F. Brinkley
(Durham, N.C.: Duke University Press, 1955), p. 449.

[36] Cf. John R. Knott, Jr., "Sir Thomas Browne and the Labyrinth of
Truth," in *Approaches to Sir Thomas Browne: The Ann Arbor Tercentary
Lectures and Essays,* ed. C. A. Patrides (Columbia, Mo.: University of
Missouri Press, 1982), pp. 19-30.

[37] "Observations upon Several Plants Mention'd in Scripture"; quoted
in Knott, p. 21.

Parables, Allegories, into real and rigid interpretation"[38] strikingly agrees with the (post)structuralist hermeneutic position found in Paul Ricoeur's seminal essays on biblical interpretation. Setting out from the basic question of why "we are deaf to the Word today," Ricoeur reaches a diagnosis which Lewis S. Mudge sums up as follows:

> The root of the problem, for Ricoeur, lies in a general loss of sensitivity to symbolic language in modern Western civilization. We construe the world in terms of the Cartesian dichotomy between the self as sovereign consciousness on the one hand, and an objectivized, manipulable nature on the other. We conceive ourselves as authors of our own meaning and being, set in the midst of a world there for us to interrogate, manipulate, and control. We make language our instrument in this project in a way that sees artful equivocation, richness of meaning, or metaphysical range as a liability to be overcome rather than a gift to be treasured. We dismiss realms of meaning beyond the literal either as confusion to be cleared up by theologian or as emotional embellishment to be kept in check. It is hard for us to see scriptural language, full as it is of figure, metaphor, vision, and myth, as having to do with reality.[39]

Joyce would probably have agreed with Sir Thomas's statement that "all things are seen quincunxially." As Hans Walter Gabler and Hugh Kenner have pointed out, Stephen in *A Portrait* lives through "a period of conspicuous indulgence in

[38]   Lewis S. Mudge, ed., *Essays on Biblical Interpretation*, (London: SPCK, 1981), p. 4.

[39]   Lewis S. Mudge, ed., *Essays on Biblical Interpretation*, (London: SPCK, 1981), p. 4.

chiasmus,"[40] and once we are put on this track, we can find plenty of chiastic structures in Joyce's works, as Riquelme has further shown.[41]

In "Grace," the person who is held in contempt by his friends, M'Coy, is moved to the center of the quincunx, as if to exemplify another famous biblical metaphor handed down by Luke in the form of a riddle: "What is this then that is written, The Stone which the builders rejected, the same is become the head of the corner?" (Luke 20:17). M'Coy has rightly been seen as a precursor and, in *Ulysses* a *Doppelgänger* of Bloom.[42] In "Grace" we get an idea of his Ulyssean potential when we come to read: "His line of life had not been the shortest distance between two points and for short periods he had been driven to live by his wits" (*D* 198). In *Ulysses* we will find Bloom, if we are ready to follow Leo Knuth's suggestive reading, "at the intersection of the X, in the central section (number X) of this episode (chapter X)," in a position which transforms Bloom into "an anthropomorphic *imago mundi* — a figure of a man, circumscribed by a circle, his arms and sometimes also his legs apart, to form either an X-shaped Saint Andrew's cross or a Y- or T-shaped Tau-cross."[43]

[40]   Hugh Kenner, *Ulysses* (London: Allen and Unwin, 1980), p. 7.

[41]   John Paul Riquelme, *Teller and Tale in Joyce's Fiction* (Baltimore: Johns Hopkins University Press), 1983.

[42]   Cf. Marvin Magalaner, "Leopold Bloom before *Ulysses*," *Modern Language Notes,* 68 (1953), 110-12.

[43]   Leo Knuth, "The Ring and the Cross in Joyce's *Ulysses*," in *Ulysses: Cinquante Ans Après,* ed. Louis Bonnerot (Paris: Didier, 1974), p. 185.

5 Peter's Scandal

If rejected stones can become cornerstones of a building the same process can also happen in reverse. In the conversation at Tom Kernan's bedside, Mr Cunningham confirms the general resolution for a retreat by the words: "We'll all renounce the devil ... together, not forgetting his works and pomps." A comic touch is added by Mr Fogarty who quotes "laughingly": "Get behind me, Satan!" (D 171) As so frequently happens with proverbial sayings, the speaker would be astonished if reminded of the original situation in which these words were spoken. In Matthew they are addressed to Peter who wants to prevent Jesus's passion by stopping him on the way to Jerusalem. Jesus' words, "Get thee behind me, Satan: thou art an offense to me: for thou savorest not the things that be of God but those that be of men" (Matt. 16:23) follow almost immediately after Peter had been chosen as the rock on which the church should be built. Exaltation is followed immediately by abasement; Peter, the solid rock, has turned into a rock of offense or, in Greek, into a *skandalon*. The whole conversation on the popes and the dogma of infallibility is thus subtly juxtaposed with this confrontation between Jesus and Peter, and another ironic touch is added to the words "crux upon crux," which according to Mr Cunningham, one of Peter's successors has chosen as a motto (D 167). Jesus's reprimand that Peter represents "not the things that be of God" foreshadows the compromise of the church diplomatic with the worldly powers, which Joyce found so offensive, and Peter's very name is a bad omen predicting the petrifaction of living faith in an institutionalized church.

6 The Charisma of the Word

Jesus reminds his listeners repeatedly that his parables require attentive listening: "He that hath ears let him hear" (Mark 4:9; 7:16). Hence, it is not without irony when, four times, Father

Purdon's congregation is called "his listeners," since the repetition drives home the point that, in fact, they have switched off inwardly and present, at the most, an "attentive face" (*D* 173).

In the sickbed scene, we are told that Tom Kernan "thought he owed it to his dignity to show a stiff neck" before he surrenders to his friends (*D* 163). Though common in the Old Testament this metaphor occurs only once in the New Testament, in a passage which must have been very significant for Joyce. When Stephen, the first martyr and prototype of Stephen Dedalus, is brought to the council to defend himself, he reprimands the elders: " Ye stiffnecked and uncircumcised in heart and ears, ye do always resist the Holy Ghost: as your fathers did, so do ye" (Acts 7:51). But while Father Purdon's listeners are quite as obstinate, he himself is just the opposite of Stephen, "a man full of faith and of the Holy Ghost" (Acts 6:5). The living spirit of the Word has turned into a dead letter and interpreting and preaching the gospel has become a routine performance. Nothing is lost if the congregation won't listen.

In the conversation about the mottoes of the popes Mr Fogarty contradicts Mr Cunningham and maintains that Leo XIII had not chosen "lux upon lux," but "lux in tenebris," to which M'Coy adds knowingly, "O yes ... *Tenebrae*" (*D* 167). This dialogue sounds like an unintended parody of the beginning of John's gospel: "Et lux in tenebris lucet, et tenebrae eam non comprehenderunt" (1:5). If we follow the English version for a few lines, we focus on the word around which the story revolves:

> And the Word was made flesh, and dwelt among us ... full of grace and truth ... John bare witness of him, and cried, saying, this was he of whom I spoke, He that cometh after me is preferred before me; for he was before me. And of his fullness have we all received, and grace for grace. For the law was given by Moses, but grace and truth came by

Jesus Christ (1:14-16).

With its emphasis on the "Word full of truth and grace," John's gospel seems to have been a kind of spiritual bequest for Joyce. We hardly need to know of Joyce's remark to Frank Budgen after listening to Bach's Matthew Passion, "I simply cannot understand how any man can mix the synoptic gospels with the gospel according to St John,"[44] to guess which gospel he preferred.

If we continue to read in John we come across a passage which has no counterpart in the synoptic gospels and which contrasts John the Baptist, who baptizes with water, and Jesus, who baptizes with the Holy Spirit. In the Acts which follow John's gospel we read about the apostles' spiritual transformation through the Pentecostal effusion of the Holy Spirit which gives them the zeal to become missionaries and baptize those who are willing to hear the Word.

In "Grace" we suspect that the resolution, "to stand up with lighted candles in our hands and renew our baptismal vows" (D 171), will not bring about any spiritual change, and before we come to the end of the story, we probably agree with Mrs Kernan's skepticism that "a man of her husband's age would not change greatly before death" (D 157). The candles to which Kernan objects as "magic lantern business" (D 171) are, in fact, associated with death from the very beginning in Dubliners: expecting the death of the priest, the young boy looks out for "the reflection of candles on the darkened blinds for I knew that two candles must be set at the head of a corpse" (D 9).

---

[44] Frank Budgen, *James Joyce and the Making of Ulysses* (Bloomington: Indiana University Press, 1961), p. 102. Incidentally, chiastic structures are so prominent in John that Peter F. Ellis calls them "the habitual and almost subconscious rhythmic movement of the Johannine thought-process," *The Genius of John*, (Collegeville, Minn.: Liturgical Press, 1985), p. 27.

The only invigorating spirit in "Grace" is Mr Fogarty's "half-pint of special whisky" (*D* 166), which is poured out in "five small measures" (*D* 167) and is not even enough to go around twice. The biblical record of Pentecost does not forget to mention the skepticism of the bystanders who mock, "These men are full of new wine" (Acts 2:13), but of course nobody could get drunk on half a pint of whisky divided five ways. Nevertheless the "gift," as it is called three times, is appreciated, especially since there is still "a small account of groceries unsettled" (*D* 166). This is probably the closest approximation to the effusion of a charismatic gift, but in spite of it there is no spiritual renewal in sight at the end of the story. Marvin Magalaner points out the "parallel" between the crowded pub and the crowded church,[45] but if both institutions in the story work hand in hand to meet the spiritual demands of their customers, they only contribute to the paralysis of Dublin life.

7 Institutionalization and Charisma

When Joyce began his stories and his autobiographical novel in 1904, Dublin appeared to him as the "centre of paralysis" and the Irish as the "most belated race in Europe." What he experienced in Dublin, however, was in many ways just a special variety of a general social and cultural situation around the turn of the century.

In *The Rise of the Modern German Novel: Crisis and Charisma*,[46] Russell A. Berman convincingly applies the category of charisma to the concept of the modern novel. This category became crucial for Max Weber, who, after a deep

[45]   Magalaner, *Time of Apprenticeship*, p. 136.

[46]   Russell A. Berman, *The Rise of the Modern German Novel: Crisis and Charisma* (Cambridge, Mass.: Harvard University Press, 1986).

personal crisis in 1898, came to see the fully rationalized and demystified world of modern capitalism as an "iron cage," which left no room for individual development and could only be shattered by a thorough charismatic renewal. As Berman explains, Weber appropriated the term from the debate among Protestant theologians about the origins of Catholicism which followed the declaration of papal infallibility. Rudolf Sohm, one of the spokesmen in this controversy, described the early Christian community as a "pneumatic anarchy" (p. 51), whose liberal spirit was throttled by the increasing institutionalization of the Church. Such a criticism of the rigid hierarchy and authoritarianism of Catholicism went together with a deep anxiety at the stifling bureaucratization of life around the turn of the century and, according to Berman, led to a "charismatic crusade" (p. 52) in the literature of the time.

In his exile, Joyce found out that life in Austrian Trieste or in Italian Rome was no less subject to paralysis than life in Dublin. In Rome, in particular, where he worked in a bank for nine and a half hours a day, and put up with the dreary conversations of his fellow clerks as well as with the monotonous work of writing up to two hundred and fifty letters per day, he began to see Dublin in a mellower light, and the Irish appeared to him as " the most civilized people in Europe ... the least burocratic [sic]" (L II 202). As we know, Joyce developed a strong interest in socialist and anarchist ideas and, according to Dominic Manganiello, shared the conviction "that the state produced an authoritarian and bureaucratic society which stifled individual initiative and spontaneity."[47]

Such a diagnosis helps us to understand why Joyce originally called his stories "a series of epicleti" (L II 55). Joyce adopted this word from the Greek *epiklesis*, which refers to the

---

[47]   Dominic Manganiello, *Joyce's Politics* (London: Routledge, 1980), p. 70-71.

invocation of the Holy Spirit in the eucharistic liturgy of the Eastern Church. Like Shelley in his "Ode to the West Wind," Joyce invokes a pneumatic spirit to inspire his stories and to help him in "the first step towards the spiritual liberation of my country" (*L* I 63). But whereas Shelley invokes his "Spirit fierce" directly and in the clear tone of "the trumpet of a prophecy," Joyce as a modern writer prefers a "style of scrupulous meanness" (*L* II 34) to foreground the absence of this pneumatic spirit in the life of his Dubliners. On the whole, the story seems to give the same answer as Mr Cunningham to Mr Kernan's question, "What's in the wind?" — "O, it's nothing" (*D* 162).

This style also distinguishes Joyce's stories from the invocation of the Holy Spirit which Gustav Mahler made about the same time in his Eighth Symphony, by integrating the old Pentecostal hymn "Veni, creator spiritus." Precisely because Joyce avoids Mahler's ecstatic tone, he is not open to Theodor W. Adorno's criticism that Mahler in this symphony denied his own idea of a radical secularization of metaphysical words, by the very use of these words. Instead, Joyce's prose confirms Adorno's view that "the substance can be better preserved through negation than through demonstration."[48]

In our story the word "grace" is used in a completely secular sense and gathers metaphysical significance only in Father Purdon's sermon. But, paradoxically enough, his attempt to explain its religious meaning makes the reader aware of the process of secularization even more poignantly. In his essay on James Clarence Mangan (1902), Joyce wrote: "Beauty, the splendour of truth, is a gracious presence when the imagination contemplates intensely the truth of its own being or the visible world, and the spirit which proceeds out of truth and beauty is the holy spirit of joy" (*CW* 83). In *Dubliners*, Joyce's realism

---

[48]   My translation from *Mahler* (Frankfurt: Suhrkamp, 1960), p. 183.

rules out such a "gracious presence" and allows an approach only through negation. As a "gnomonic allusionist,"[49] he does not quote the passage from John directly, in which "the Word ... full of grace and truth" is mentioned, nor the poem by Pope Leo XIII on "the invention of the photograph," mentioned by Mr Cunningham. As Richard Brown rightly remarks, the poem "claims that the photograph captures, when it is present, just what Joyce's story captures in its absence, that is 'gratiam' — grace."[50] Nor does Joyce include the prayer which follows the parable of the unjust steward on the Eighth Sunday after Pentecost, In the *Missal*:

> Accept, we pray thee, Lord the gifts we bring thee out of thy own bounty, so that, by the powerful working of thy grace, these holy rites may sanctify our conduct in this present life and bring us finally to everlasting joy: through our Lord (p. 573).

In all the other stories pneumatic powers and charismatic gifts exist only in absence or, to use Fritz Senn's word, in the form of dislocution.[51] In "The Sisters," the handkerchief with which the priest tries to wipe off the stains of snuff is called "inefficacious," a word that points towards the absence or "efficacious grace" (*D* 12). When one of the sisters talks about "one of them newfangled carriages that make no noise ... them with the rheumatic wheels," (*D* 17) her malapropism indicates

---

[49] Bernard Benstock, "Text, Sub-Text, Non-Text," 357.

[50] Richard Brown, "A Grace Beyond the Reach of Art," *James Joyce Broadsheet*, 5 (1981), 1.

[51] See Fritz Senn, *Joyce's Dislocutions: Essays on Reading as Translation,* ed. John Paul Riquelme (Baltimore: Johns Hopkins University Press, 1984).

that in Joyce's Dublin, pneuma, like everything else, exists only in the form of paralysis or a similar disease. In "Araby" the boy takes along to the bazaar a "florin," of all possible coins the one which, as Harry Stone remarks, was known as "godless and graceless," because the inscription "Dei gratia, F.D." had been forgotten when it went into circulation.[52]

In "A Little Cloud" Little Chandler anticipates in his mind the reviews of his first poems, "Mr Chandler has the gift of easy and graceful verse" (*D* 74), but these poems remain unwritten in the story and the reader strongly doubts that they will ever be written. In "The Dead," Aunt Julia, one of the "Three Graces of the Dublin musical world," (*D* 204) tackles her song "with great spirit" and does not "miss even the smallest of grace notes" (*D* 193). Although Gabriel prefers it to Mary Jane's "academy piece ... full of runs and difficult passages" (*D* 186), the reader doubts whether it gains much in grace by following each grace note pedantically.

Joyce ends his essay "Drama and Life" with Lona's answer to Rörlund's question in Ibsen's *Pillars of Society*: "what will you do in our society, Miss Hessel?" "I will let in fresh air, Pastor" (*CW* 46). In his essay on *When We Dead Awaken*, he comments upon the tendency in Ibsen's later work "to get out of closed rooms" (*CW* 66) and quotes from the dialogue:

> Ulfheim. But don't you see that the storm is upon us? Don't you hear the blasts of wind?
> Rubek (*listening*). They sound like the prelude to the Resurrection Day (*CW* 61).

Joyce's stories show an abundance of dusty, musty and rusty objects, as well as of dark and unaired rooms. Thus "Grace"

[52] Harry Stone,"'Araby' and the Writings of James Joyce," in *Dubliners*, Viking Critical Edition, pp. 358-9.

moves from the pub to the bedroom and to the church, and if there is any fresh air, it is a "keen east wind ..., blowing from the mouth of the river" (*D* 153) on the way home from the pub. This cold wind, which heralds the snowfall at the end of "The Dead," might be some "distant music" (*D* 210) or the prelude to Resurrection Day, and might suggest the hopeful question at the end of Shelley's poem, "O, Wind, if Winter comes, can Spring be far behind?" Even readers who deny that Joyce's stories offer such a perspective of hope would probably agree that, like Ibsen in his plays, he admits fresh air into the stifling atmosphere of the *fin de siècle*.

University of Erlangen

Index

CONSTELLATION CALIBAN
Figurations of a Character
Ed. by Nadia Lie and Theo D'haen
Amsterdam/Atlanta, GA 1997. 356 pp. With ill.
(Textxet 10)

ISBN: 90-420-0244-1   Bound Hfl. 175,-/US-$ 92.-
ISBN: 90-420-0238-7   Paper Hfl. 50,-/US-$ 26.-

"We are now in the Age of Caliban rather than in the Time of Ariel or the Era of Propero," Harold Bloom claimed in 1992. Bloom was specifically referring to Caliban's rising popularity as the prototype of the colonised or repressed subject, especially since the 1980s. However, already earlier the figure of Caliban had inspired artists from the most divergent backgrounds: Robert Browning, Ernest Renan, Aimé Césaire, and Peter Greenaway, to name only some of the better known.

Much has already been published on Caliban, and there exist a number of excellent surveys of this character's appearance in literature and the other arts. The present collection does not aim to trace Caliban over the ages. Rather, Constellation Caliban intends to look at a number of specific refigurations of caliban. What is the Caliban-figure's role and function within a specific work of art? What is its relation to the other signifiers in that work of art? What interests are invested in the Caliban-figure, what values does it represent or advocate? Whose interests and values are these?

These and similar questions guided the contributors to the present volume. In other words, what one finds here is not a study of origins, not a genealogy, not a reception-study, but rather a fascinating series of case studies informed by current theoretical debate in areas such as women's studies, sociology of literature and of the intellectuals, nation-formation, new historicism, etc.

Its interdisciplinary approach and its attention to matters of multi-culturalism make Constellation Caliban into an unusually wide ranging and highly original contribution to Shakespeare-studies. The book should appeal to students of English Literature, Modern European Literature, Comparative Literature, Drama or Theatre Studies, and Cultural Studies, as well as to anyone interested in looking at literature within a broad social and historical context while still appreciating detailed textual analyses.

EDITIONS RODOPI B.V.

USA/Canada: **All Other Countries:**
2015 South Park Place   Keizersgracht 302-304
Atlanta, GA 30339   1016 EX Amsterdam
Tel. (770) 933-0027   The Netherlands
Fax (770) 933-9644   Tel. ++ 31 (0)20 622 75 07
Call toll-free (U.S.only) 1-800-225-3998   Fax ++ 31 (0)20 638 09 48
e-mail: orders-queries@rodopi.nl — http://www.rodopi.nl

SJEF HOUPPERMANS

Claude Ollier cartographe

Amsterdam/Atlanta, GA 1997. 237 pp.
(Collection Monographique Rodopi en Littérature Française
Contemporaine 29)
ISBN: 90-420-0242-5   Hfl. 70,-/US-$ 36.50

De *La Mise en scène* et *Le Maintien de l'ordre* jusqu'à
Déconnection, Outback ou l'arrière-monde et au-delà, l'oeuvre
aujourd'hui vaste et labyrinthique, de Claude Ollier est considérée
comme une des plus richement novatrices des quarante dernières
années. Fondée sur une poétique de l'éclatement de l'unité de la
personne/du personnage, sur une esthétique du non-fixe, de l'illimité,
de la "question" généralisée dans l'ubiquité de ses pertinences, sur
une appréciation du rôle déterminant mais incompris du langage dans
l'expérience de l'être, l'oeuvre d'Ollier s'élabore, consciente de ses
tensions implicites mais planant magistralement sur elles, entre échec
et jeu (d'échec/s), réel insaisissable et saisie onirique, phantasmatique,
imaginaire, entre le haut sérieux de tout ce qui est troué, futile,
déroutant et ce qui, par le biais du "champ transférentiel" de l'écrit,
permet ironiquement mais sûrement de tout replénifier. C'est ainsi,
comme l'explique Sjef Houppermans dans cette très belle étude
d'une oeuvre à la fois difficile et exemplaire, qu'un nouveau pacte
entre livre et lecteur/lectrice, et auteur peut-être aussi, parvient à
s'établir. Si le livre n'est pas le lieu idéal d'une "vraie vie", la vraie
mort, celle du désir, réussit à se différer indéfiniment dans ces beaux
<u>fuzzy sets</u> que sont les créations admirables de Claude Ollier.

Editions Rodopi B.V.
USA/Canada: 2015 South Park Place, ATLANTA, GA 30339, Tel. (70) 933
0027 / Fax (70) 933 9644. *Call toll-free* (U.S.only) 1-800-225-3998
All Other Countries: Keizersgracht 302-304, 1016 EX AMSTERDAM, The
Netherlands. Tel. + +31 (0)20 622 75 07 / Fax (0)20 638 09 48
E-mail: orders-queries@rodopi.nl —— http://www.rodopi.nl

LITERATURE AND ETHNIC DISCRIMINATION

Ed. by Michael J. Meyer

Amsterdam/Atlanta, GA 1997. XIII,240 pp.
(Rodopi Perspectives on Modern Literature 18)
ISBN: 90-420-0222-0   Bound Hfl. 125,-/US-$ 65.50
ISBN: 90-420-0221-2   Paper Hfl. 35,-/US-$ 18.-

EDITIONS RODOPI B.V.

USA/Canada:
2015 SouthPark Place
Atlanta, GA 30339
Tel. (770) 933-0027
Fax (770) 933-9644
Call toll-free (U.S.only) 1-800-225-3998

All Other Countries:
Keizersgracht 302-304
1016 EX Amsterdam
The Netherlands
Tel. ++ 31 (0)20 622 75 07
Fax ++ 31 (0)20 638 09 48

e-mail: orders-queries@rodopi.nl — http://www.rodopi.nl

PARODY
Dimensions and Perspectives

Ed. by Beate Müller

Amsterdam/Atlanta, GA 1997. IV,313 pp.
(Rodopi Perspectives on Modern Literature 19)
ISBN: 90-420-0181-X   Bound Hfl. 150,-/US-$ 78.50
ISBN: 90-420-0217-4   Paper Hfl. 45,-/US-$ 23.50

Parody is a most iridescent phenomenon: of ancient Greek origin, parody's very malleability has allowed it to survive and to conquer Western cultures. Changing discourse on parody, its complex relationship with related humorous forms (e.g. travesty, burlesque, satire), its ability to cross genre boundaries, the many parodies handed down by tradition, and its ubiquity in contemporary culture all testify to its multifaceted nature. No wonder that 'parody' has become a phrase without clear meaning.

The essays in this collection reflect the multidimensionality of recent parody studies. They pay tribute to its long and varied tradition, covering examples of parodic practice from the Middle Ages to the present day and dealing with English, American, postcolonial, Austrian, and German parodies. The papers range from the Medieval classics (e.g. Chaucer), parodies of Shakespeare, and the role of parody in German Romanticism, to parodies of fin-de-siècle literature and the intertextual puzzles of the late twentieth century (such as cross-dressing, Schwab's *Faust* parody, and Rushdie's *Satanic Verses*). And they have transformed the contentious nature of parody into a diverse range of methodologies. In doing so, these essays offer a survey of the current state of parody studies.

EDITIONS RODOPI B.V.

USA/Canada: **All Other Countries:**
2015 South Park Place   Keizersgracht 302-304
Atlanta, GA 30339   1016 EX Amsterdam
Tel. (770) 933-0027   The Netherlands
Fax (770) 933-9644   Tel. ++ 31 (0)20 622 75 07
Call toll-free (U.S.only) 1-800-225-3998   Fax ++ 31 (0)20 638 09 48
e-mail: orders-queries@rodopi.nl — http://www.rodopi.nl

MICHAEL BROPHY

Voies vers l'autre
DUPIN * BONNEFOY * NOËL * GUILLEVIC.

Amsterdam/Atlanta, GA 1997. 197 pp.
(Chiasma 5)
ISBN: 90-420-0231-X   Hfl. 60,-/US-$ 31.50

Si la poésie contemporaine continue à sonder ses propres carences, à creuser sans répit tout ce qui se prolonge en elle comme absence et manque, ses humbles conquêtes ne s'affirment le plus souvent qu'au moment d'une immense dissolution qui oppose à tout geste d'appropriation définitive une communion fuyante, ouverte et vitale. Dans la trame déliée de l'écriture se dessine non point l'image achevée, le reflet immobilisé de l'autre, mais quelques traces de son bref, de son infixable passage qui rejoint dans le monde la sombre vérité, l'en aller irrévocable, de toute existence mortelle. Voie vers l'autre, la poésie demeure de nos jours voie terrestre, voie incertaine, qui arrache l'être à la fixité et aux fixations du moi pour qu'il s'atteigne, sans cesse refait, dans la précarité immédiate de ce qui surgit, s'offre et s'efface. Notre étude interroge les œuvres de quatre poètes qui avancent courageusement dans cette voie, qui mesurent entre soi et l'autre, signe et présence, idée et monde, non seulement ruptures et écarts, mais l'espace tremblant d'un entre-deux susceptible de se muer subitement et comme inauguralement en cri et accès.

EDITIONS RODOPI B.V.

USA/Canada:	All Other Countries:
2015 South Park Place	Keizersgracht 302-304
Atlanta, GA 30339	1016 EX Amsterdam
Tel. (770) 933-0027	The Netherlands
Fax (770) 933-9644	Tel. ++ 31 (0)20 622 75 07
Call toll-free (U.S.only) 1-800-225-3998	Fax ++ 31 (0)20 638 09 48

DAVID T. LLOYD

Writing on the Edge
Interviews with Writers and Editors of Wales

Amsterdam/Atlanta, GA 1997. 155 pp.
(Costerus NS 112)
ISBN: 90-420-0248-4   Hfl. 50,-/US-$ 26.-

Complex and controversial issues have accompanied the development of English-language literature in Wales, generating a continuing debate over the nature of Welsh writing in English. The main issues include the claim of some Welsh-language writers to represent the only authentic literature of Wales, the question of whether or not an extended literary tradition in English has existed in Wales, the absence (until fairly recently) of a publishing apparatus for English-language writers, the rise of a Welsh nationalism committed to preserving the Welsh language, and the question of whether English-language literature in Wales can be distinguished from English literature proper. The primary impulse for the interviews with the thirteen writers and editors in *Writing on the Edge* was to explore these and other issues relating to the literary and cultural identity in Wales in the last decade. The book's title reflects these ongoing debates about the nature and direction of contemporary Welsh literature in English, which is often perceived as peripheral both to Welsh-speaking Wales and to the literary culture of England. As one of the contributors to the volumes says "This is what it is to be Welsh ... It's an edge. There's no moment of life in Wales that hasn't got that edge, unless you decide you're not Welsh."

EDITIONS RODOPI B.V.

USA/Canada: All Other Countries:
2015 South Park Place   Keizersgracht 302-304
Atlanta, GA 30339   1016 EX Amsterdam
Phone (770) 933-0027   The Netherlands
Fax (770) 933-9644   Tel. ++ 31 (0)20 622 75 07
Call toll-free (U.S.only) 1-800-225-3998   Fax ++ 31 (0)20 638 09 48
          e-mail: orders-queries@rodopi.nl — http://www.rodopi.nl

CLARA ORBAN

The Culture of Fragments
Words and Images
in Futurism and Surrealism

Amsterdam/Atlanta, GA 1997. 210 pp.
(Textxet 11)
ISBN: 90-420-0111-9   Hfl. 65,-/US-$ 34.-

Works of art such as paintings with words on them or poems shaped as images communicate to the viewer by means of more than one medium. Here is presented a particular group of hybrid art works from the early twentieth century, to discover in what way words and images can function together to create meaning.
The four central artists considered in this study investigate word/image forms in their work. F.T. Marinetti invented *parole in libertà*, among other ideas, to free language from syntactic connections. Umberto Boccioni experimented with newspaper clippings on the canvas from 1912-1915, and these collages constitute an important exploration into word/image forms. André Breton's collection of poems *Clair de terre* (1923) contains several typographical variations for iconographic effect. René Magritte explored the relationship between words and images, juxtaposing signifiers to contradictory signifieds on the canvas. A final chapter introduces media other than poetry and painting on which words and images appear. Posters, the theater, and the relatively new medium of cinema foreground words and images constantly.
This volume will be of interest to scholars of twentieth-century French or Italian literature or painting, and to scholars of word and image studies.

EDITIONS RODOPI B.V.

USA / Canada: **All Other Countries:**
2015 South Park Place   Keizersgracht 302-304
Atlanta, GA 30339   1016 EX Amsterdam, The Netherlands
Phone (770) 933-0027 / **Fax** 933-9644   **Tel.** ++ 31 (0)20 622 75 07
Call toll-free (U.S.only) 1-800-225-3998   **Fax** ++ 31 (0)20 638 09 48
e-mail: orders-queries@rodopi.nl — http://www.rodopi.nl

WORD & IMAGE

The Pictured Word: Interactions II
A Selection of Papers Given at the Third International Conference on Word and Image. University of Ottawa, August 16 - 21, 1993

Ed. by Martin Heusser, Claus Clüver, Leo Hoek and Lauren Weingarden

Amsterdam/Atlanta, GA 1997. 356 pp. (Textxet 12)
ISBN: 90-420-0203-4   Bound Hfl. 175,-/US-$ 92.-
ISBN: 90-420-0190-9   Paper Hfl. 50,-/US-$ 26.-

Table of Contents: REFLECTIONS ON THEORY AND METHODOLOGY. Claus CLÜVER: On Representation in Concrete and Semiotic Poetry. Áron Kibédi VARGA: L'image pensée. Lauren WEINGARDEN: Art Historical Iconography and Word & Image Studies: Manet's *A Bar at the Folies-Bergère* and the Naturalist Novel. ON INTER-TEXTUAL RELATIONS. Giselle de NIE: Seeing and Believing in the Early Middle Ages: A Preliminary Investigation. Else JONGENEEL: La bible d'images de Saint Marc à Venise. Pierre DEMAROLLE: Mots et images, ecriture et espaces dans un roman français du XVe siècle. Marian ROTHSTEIN: The Commemorative Images of *Amadis de Gaule*. Kathryn PORTER AICHELE: Paul Klee's *Composition with Windows*: An Homage and an Elegy. SEMIOTICS, PAINTING, AND POETRY. Dee REYNOLDS: Imagination and Semiotic Interactions in Painting and Poetry. Eric VOS: Visual Literature and Semiotic Conventions. Francis EDELINE: L'éspace-temps dans la poésie sémiotique. Eduardo KAC: Holopoetry and Hyperpoetry. ON MONUMENTS. Michael GARVAL: The Rise and Fall of the Literary Monument in Post-Revolutionary France. Charles VANDERSEE: Contesting "Meaning" in the Late 19th Century: A Site of American Art, Autobiography, and Ambition. Charlotte SCHOELL-GLASS: The Medium is the Message: Ian Hamilton Finlay's Garden *Little Sparta*. CARTOONS AND CARICATURE. Mirela SAIM: "Faire comprendre au peuple": représentation caricaturale et éloquence democratique dans la culture politique française de 1848. Eric HASKELL: Fusing Word and Image: The Case of the Cartoon Book, Wilde and Shelton. WORD-IMAGE INTERACTIONS IN FAR-EASTERN PRACTICES. Mingfei SHI: "The Three Perfections": Isomorphic Structures in Works of Late Chinese Poet-Calligraphers-Painters. Aiko OKAMOTO-MACPHAIL: Interacting Signs in the *Genji* Scrolls. Fumiko TOGASAKI: The Assertion of Heterodoxy in Kyoden's Verbal-Visual Texts. BEYOND CONVENTIONAL BOUNDARIES. David SCOTT: Semiotics and Ideology in Mixed Messages: The Postage Stamp. Lewis DIBBLE: Harry Wilmer's Drawings: Visual Communication and Violation of Outline Conventions. Hans LUND: From Epigraph to Iconic Epigram: The Interaction Between Buildings and Their Inscriptions in the Urban Space. Monique MOSER-VERREY: Images du corps et communication non verbale dans l'écriture de Franz Kafka. Jürgen E. MÜLLER: Video - or the Intermedial State of the Art.

EDITIONS RODOPI B.V.

USA / Canada: **All Other Countries:**
2015 South Park Place   Keizersgracht 302-304
Atlanta, GA 30339   1016 EX Amsterdam, The Netherlands
Phone (770) 933-0027 / **Fax** 933-9644   **Tel.** ++ 31 (0)20 622 75 07
Call toll-free (U.S.only) 1-800-225-3998   **Fax** ++ 31 (0)20 638 09 48
e-mail: orders-queries@rodopi.nl — http://www.rodopi.nl

TRANSLATING SENSITIVE TEXTS: LINGUISTIC ASPECTS

Ed. by Karl Simms

Amsterdam/Atlanta, GA 1997. 342 pp.
(Approaches to Translation Studies 14)
ISBN: 90-420-0270-0   Bound Hfl. 175,-/US-$ 92.-
ISBN: 90-420-0260-3   Paper Hfl. 50,-/US-$ 26.-

This volume brings together twenty-two of the world's leading translation and interpreting theorists, to address the issue of sensitivity in translation. Whether in novels or legal documents, the Bible or travel brochures, in translating ancient texts or providing simultaneous interpretation, sensitive subject-matter, contentious modes of expression and the sensibilities of the target audience are the biggest obstacles to acceptance of the translator's work. The contributors bring to bear a wide variety of approaches - generative, cognitive, lexical and functional - in confronting this problem, and in negotiating the competing claims of source cultures and target cultures in the areas of cultural, political, religious and sexual sensitivity. All of the articles are presented here for the first time, and in his Introduction Karl Simms gives an overview of the philosophical and linguistic questions which have motivated translators of sensitive texts through the ages. This book will be of interest to all working translators and interpreters, and to teachers of translation theory and practice.

EDITIONS RODOPI B.V.

USA / Canada:	All Other Countries:
2015 South Park Place	Keizersgracht 302-304
Atlanta, GA 30339	1016 EX Amsterdam, The Netherlands
Phone (770) 933-0027 / **Fax** 933-9644	**Tel.** ++ 31 (0)20 622 75 07
Call toll-free (U.S.only) 1-800-225-3998	**Fax** ++ 31 (0)20 638 09 48

e-mail: orders-queries@rodopi.nl — http://www.rodopi.nl

INTERART POETICS
Essays on the Interrelations of the Arts and Media

Ed. by Ulla-Britta Lagerroth, Hans Lund and Erik Hedling

Amsterdam/Atlanta, GA 1997. 354 pp.
(Internationale Forschungen zur Allgemeinen und Vergleichenden Literaturwissenschaft 24)
ISBN: 90-420-0202-6   Bound Hfl. 175,-/US-$ 92.-
ISBN: 90-420-0210-7   Paper Hfl. 50,-/US-$ 26.-

In this anthology are gathered 28 essays, devoted to the interrelations of the arts and media. They present together the current state of the emerging field of Interart Studies. The contributors — Stephen Greenblatt, Claus Clüver, Erika Fischer-Lichte, John Neubauer, Steven Paul Scher, Walter Bernhart, Ulrich Weisstein, Eric T. Haskell, Eric Vos, Thomas Elsaesser, among others — are leading international scholars in the fields of Art History, Literary Criticism, Musicology, Film, Theatre and Media Studies. In challenging ways they promote interdisciplinary strategies in the study of the traditional arts: dance, literature, music, painting, sculpture, theatre etc, as well as of the modern media: film, TV, video, computer-generated arts, etc.
The essays collected engage in a broad perspective of topics, approached from varying theoretical, methodological or ideological viewpoints. No single thread runs through the diversely conceived essays, yet it is evident that what all contributors appear to envision is the importance today of investigations into the problems of what might be called the interart — or intermedia — discourse. Aimed at university teachers, scholars, students and even artists, this book will meet the demands from those interested in modern modes of interart and intermedia analysis.

USA/Canada:
   Editions Rodopi B.V., 2015 South Park Place, Atlanta, GA 30339, Tel. (70) 933-0027, *Call toll-free* (U.S.only) 1-800-225-3998, Fax (770) 933-9644
All Other Countries:
   Editions Roopi B.V., Keizersgracht 302-304, 1016 EX Amsterdam, The Netherlands. Tel. ++ 31 (0)20-622 75 07, Fax ++ 31 (0)20-638 09 48
E-mail: orders-queries@rodopi.nl —— http://www.rodopi.nl

CONRAD:
INTERTEXTS & APPROPRIATIONS
Essays in Memory of Yves Hervouet

Ed. by Gene M. Moore, Owen Knowles and J.H. Stape

Amsterdam/Atlanta, GA 1997. IX,163 pp.
(Textxet 9)
ISBN: 90-420-0218-2   Bound Hfl. 80,-/US-$ 50.-

Contents: Notes on Contributors. A Bibliography of Works by Yves Hervouet. Paul KIRSCHNER: The Legacy of Yves Hervouet: An Introduction. Susan JONES: Conrad's Debt to Marguerite Poradowska. Amy HOUSTON: Conrad and Alfred Russel Wallace. Gene M. MOORE: Conrad's 'The Idiots' and Maupassant's 'La Mère aux monstres'. J.H. STAPE: 'Gaining Conviction': Conradian Borrowing and the *Patna* Episode in *Lord Jim*. Owen KNOWLES: Conrad, Anatole France, and the Early French Romantic Tradition: Some Influences. J.H. STAPE: 'One can learn something from Balzac': Conrad and Balzac. Hugh EPSTEIN: *Bleak House* and Conrad: The Presence of Dickens in Conrad's Writing. Hans van MARLE and Gene M. MOORE: The Sources of *Suspense*.

USA/Canada:
   Editions Rodopi B.V., 2015 South Park Place, Atlanta, GA 30339, Tel. (70) 933-0027, *Call toll-free* (U.S.only) 1-800-225-3998, Fax (770) 933-9644
All Other Countries:
   Editions Roopi B.V., Keizersgracht 302-304, 1016 EX Amsterdam, The Netherlands. Tel. ++ 31 (0)20-622 75 07, Fax ++ 31 (0)20-638 09 48
E-mail: orders-queries@rodopi.nl —— http://www.rodopi.nl

FIEKE SCHOOTS

"Passer en douce à la douane".
L'Écriture minimaliste de Minuit:
Deville, Echenoz, Redonnet et Toussaint

Amsterdam/Atlanta, GA 1997. 234 pp.
(Faux Titre 131)
ISBN: 90-420-0283-2   Hfl. 75,-/US-$ 39.-

Les quatre auteurs réunis ici, Deville, Echenoz, Redonnet et Toussaint, ont beaucoup attiré l'attention de la critique littéraire depuis la fin des années 80. Or, l'objectif de cette étude est, tout en respectant leur singularité, d'analyser leurs romans à partir de traits communs. Publiés aux Éditions de Minuit, ils représentent une pratique de l'écriture caractéristique de la littérature française actuelle, que l'on qualifie ici d''écriture minimaliste'.

Outre ce minimalisme, les recherches romanesques de ces auteurs se rejoignent sur un certain nombre de points. Ainsi, le jeu citationnel qu'ils pratiquent ne manque pas de mettre en cause la représentation de la réalité. De plus, l'organisation de leurs récits témoigne d'une réflexion sur les notions d'ordre et de chaos, de hasard et de nécessité. Enfin, l'étude de leur vision du monde montre que la réalité y fait tout de même sa rentrée 'en douce'.

Le jeu d'ensemble que propose ce livre s'attache à repérer, à la lumière du Nouveau Roman et du postmodernisme, un nouveau territoire dans le paysage littéraire français et souligne en même temps quelques affinités entre la littérature et la pensée actuelles.

EDITIONS RODOPI B.V.

USA / Canada: **All Other Countries:**
2015 South Park Place   Keizersgracht 302-304
Atlanta, GA 30339   1016 EX Amsterdam, The Netherlands
Phone (770) 933-0027 / **Fax** 933-9644   **Tel.** ++ 31 (0)20 622 75 07
Call toll-free (U.S.only) 1-800-225-3998   **Fax** ++ 31 (0)20 638 09 48
e-mail: orders-queries@rodopi.nl — http://www.rodopi.nl